# JOURNEY
# TO
# JUSTICE

# JOURNEY TO JUSTICE

*The Inside Story of the Chinese Prosecutor Hsiang Che-chun and His Team in the Tokyo Trial*

XIANG Longwan

上海交通大學出版社
SHANGHAI JIAO TONG UNIVERSITY PRESS

naturalogic

Journey to Justice:
The Inside Story of the Chinese Prosecutor Hsiang Che-chun and His Team in the Tokyo Trial

XIANG Longwan



上海交通大學出版社
SHANGHAI JIAO TONG UNIVERSITY PRESS

Published by NATURALOGIC PUBLISHING INC., under an exclusive license with Shanghai Jiao Tong University Press.



First English Edition 2023
ISBN: 978-1-4878-1077-1

naturalogic | NATURALOGIC
*Passion is the genesis of genius.*
www.naturalogicpublishers.com

19-1235 Johnson St. Coquitlam, BC, Canada V3B 7E2

# Preface I

**GAO WENBIN** (William V.P.KAW), Professor of Shanghai Maritime University, translator, and secretary of the Chinese Prosecutor from the International Military Tribunal for the Far East

All memories crowded upon my mind when I participated in the feature film Tokyo Trial premiere in Shanghai with Mr. HSIANG Che-chun's son XIANG Longwan and Judge MEI Ju-ao's son MEI Xiao'ao twelve years ago. On the one hand, with the exciting and vivid plots from the memoirs of Judge MEI Ju-ao and the Chief Counsel of the Prosecutor NYI, Judson T.Y., this movie aroused people's attention to this important historical event. However, it is a pity that there are some fabricated plots in the film. I remember that Mr. HSIANG and I brought back two large boxes of court records and court evidence from Tokyo in August 1948. I believe the film could have been made more real and exciting if the first-hand material had been used in its production.

Happily, Mr. XIANG Longwan has visited the United States many times with his wife JIANG Fu and copied many first-hand materials such as Mr. HSIANG's statements at the tribunal and translated them into Chinese after returning to China. They published *The Tokyo Trial, Chinese Prosecutor HSIANG Che-chun* with Shanghai Jiao Tong University Press in 2010. I wrote a preface to this book at the request of Mr. XIANG Longwan, reviewing Mr. HSIANG Che-chun's visit to Tokyo and the hard work at that time.

Unexpectedly, this book has some significant implications. Center for the Tokyo Trial Studies was established in Shanghai Jiao Tong University on May 3, 2011, the 65th anniversary of the Tokyo Trial. I am honored to be invited to the inauguration ceremony and express my congratulations and sincere hope. A significant amount of research was conducted on the Tokyo Trial within the past seven years. All the available court records and evidence have finally been published in China, and the study books have been published one after another. It is a blessing for me to witness it in my lifetime.

To commemorate the 70th anniversary of the closure of the Tokyo Trial, Mr. XIANG Longwan wrote another book about the Chinese prosecution team, which reminded me of those years and moved me to tears. As a historical event, the Tokyo Trial still has great significance today. It should be integrated into our national education so that the general public, especially the young people, can learn more about it. At Mr. XIANG Longwan's request, I've written a few words for this book as a preface at age 96. I believe this informative and vivid book will be popular.

GAO Wenbin

# Preface II

CHENG Zhaoqi, Professor of Shanghai Jiao Tong University, Director of Center for the Tokyo Trial Studies

Two years ago, Mr. XIANG Longwan invited me to write a preface before writing the book. I found that my name was specifically marked in the preface after the manuscript was completed. It stands to reason that it's an obligation I cannot decline. However, I can't help but hesitate because no matter what, the most suitable one for the preface is Mr. GAO Wenbin, a secretary of Mr. HSIANG Che-chun, the only one still alive in China who has participated in the whole process of the Tokyo Trial. Therefore, I feel it would be redundant to write it again when Mr. Gao Wenbin's wonderful preface already exists. However, Mr. XIANG has been very helpful to the Center for the Tokyo Trial Studies over the years as well as to me personally. I should try my best to say a few words relating to the topic to show my gratitude to Mr. XIANG even if I can't contribute too much to the book.

During a lecture a few years ago, an audience member asked a question in the question-and-answer session. "Who played a greater role in the Tokyo Trial, the judge or the prosecutor?" Generally speaking, it was not difficult to answer because the prosecutor prosecutes, and the judge judges the case. Each performs its own functions, and they cannot be compared. However, for a Chinese who is deeply affected by *Creation of the Gods* and *Outlaws of the Marsh* where everything has to be ranked, he must think that I didn't answer his question. Writing this short preface, I couldn't help but think of that. I am not trying to answer this question and rank them here because I have realized that even I, who have done a large amount of research on the Tokyo Trial, have not been very clear about the answer. Although Judge MEI Ju-ao's writings on the Tokyo Trial are incomplete, he gave us some important first-hand documents, such as half of the overview drafts and some diary fragments. In comparison, Mr. HSIANG Che-chun gave us nothing except his "confession" and short speeches during the Cultural Revolution. It is even more challenging to get into it.

It has changed a lot over the recent years. The role of the Chinese judge and prosecutor has generally become clearer after the establishment of the Center for the Tokyo Trial Studies. We know the judge's role from *The Tokyo Trial Manuscript of MEI Ju-ao* compiled by MEI Xiaokan and MEI Xiao'ao. The contribution of the prosecutor is fully demonstrated through *HSIANG Che-chun's Letters, Telegrams, and Statements at the Tokyo Trial,* as well as this book written by Mr. XIANG Longwan. We had been bullied by foreign powers before the foundation of the People's Republic of China. Our first real victory finally arrived after the arduous struggle with our allies in World War II. The trial of Japanese war criminals is indispensable of this victory. Looking through the dusty archives from 70 years ago, we can see that the role played by the Chinese prosecutor and the Chinese judge was really important. I won't say the details here because this book has excellent explanations. I want to say a few words about Mr. Qiu Shaoheng's (Henry CHIU) recollection of Mr. HSIANG Che-chun's "cowardice" and "submission" to the United States.

Mr. CHIU was the secretary of Mr. HSIANG Che-chun at the beginning of the Tokyo Trial but later returned to China for some reason. He participated in the trial of the LIN Biao and JIANG Qing Group and the drafting of *The Basic Law of the Hong Kong Special Administrative Region of the People's Republic of China* after the Cultural Revolution. Since the end of the 1980s, he had been interviewed and mentioned in the Tokyo Trial many times. His words on trial are quite inaccurate due to the long lapse of time. Especially for the part involving Mr. HSIANG Che-chun, it's incredibly wrong. For example, he said that Mr. HSIANG refused to appear at the tribunal because "he is not confident in himself." (You Junyi February 2006, "The Colorful Life of Professor CHIU Shaoheng, Honorary President of the Shanghai Law Society," *Oriental Law*, no.

2, 146) *"He refused to appear at the tribunal in accordance with the instructions of the National Government of Republic of China."* (Ma Lingguo 1999, "CHIU Shaoheng, the Chinese Prosecutor in the International Military Tribunal for the Far East," *The Essence of Literature and History*, no. 5, 12) All in all, he stated several different reasons why Mr. HSIANG refused to appear at the tribunal. As a result, Mr. CHIU had no alternative but to become *"the first Chinese prosecutor to appear at an international tribunal."* (Zhu Chengshan 1995, "Searching for Witnesses for the International Military Tribunal for the Far East—Prosecutor CHIU Shaoheng," *The Good Years*, no. 1, 35)

The reason why "it's incredibly wrong" is that, firstly, the National Government had no "instruction" to oppose the court appearance. Secondly, Mr. HSIANG Che-chun appeared at the tribunal long before Mr. Qiu. Thirdly, Mr. HSIANG Che-chun showed no cowardice, whether from the literature or the video material. Actually, he was not only upright and sharp but also calm and personable. Soon after the Tokyo Trial started, the prosecutor launched a fierce attack, and the defendant defended intensely. Mr. HSIANG Che-chun came on stage after Chief of Counsel Joseph B. Keenan and British prosecutor Arthur S. Comyns Carr. He fervently refuted the defendant's statement that Japan's actions against China were not aggression. During the rebuttal, President of the tribunal William F. Webb even reminded him not to be too blistering. SHIMADA Shigetaro's attorney TAKIKAWA Masajiro wrote in his work that *"Mr. HSIANG is really a gallant Chinese man"* (TAKIKAWA, M. 2006, *To try the Tokyo Trial*, Keibunsha Press), in *To Try the Tokyo Trial* published shortly after the Allies lifted the restrictions. As a secretary of Mr. HSIANG, Mr. CHIU was in Tokyo at that time, even if he didn't show up at the tribunal from the beginning. He should know Mr. HSIANG's appearance at the tribunal. Although it is possible that he had a vague memory or completely forgot about it due to the long lapse of time, it is confusing that what he said is completely the opposite of the fact.

I don't think Mr. CHIU did it deliberately. Maybe it stemmed from his misunderstanding of Mr. HSIANG. I would like to say a few more words on this topic here. The victory of World War II was a concerted effort of the Allies. Similarly, the success of the Tokyo Trial was also a concerted effort of China, the United States, and other countries. Since different countries have different interests and demands, the success couldn't have been achieved if they hadn't compromised. Whether during the preparation of the United Nations War Crimes Commission or the actual trial, every claim made by China was achieved through consultations with other countries, especially the United States. Mr. HSIANG was fifty-five years old at the time of the Tokyo Trial. From the correspondence he sent to China during the trial and Mr. GAO Wenbin's recall afterward (GAO Wenbin 2008, "My Experience during the Tokyo Trial," *Life Week*, no. 21). We can see he had a deep understanding of the way of the world due to the domestic trouble and foreign invasion and his drifting from place to place. On the one hand, as we said earlier, we could not get any proof from the original files and video material that Mr. HSIANG was "weak" to the United States though Mr. CHIU said that many times. On the other hand, I think Mr. CHIU's stereotype of him resulted from Mr. HSIANG's general perspective on the situation when he was in dilemmas. That couldn't be understood by Mr. CHIU, who had just entered his thirties at that time.

I want to point out here that the Tokyo Trial participants tended to distort the Sino-U.S. relation at the Tokyo Trial due to the deterioration of their relation during the Cold War. China and the United States both belonged to the majority during the trial, despite their differences. They were not rivals everywhere. Moreover, we cannot find any proof to show that China's major demands have not been fulfilled due to the obstruction of the United States. From this point of view, it's not easy to say whether it's a good thing or a bad thing that Mr. HSIANG didn't leave us any material of the Tokyo Trial.

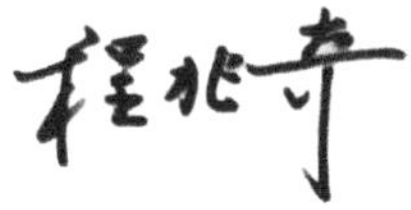

CHENG Zhaoqi

# Author's Note

**XIANG** **Longwan**,
Mathematics Professor of Shanghai Jiao Tong University, Honorary Director of the Center for the Tokyo Trial Studies

I was only an elementary school kid when my father served as the prosecutor for China in the Tokyo Trial in the 1940s. Up to this day, I can still vaguely recall the scene of my father returning home from Tokyo for a short stay on several occasions. Often he had to work at the typewriter overnight and left in a hurry the next day. I also remember when I went to the airport with my mother to see him off. It's a pity I don't recall anything about the Tokyo Trial other than those fragmentary memories. My father was 49 years older than me and was already in his twilight years after I had grown up. He very seldom talked to me about the Tokyo Trial. It wasn't until 2004, when I worked with CCTV on the documentary *For Whom the Bell Tolls*, and 2006 when I attended the feature film Tokyo Trial premiere did I realize my lack of knowledge about the Tokyo Trial.

During my visit to the United States as a member of the delegation from the Shanghai Overseas Returned Scholars Association (SORSA) in early 2006, I saw microfilm and printed trial records of the International Military Tribunal for the Far East at the Library of Congress in Washington for the first time.

My wife Jiang Fu and I also visited the US in the late spring of 2006 to attend the commencement of our younger son, and in the fall of 2007 again to meet relatives and friends there. During these two visits, we went to the Library of Congress, the National Archives of the United States, and the East Asian Library of Columbia University, where I copied the English manuscripts of my father's ten statements in court and took some photos of related documents. After returning to China, I translated my father's ten statements into Chinese. I had it compiled and published by Shanghai Jiao Tong University Press in 2010 in a collection that includes my mother's memoir *A Good Mentor and a Good Husband* and some media reports at the time. The book was *The Tokyo Trial: the Story of the Chinese Prosecutor HSIANG Che-chun.*

It quickly caught the attention of people interested in the Trial, although only a small number of the Trial records were cited in the book. On May 3, 2011, the Center for the Tokyo Trial studies was established at Shanghai Jiao Tong University on the 65th anniversary of the Tokyo Trial. Since then, many scholars have shown interest in collecting, analyzing, editing, and publishing documents related to the Trial, and research findings in the field have come forth in large numbers.

Shanghai Jiao Tong University and the National Library of China have worked together to edit and publish 83 volumes of *Transcripts of the Proceedings of International Military Tribunal for the Far East* (English version and the indexes & appendices in Chinese, English and Japanese), 53 volumes of *A Collection of Court Exhibits of the International Military Tribunal for the Far East* (Japanese version and the indexes & appendices in Chinese, English and Japanese), 73 volumes of *Numerical Case Files Relating to Particular Incidents and Suspected War Criminals, International Prosecution Section (1945–1947)* (English version and the indexes & appendices in Chinese, English and Japanese), 12 volumes of *Transcripts of the Proceedings of the International Military Tribunal for the Far East: the China Related* (Translated version in Chinese) and 10 volumes of *Transcripts of the Proceedings of International Military Tribunal for the Far East, Integral Translation(First Series)* The publication of these books filled the void in the study of Tokyo Trial in China. The Center has frequent collaboration and exchanges with scholars at home and abroad. It has so far compiled and translated more than 20 books for publication, making the voice of Chinese scholars heard beyond China. The Center also plays the role of a think tank whose advisory reports have been highly valued by the relevant authorities in China.

As a Mathematics professor, I have learned a lot about history and law while searching for information about the Tokyo Trial. Now I have a general understanding of it and its significance, and the contribution of the Chinese delegation. I am glad to share my thoughts and feelings with readers who wish to learn about it. I have delivered relevant lectures in Shanghai, Beijing, Tianjin, Xi'an, Nanjing, Suzhou, Chengdu, Shenzhen, Hong Kong, Macau, New York, Washington, Chicago, San Francisco, Los Angeles, Tokyo, Melbourne, Paris, Hague, Amsterdam, etc. In schools, colleges, and social groups in recent years, I, along with ZHAO Yuhui, a young teacher, and other colleagues, have offered general education courses on the Tokyo Trial at Shanghai Jiao Tong University since 2013. I have been invited to give five lectures (2015) and eighteen lectures (2021) on CCTV and have participated in two seasons of a documentary on the trial made by The International Channel Shanghai (ICS) since 2015. These courses, lectures, and documentaries have been warmly welcomed, which has greatly benefited and inspired me.

Friends in education told me that there's barely any content on the Tokyo Trial in our existing textbooks for middle schools, colleges, and universities. A very important reason is that teachers, especially textbook writers, are not knowledgeable in this area. They suggested that I write a popular book based on the lectures, which can be used as a textbook and a reading material. Despite my limited knowledge, I mustered up the courage to try to fulfill the task in 2018, the 70th anniversary of the Tokyo Trial.

This book, *Journey to Justice*, is mainly about the Chinese prosecutor and his team's contribution to the trial. Part of its content is similar to that in *My personal experience at the Tokyo Trial,* wrote by Judge MEI Ju-ao and compiled by his daughter MEI Xiaokan and his son MEI Xiao'ao. I have set three writing principles for myself: one is to cover sufficient information and not to use any language like an angry young man; the second is to provide enough proof for the argument; the third is to consider both the seriousness of historical material and the readability.

First-hand court records and international treaties are the most convincing. The recall of the parties and the media reports at that time are also strong evidence. This book has frequently quoted the above documents. Additionally, the study achievements of Chinese and foreign scholars have also been of great help. If some citations are too long, you may skip them. A note indicates the citation source at the end of each chapter for reference.

My intention is that readers can judge by themselves the crimes committed by Japanese war criminals through the quotation and rational analysis of a large number of historical materials. However, when I saw the evidence that the Japanese militarists had conspired and caused trouble despicably again and again and the heinous atrocities committed by the Japanese invaders in places such as Nanjing, Hankou, Guangzhou, Hong Kong, and the Philippines, it was tough for me to keep calm. Please forgive me if there are still some radical words in the book.

Professor KAO Wen-pin, who participated in the Tokyo Trial from the start to the end and is still alive today, is not only my father's colleague but also his close friend regardless of age. He has always cared for and inspired our work. It is my great honor that he has written a preface to this book at the age of ninety-six.

Professor CHENG Zhaoqi is a leading scholar in the Tokyo Trial study. The Center for the Tokyo Trial Studies has achieved much in the past seven years and has attracted the attention of scholars at home and abroad under his leadership. I had learned a lot from him when we worked together. He also wrote a preface to the book, which is very kind.

I've received help from many people from the Academic Affairs Office of Shanghai Jiao Tong University, the Shanghai Jiao Tong University Press, and the Center of Tokyo Trial Studies in the process of writing. The content, style, and even the book's title has been revised many times. Dr. ZHAO Yuhui verified the material used in the book. Director of the Press LIU Peiying, senior editor YU Jinbao and Ms. CUI Xia's pertinent opinions have played an important role in determining the book's framework. Ms. WANG Xuan provided detailed information to show the relation between Japan's use of biological weapons and the Tokyo Trial. Moreover, several close friends such as Professor ZONG Liwen, Miss CHEN Zhuojun, JIN Yun'an, and LIU Feng, who are also senior editors and media professionals, proofread the book. Mr. LI Bin, a famous artist, is creating a huge oil painting named *Tokyo Trial*. He generously agreed that part of the painting could be used as the book's cover. Many of the photos and documents used in this book came from Professor JIA Hao, Mr. LI Bin, and the descendants of MEI Ju-ao, NYI, Judson T.Y., and E Sen. They are Ms. MEI Xiaokan, Mr. MEI Xiao'ao, Ms. NI Naixian, and Ms. E Yinhua. The National Library of China, The Memorial Hall of the Victims in Nanjing Massacre by Japanese Invaders, the Shanghai Songhu Memorial Hall for the War of Resistance Against Japanese Aggression, The International Channel Shanghai, and the National Archives of the United States also helped me with much material. Friends such as LI Yan,

ZHOU Qi, JIANG Xiongyi, WANG Xiaodong, XIANG Yucheng, and XIANG Yuming have sent me valuable photos from all over the world. The group photo of the Chinese delegation that attended the Tokyo Trial by Mr. KAO Wen-pin is vital to the book. The English version of the catalog and the Index were translated and proofread by Professor TAO Qing, Dr. GONG Zhiwei, and Miss Marquise Lee. The editors, Dr. BAO Suo and Ms. FENG Yuan, and the art editor Ms. SUN Min devoted themselves to the final work of this book. I would like to express my gratitude here to them all.

One discovers his ignorance only through learning. I was not relaxed but felt anxious when the book was completed. After finishing this book, I realized my limited understanding of the Tokyo Trial and my limited knowledge of history and law. Please let me know if there is any defect in it.

向隆万

XIANG Longwan

# Preface to the English Edition

More than seven decades have passed since the trial of Japanese Class A war criminals in Tokyo by the International Military Tribunal for the Far East was concluded. Justice was eventually meted out to the culprits who committed the war crime. Millions of people in dozens of countries also received the punishment they deserved by the international tribunal. The common aspiration of peace-loving people for restoring human dignity became a reality at long last. Both the team of the Chinese judge and the team of Chinese prosecutor had made tremendous contributions to the success of the trial during the two-and-a-half-year court process, from identifying war criminals, collecting evidence, arranging witnesses for a court hearing, all the way through to participating in the drafting of the *Indictment* by the Chinese Prosecution Team and the *Judgement* by the Chinese judge Team. China had suffered the longest and the heaviest loss among countries invaded by Japan during WWII. Consequently, it came as no surprise that the Tokyo Trial spent most of its time in the China part. In fact, 44 out of the 55 counts of war crimes listed in the *Indictment* were linked to Japan's invasion of China, and the verdicts on the Japanese crimes against China took the largest portion of the *Judgement*.

Regrettably, most of the work of the Chinese teams had not been referred to or included by scholars in their research on the Tokyo Trial. I wrote this book with the primary goal of filling the void. The materials I used in this book to present the great contributions of the Chinese judge team and Chinese prosecutor team to the Tokyo Trial were largely drawn from the research by my colleagues at the Center for the Tokyo Trial Studies in Shanghai Jiao Tong University. These included data and information they collected from across the globe in the past ten years, including Nanking, Beijing, Shanghai, Taipei, New York, Washington D.C., Boston, Canberra, and Tokyo, to name but a few. I hope the English edition of the book, scheduled to be published on the 76th anniversary of the opening of the Tokyo Trial, will help readers understand better the trial and that chapter of history in general. The publication of the book will also serve as another celebration of the victory of justice in modern history.

The book cites the court records of the Tokyo Trial extensively. Due to the space limitation, I could not exhaust all the references. For researchers interested in finding out more, a complete text of the *Proceedings of the International Military Tribunal for the Far East* is available at the Center for the Tokyo Trial Studies in Shanghai Jiao Tong University. The Chinese names in this book are mostly spelt in Hanyu Pinyin; However, Chinese names that appeared in the trial records, especially names of the judges, prosecutors, defendants, and witnesses, were arranged according to Wittoma Pinyin to be consistent with their original appearances in historical documents.

My thanks go to Ye Xingguo, President of Zhejiang Yuexiu University, for his generous support; Yang Aijun, Li Dan, and Huang Danhua, for translating the book into English; Tao Qing, for polishing and sharpening the English manuscript; Chris Q.K. Tang, Aaron Y.P. Li, Zhou Jingwen, Gary Lee, Amy Lee, Yang Daqing, and Mei Xiaokan, for the helpful comments informed by their expertise in English and/or the law; Cui Xia and Sun Ying from Shanghai Jiao Tong University Press, for the meticulous editing and review of the book. This book would not have been possible without their strenuous efforts.

*Xiang Longwan*

XIANG Longwan

# Contents

# CHAPTER I

# Mission Accepted

## *Surrender of the Japanese*

At 7:00 a.m. on August 15, 1945, China, the United States, the United Kingdom, and the Soviet Union simultaneously issued a statement that Japan officially surrendered unconditionally.

At noon on the same day, a rigid and slightly trembling voice was heard on the radio throughout Tokyo.

> *After pondering deeply, the general trends of the world and the actual conditions obtaining in Our Empire today, we have decided to effect a settlement of the present situation by resorting to an extraordinary measure. We have ordered Our Government to communicate to the Governments of the United States, Great Britain, China and the Soviet Union that Our Empire accepts the provisions of their Joint Declaration.*
>
> *To strive for the common prosperity and happiness of all nations as well as the security and well-being of Our subjects is the solemn obligation which has been handed down by Our Imperial Ancestors and which lies close to Our heart. Indeed, We declared war on America and Britain out of Our sincere desire to ensure Japan's self-preservation and the stabilization of East Asia, it being far from Our thought either to infringe upon the sovereignty of other nations or to embark upon territorial aggrandizement. But now the war has lasted for nearly four years. Despite everyone doing their best- the gallant fighting of the military*

*and naval forces, the diligence and assiduity of Our servants of the State, and the devoted service of Our one hundred million people – the war situation has not developed to Japan's advantage, and the general trends of the world have all turned against her interest. Moreover, the enemy has begun to deploy a new and cruel bomb, whose power will do, incalculable damage, taking the toll of many innocent lives. Should we continue to fight, not only would it result in an ultimate collapse and obliteration of the Japanese nation, but also it would lead to the total extinction of human civilization...* [1]

The breaking news of the Japanese surrender quickly spread to every corner of the world. Journalistic reports from around the world depicted huge celebrations across China and the whole world, where masses of people congregated, decorated the streets, and set off fireworks.

People excitedly spread the news when it was broadcasted repeatedly in China. Streets were crowded with people celebrating with fireworks and decorations from morning until night everywhere across the country. CHIANG Kai-shek delivered a radio speech immediately on August 15: "*We won our war against Japan today. It finally got its proof that justice would triumph over power ultimately.*"

A poet named Ai Qing captured it in Yan'an in his improvised poem *The People's Carnival*: "*This is a great carnival! A triumphant carnival! A liberating carnival!*" New dishes such as the "Bombing Tokyo," the "National Unity," and the "Joy to the World" were introduced by restaurants in Chungking, showing the true feelings of Chinese people at that time. After the Mukden Incident in 1931, China was almost a hell on earth under the invasion of Japanese fascists; cities were bombed, villages were burned, and people were tyrannized and slaughtered. However, Chinese soldiers and civilians never yielded, vowing to "Let our flesh and blood forge our new Great Wall!" With huge national sacrifices, the Chinese people supported the main battlefield of the East in World War II and contributed to the victory of the Anti-Fascist War in the world. How could victory not be celebrated?

However, people in Tokyo had a different response. When they heard the Emperor's speech would be broadcast, they flocked to the square outside the imperial palace. As the Emperor was considered a deity, most people had never heard his voice, and they did not entirely understand his use of ancient Japanese.

"*Is it really his Majesty's voice?*" "*Did he really admit defeat? Did Japan surrender?*" People were confused.

"*The Empire of Japan is invincible!*" "*His Majesty said, 'to end the war' instead of 'surrender'!*" Those who opposed surrender refused to admit failure, but more people were thinking in silence. Didn't his Majesty admit to "accept the provisions of the *Joint Declaration*" in the edict? The *Joint Declaration* refers to the "*Potsdam Proclamation*" signed by the heads of China, the United States, and Great Britain on July 26, where in article 13th, Japan was urged to surrender unconditionally: "We call upon the government of Japan to proclaim now the unconditional surrender of all Japanese armed forces, and to provide proper and adequate assurances of their good faith in such action. The alternative for Japan is prompt and utter destruction."[2]

However, those words fell on deaf ears of the Japanese policymakers. On July 28, the government of Japan refused to accept the *Potsdam Proclamation* officially and vowed that their military would conduct special operations in Japan, threatening to fight to the last person. On the same day, U.S. President Truman learned this news from the radio and finally decided to drop atomic bombs on Japan to end the war quickly.

"*If Japan had surrendered earlier, there would have been no atomic bombs! What had his Majesty done?*" This was the accusation from the Japanese people.

However, intransigents brainwashed by militarism were still stubbornly fighting. The pro-war contingent in the Japanese government was still clamoring to "continue the war." In fact, the Emperor recorded the edict in advance on August 14. Some radical young Japanese military officers broke into the imperial palace, searched for the recording, and destroyed it late that night. What's worse, they killed Lieutenant General MORI Takesi, commander of the Guards Divisions, who was unwilling to join them in mobilizing the army to initiate a rebellion in his name. The rebels occupied the radio station, and the residences of Japanese Prime Minister SUZUKI Kantaro, Minister KIDO Koichi, and former Prime Minister HIRANUMA Kiichiro were also attacked before dawn on August 15. Many diehards expressed their fanaticism, disappointment, and resentment with extreme methods such as hara-kiri when the rebellion was put down later.

The diehards included not only fanatical young officers but also commanders. The representative was ANAMI Korechika, who served as the War Minister in the cabinet of SUZUKI Kantaro in April 1945. He was defeated by General Xue Yue in the Battle of Changsha and fled away. In the month when he took office as the War Minister, the Japanese "Kamikaze" suicide planes attacked more than 2,500 times, sinking more than 40 U.S. ships, including aircraft carriers in the Pacific War. He refused the *Potsdam Proclamation* and advocated again for a "local showdown" when Allied forces attacked the border. Not wanting to hear the Emperor's edict of defeat, he committed hara-kiri at his home in the early morning of August 15. According to the statistics, from ANAMI Korechika to low-ranking officers and soldiers, more than 200 people committed suicide by hara-kiri before and after hearing the surrender edict. However, compared to "fighting to the last person" advocated by the war maniacs, this number is minimal.

The Japanese surrender ceremony was held at 9 a.m. on September 2 on USS Missouri, anchored in Tokyo Bay. The Japanese *Instrument of Surrender* reads clearly: "We hereby proclaim the unconditional surrender to the Allied Powers of the Japanese Imperial General Headquarters and of all Japanese Armed Forces and all Armed Forces under Japanese control wherever situated."

The government of Japan said clearly their acceptance of the terms and conditions of the *Potsdam Proclamation* in the *Instrument of Surrender*:

> *"We hereby undertake for the Emperor, the Japanese Government, and their successors to carry out the provisions of the Potsdam Declaration in good faith and to issue whatever orders and take whatever action may be required by the Supreme Commander for the Allied Powers or by any other designated representative of the Allied Powers for the purpose of giving effect to that declaration."*

At the end of the *Instrument of Surrender*, it says, "*The authority of the Emperor and the Japanese Government to rule the State shall be subject to the Supreme Commander for the Allied Powers, who will take such steps as he deems proper to effectuate these terms of surrender.*"[3]

MAMORU Shigemitsu, Japan's new Minister of Foreign Affairs, was the first to sign the *Instrument of Surrender* on behalf of the Japanese government. Then UMEZU Yoshijiro, Chief of the Army General Staff, signed on behalf of the Japanese Imperial General Headquarters. After that, Admiral MacArthur, Supreme Commander for the Allied Powers, American Admiral Chester William Nimitz, Chinese Admiral HSU Yung-chang (Xu Yongchang), English Admiral Bruce Fraser, Soviet Union's Lieutenant Admiral Kuzma Derevyanko, and representatives of Australia, Canada, France, the Netherlands, and New Zealand signed in that respective order. Thousands of U.S. military planes celebrating the victory flew by Tokyo Bay when MAMORU Shigemitsu, whose leg had been badly hurt in Shanghai 13 years ago, limped off USS Missouri. This day is the official end date of the Second World War. September 3 is the "Victory of the World Anti-Fascist War Day" for many countries, including China and the United States.

An impressive parade lasted from noon to night after the news of the victory reached Chungking. CHIANG Kai-shek invited MAO Tse-tung (Mao Zedong) to conduct an important negotiation at that time. On September 3, *Jiefang Daily* in Yan'an reported the good news on the front page with the title "Japanese Invaders Signed the *Instrument of Surrender*" and published the news from Xinhua News Agency:

"*September 2, Xinhua News Agency, Chungking:*

*Japan officially surrendered on September 2. Mr. CHIANG Kai-shek, Chairman of the National Government of the Republic of China, hosted a banquet at his official residence for Chairman MAO, CHOU En-lai* (Zhou Enlai), *and WANG Jo-fei* (Wang Ruofei) *at 8:30 p.m. on the day. SUN Ko* (SUN Ke), *FENG Yu-hsiang* (Feng Yuxiang), *Wu Tieh-cheng* (Wu Tiecheng), *HSIUNG Shih-hui* (Xiong Shihui), *CHANG Po-ling* (Zhang Boling), *MO Te-hui* (MO Dehui), *CHIANG Jung* (Jiang Yong), *WANG Yun-wu* (Wang Yunwu), *CHANG Chun* (Zhang Qun), *TSO Shun-sheng* (Zuo Shunsheng), *FU Szu-nien* (Fu Sinian), *LENG Chueh* (Leng Jue), *HUANG Yen-pei* (Huang Yanpei), *SHAO Li-tzu* (Shao Lizi), *WU Ting-chang* (Wu Dingchang), *WANG Shih-chieh* (Wang Shijie), *CHANG Chih-chung* (Zhang Zhizhong), *CHEN Li-fu, KAN Nai-kuang* (Gan Naiguang), *WU Kuo-chen* (Wu Guozhen), *CHOU Chih-jou* (Zhou Zhirou), *LEI Chen* (Lei Zhen), *PAI Chung-his* (Bai Chongxi), *WENG Wen-hao, HSU Hsiao-yen* (Xu Xiaoyan), *etc., were also there. Mr. CHIANG Kai-shek said at the banquet: "Today is the day of the Japanese surrender. I am very happy to have Mr. MAO Tse-tung here to celebrate the victory together." Chairman MAO expressed his gratitude to Mr. CHIANG for his hospitality, and then they celebrated the victory together.*"

Chairman MAO gladly inscribed for *Xinhua Daily* published that day:

*Celebration of the victory of the War of Resistance against Japan and liberation of the Chinese nation!*

Since then, several Japanese surrender ceremonies had been held in various parts of Asia and the Pacific. On August 21, eight people, including IMAI Takeo, Vice-Chief of the General Staff of the China Expeditionary Army, were sent to Zhijiang, Hunan Province, to confirm the surrender details. The Japanese surrender ceremony in the China Theater was held in the old auditorium of R.O.C. Military Academy in Nanking on the morning of September 9. OKAMURA Yasuji, commander-in-chief of the China Expeditionary Army, signed the instrument of surrender and handed over his personal sword, indicating that the Japanese invaders surrendered to China officially. General HO Ying-chin (HE Yingqin), Commander-in-chief of the Chinese Army, accepted the instrument of surrender submitted by KOBAYASHI Asasaburo, Chief of Staff of the China Expeditionary Army, in the auditorium of the Command Headquarters in Nanking.

The Japanese surrendered! And it will be remembered forever. President XI Jinping of the People's Republic of China mentioned it again at the military parade seventy years later on September 3, 2015:

> *Seventy years ago today, the Chinese people, having fought tenaciously for 14 years, won the great victory of our War of Resistance Against Japanese Aggression, marking the full victory of the World Anti-Fascist War. On that day, the world was once again blessed by the sunshine of peace. Let us bear in mind the great truth of history: Justice will prevail! Peace will prevail! The people will prevail!*

## *Lessons from History*

In the Second World War, the Fascist Axis had brought unprecedented disasters to mankind. How should we deal with the culprits who launched the war of aggression? How should the executioners who plunged people into misery and suffering be punished?

Looking back at history, the leaders of a defeated country had never been punished or tried by the court before the establishment of IMTFE, even if they were culpable for launching wars of aggression. No head of state was killed or imprisoned after defeat, even though Napoleon Bonaparte was exiled to St. Helena with life imprisonment. None of them has been tried by any international or domestic court.

As for weaker countries, they had to cede territory and pay compensation if they suffered a defeat even though they fought against the aggression. The aggressors dared not attend the trial because they were in the wrong.

Take modern China as an example. The *Treaty of Shimonoseki* was signed between Japan and the Qing Empire of China in 1895. China was forced to concede much in the way of territory, including the Liaodong Peninsula (The government "redeemed" it with 30 million taels of silver later.), Taiwan and the Penghu Islands, as well 200 million taels of silver.

The *Boxer Protocol* was signed by the Qing government and the Eight-Nation Alliance in 1901. China was forced to pay 450 million taels of fine silver as indemnity to the eight nations involved, and Japan got 7.73% of it. Moreover, there were other clauses, such as the destruction of Taku Forts. Chinese would not have the right to reside in the Legation Quarters. China would concede the right and power to station troops in 12 strategic places. Boxer and Government officials were to be punished for crimes or attempted crimes against the foreign Governments or their nationals. These unequal treaties were the "Victor's justice" of the great powers to China. This is not civilized justice.

After the end of the First World War, people had imagined that the German head of state and high-ranking officials who started the war would be tried by an international tribunal, and the call for "hanging Kaiser Wilhelm II" once pervaded Europe. However, due to the friction and suspicion among some countries, especially after the October Revolution victory in Russia, countries such as Britain and France had turned most of their attention to the issue of how to deal with the Soviet Union. In addition, the German government didn't want to extradite war criminals and hand them over to the international tribunal, which made the provisions of the *Treaty of Versailles* to punish William II and other major war criminals exist only in name. In the end, the international tribunal was not organized successfully, and the Allied Powers, as the victors, handed over the trial to the German government.

The German government, which overtly agreed but covertly opposed, delayed the trial in Leipzig until two and a half years after the end of the war. The number of important war criminals proposed by the Allies was reduced by Germany from 896 to 45. Only 12 were tried of the 45, and of that number, only six were convicted. Their sentences ranged from six months to four years, which was really exiguous. Two of the prisoners even escaped from prison. Therefore, the final result of the Leipzig Trial showed that only minor punishments were given to four minor war criminals. Unexpectedly, General Karl Stenger, who killed many wounded and sick prisoners, was acquitted. On July 8, 1921, *The New York Times* reported it. "People cheered when General Stenger was acquitted and released while the four Frenchmen who participated in the trial on behalf of the French government were insulted."[4] As for Wilhelm II, he fled to the Netherlands a long time ago, and the government of the Netherlands refused to extradite him on the grounds of its own laws and traditions. In this way, the one who should be held responsible for the war was never punished, and the Leipzig Trial became a farce.

Lessons learned from the First World War, as early as two years before the Japanese surrender, that is, in late November 1943, CHIANG Kai-shek (Jiang Jieshi) of China, Franklin D. Roosevelt of the United States, and Winston Churchill of the United Kingdom met in Cairo, Egypt, to discuss the tactics against Japan and its punishment after the war. On December 1 of the same year, the *Cairo Declaration* was issued in Chungking, Washington, and London, respectively. The main content was that China, the United States, and the United Kingdom pledged themselves to persevere in the prolonged operations necessary to procure the unconditional surrender of Japan. Japan should give back all islands occupied in the region of the Pacific Ocean since World War I. Following the war, Northeast China, Taiwan, and the Penghu Islands would be returned to China, and Korea would gain independence. The *Cairo Declaration* specifically pointed out that "The Three Great Allies were fighting this war to restrain and punish the aggression of Japan. They coveted no gain for themselves and have no thought of territorial expansion."[5]

The *Cairo Declaration* showed that the determination of anti-fascist allies to defeat Japan boosted people's morale in the anti-fascist war and frustrated the aggression of Japanese invaders. It has become one of the international laws that all relevant countries should follow after the war.

Then *Potsdam Proclamation* was issued by U.S. President Harry S. Truman, British Prime Minister Winston Churchill, whose place was taken by Clement Richard Attlee later, and Soviet leader Stalin after they held a meeting in Potsdam, Germany on July 26, 1945. CHIANG Kai-shek signed with the heads of the United States and the United Kingdom together, although he did not attend the meeting. The Soviet Union did not sign it at first because it had not declared war on Japan. It was not until August 8 that Stalin's name was added to the *Potsdam Proclamation*.

The *Potsdam Proclamation* is a continuation of the *Cairo Declaration*. It declared that China, the United States, and the United Kingdom would work together to defeat the Japanese after the victory over Germany. It involved the implementation of the *Cairo Declaration* and other decisions on how to punish the Japanese after the war.

There are 13 articles in the proclamation. In addition to Article 13 cited before, Article 10 specifically states that "*We do not intend that the Japanese shall be enslaved as a race or destroyed as a nation, but stern justice shall be meted out to all war criminals, including those who have visited cruelties upon our prisoners.*"[6]

## *Arrest of the War Criminals*

Four groups of suspects were arrested by the Allies from September to December 1945.[7]

The first warrant was issued on September 11. Twenty-seven out of a total of 39 suspects were Japanese. The first one was the former Japanese Prime Minister TOJO Hideki, one of the three fascist heads on par with Benito Amilcare, Andrea Mussolini, and Adolf Hitler. Many former high-ranking officials were also arrested, including the Minister of Foreign Affairs TOGO Shigenori, the Minister of the Navy SHIMADA Shigetaro, the Minister of Finance KAYA Okinori, and the Minister of Commerce and Vice Minister of Munitions KISHI Nobusuke. KISHI Nobusuke was an "old acquaintance" of the Chinese people. In the Japanese puppet state Manchukuo in Northeast China, he was one of the five Japanese officials in power and was known as the "Monster of Manchuria."

Moreover, there were military officers and spies who committed many crimes in various parts of the Asia-Pacific region, such as DOIHARA Kenji, who had been engaged in spy activities in China for a long time, HASHIMOTO Kingoro, who advocated fascist theories and was the initiator of the secret society "Sakurakai" (Cherry Blossom Society), and HONMA Masaharu, a lieutenant general who commanded the Japanese 14th Army to invade the Philippines. Additionally, there were 12 non-Japanese who served the Japanese government during the war. Among the 27 Japanese suspects, except for two who had committed suicide, the remaining 25 were either arrested by the Allies or turned themselves in.

TOJO Hideki's arrest was undoubtedly the most dramatic. He knew that he would be subjected to severe punishment after Japan's surrender, so he locked himself in a small room and hovered between life and death all day long until the Allies arrived in Japan.

During TOJO's tenure as the Minister of War, he set a rule of "never be humiliated as prisoners." Many Japanese soldiers brainwashed by the "Bushido" would rather commit suicide than surrender. In the Battle of Midway in 1942, the Battle of Saipan in 1944, and the Battle of Iwo Jima in 1945, those Japanese soldiers fought fervently at an absolute disadvantage but were rarely captured. Now it was TOJO's turn to choose between life and death; he knew he would be laughed at if he cravenly clung to life, but he was not brave enough to commit suicide. He didn't make his decision until the military police of the Allies surrounded his house. Left-handed TOJO picked up a pistol with his right hand and shot himself on the left side of his chest, missing his heart but leaving him drenched in blood. The U.S. military police immediately sent him to the hospital, and a U.S. soldier even gave him a blood transfusion to rescue him. As one of the three biggest culprits in the world, he must be alive to stand trial. He had to be brought to justice.

The second warrant was issued on November 19, 1945. Eleven Japanese war criminals were mentioned this time, including ARAKI Sadao, an extreme militarist who served as the Minister of the War and the Minister of Education, HONJO Shigeru, the commander of the Kwantung Army and the one who was responsible for the Mukden Incident, MINAMI Jiro, Minister of the War during the Mukden Incident, MATSUI Iwane, Japanese commander during the Nanking Massacre, KOISO Kuniaki who advocated Japan's invasion, MATSUOKA Yosuke, Minister of Foreign Affairs who signed the alliance among Germany, Japan, and Italy. Nine of these eleven suspects turned themselves in except for HONJO Shigeru, who had committed suicide, and MATSUOKA Yosuke, who had been seriously ill.

The third warrant was issued on December 2, 1945, and a total of 59 suspects were arrested this time. In addition to high-ranking officials in political and military circles, such as the former Prime Ministers HIROTA Koki and HIRANUMA Kiichiro, the Chief Cabinet Secretary HOSHINO Naoki was also one of the five real powers in the puppet state of the Empire of Manchuria, the Chief of the Military Affairs Bureau SATO Kenryo, the commander of the North China Area TADA Hayao, the commanders-in-chief of the China Expeditionary Army HATA Shunroku and NISHIO Toshizo, and the Second Deputy Chief of Army General Staff of the Kwantung Army HATA Hikosaburo; it also included some Japanese financial and industrial magnates who supported the invasive war, such as the president of the Manchurian Industrial Development Company AIKAWA Gisuke and the Mitsubishi Heavy Industries President GOKO Kiyoshi. There were also individuals or media workers enthusiastic about militarism, such as the "Japanese Goebbels" OKAWA Shumei, the *Hochi Shimbun* president OTA Masataka, and the *Asahi Shimbun* vice president SHIMOMURA Hiroshi. Several relatives of the emperor were also on the arrest list.

The fourth warrant was issued on December 6, 1945. This was the last arrest of nine major Japanese war criminals. Among them were two important personnel in Japanese politics. One was the nobleman KONOYE Fumimaro who served as Prime Minister three times. He presided over the Japanese invasion of China in 1937. Another was also a nobleman, Marquis KIDO Koichi, a close associate of the Emperor. He had served successively as the Minister of Education, the chief secretary of the Home Ministry, the Minister of Health and Welfare, the Home Minister in the Cabinet, and the chairperson of the Council of Ministers. He was the bridge between the Cabinet and the Japanese Emperor.

## *Creation of the Tribunal*

A tribunal to try them was under preparation while those war criminals were arrested. On December 26, 1945, the foreign ministers of the Soviet Union, the United States, and the United Kingdom held a meeting in Moscow. They passed a resolution stating that the supreme commander of the Allies in Japan should take all measures to acknowledge a Japanese surrender and to implement provisions for occupying and controlling Japan. This resolution was also approved by the Chinese government afterward.

Immediately after the Moscow Conference, the establishment of the Far Eastern Commission in Washington was announced. According to the Commission, the powers that be were to make policy recommendations to the U.S. government in enforcing the provisions of the instrument of surrender. On January 19, 1946, in accordance with the resolution of the Moscow Conference, a special proclamation was issued by the Supreme Commander of the Allied Powers for the establishment of an International Military Tribunal for the Far East, stating that *"There shall be established an International Military Tribunal for the Far East for the trial of those persons charged individually, or as members of organizations, or in both capacities, with offenses which include crimes against peace."*

On the same day, General MacArthur approved the *Charter of the International Military Tribunal for the Far East* with 17 articles in 5 sections, which was the basic legal provision of the Tokyo Trial. It clearly stated the tribunal mechanism and jurisdiction and established litigation procedures based on the Common Law.

This way, the Tokyo Trial, which had attracted worldwide attention, was almost ready to begin. Those Chinese soldiers and civilians who made tremendous sacrifices and significant contributions to the victory of the anti-fascist war and all the Chinese people sincerely hoped to see the war criminals brought to justice. In fact, preparations for the trial of the Japanese war criminals had already begun.

The President of the International Military Tribunal for the Far East, Sir William Flood Webb, was also the president of the Queensland Court of Australia. In 1943, he was the chairman of the Japanese War Crimes Investigation Commission in Australia. The attorney general of the tribunal was Judge Joseph B. Keenan, who was the United States Assistant Attorney General. He had been appointed as the head of the legal advisory group to search for Japanese war criminals. He was also the director of the International Prosecution Section before the tribunal's establishment.

Representatives of the Allied Powers were recommended by their governments and approved by General MacArthur.

In 1945, Mr. WEI Tao-ming (Wei Daoming), the Ambassador of the National Government to the United States, telegraphed the Ministry of Foreign Affairs at Chungking:

> *I received a letter from the U.S. Department of State regarding establishing the International Tribunal for the trial of the Far East war criminals. The commander-in-chief of the allied forces requests all the countries concerned to recommend suitable personnel for selection. The U.S. government invites China, Britain, and the Soviet Union each to recommend five people, and Australia, Canada, France, the Netherlands, and New Zealand each to recommend three. It hopes that there will be civil officials among them and that the recommended civil and military officials had better be proficient in English.*[8]

Upon receiving the telegram, the Ministry of Foreign Affairs immediately issued a document to the departments concerning the request for the recommendation of candidates to Japan. On November 9, Military Orders Minister (MOM)

HO Cheng-chun (HE Chengjun) wrote to Foreign Minister WANG Shih-chieh recommending LU Chieh (LU Jie), Supervisor from the Yunnan-Myanmar Railway Department of Military Law Supervision, and SHI Yu-sung (SHI Yushong), Second Secretary. On November 15, the Ministry of Justice and Administration wrote to the Ministry of Foreign Affairs recommending HSIANG Che-chun (XIANG Zhejun) and NYI, Judson T.Y. (NI Zhengyu). Later, the Ministry of Military Orders also recommended LIU Fang-chu (LIU Fangju). The Ministry of Foreign Affairs conducted a preliminary examination of the five candidates and found that their overall qualifications were not satisfactory. It recommended three well-known jurists, WU Ching-hsiung (WU Jingxiong), YEN Shu-tang (YAN Shutang), and MEI Ju-ao (Mei Ruao), in addition to the five candidates already recommended.

In accordance with the request for recommending five candidates, the Ministry of Foreign Affairs selected five from the eight recommended list of candidates, namely MEI Ju-ao, HSIANG Che-chun, NYI, Judson T.Y., LIU Fang-chu, and Lu Chieh. Foreign Minister WANG Shih-chieh submitted the selection report to CHIANG Kai-shek, Chairman of the National Government, on November 29.

As the Second World War had just ended and many countries were facing hardships in rebuilding their war-torn land, the progress of the selection was very slow. In order to set up a court to try Japanese Class A war criminals as soon as possible, the Allies' headquarters requested that all the concerned countries should send one or two representatives first. In early December, the Ministry of Foreign Affairs once again submitted the selection report to CHIANG Kai-shek: "*After considering the people recommended by the Ministry of Justice and Administration, the Ministry of Military Orders, the Ministry of Military Law Supervision, and other functional departments, we have selected Hsiang Che-chun and MEI Ju-ao as our country's representatives.*"[9]

CHIANG Kai-shek finally decided on HSIANG Che-chun and MEI Ju-ao. On December 8, the Executive Yuan replied to the Ministry of Foreign Affairs on his behalf:

*Dear Foreign Minister Wang Shih-chieh,*

*I have received and read the brief document and its attachment submitted on December 7. Regarding the proposed selection of HSIANG Che-chun and MEI Ju-*

*ao as our country's representatives to the International Tribunal for the Far East, I approve the proposal, and the Executive Yuan will act accordingly.*

*Sincerely,*
*CHANG Kai-shek*[10]

HSIANG Che-chun (1892–1987), Ming Si (courtesy name), was born in Ningxiang, Hunan Province, in 1892. MEI Ju-ao (1904–1973), Ya Hsuan (courtesy name), was born in 1904 in Nanchang, Jiangxi Province. Because of the *Boxer Protocol*, both of them had studied at the former Tsinghua University and then went on to prestigious American universities for further studies. After getting a Bachelor of Arts degree from Yale University, HSIANG Che-chun entered Yale Law School and then transferred to George Washington University to obtain a Bachelor of Laws degree. He was the president of the World Student Union of Yale University. During the May Fourth Movement, CHA Liang-chao (Zha Liangzhao) was selected as the representative of Chinese students. They held a meeting with compatriots in the United States to oppose Japan's unreasonable demands to occupy Shandong Province. He also served as a secretary of eight Chinese organizations at the Washington Naval Conference in 1920. MEI Ju-ao received a Bachelor of Arts degree from Stanford University and a Doctor of Laws degree from the University of Chicago. During his stay in the United States, he and his fellow students SHIH Huang (Shi Huang), CHI Chao-ting (Ji Chaoding), HSU Yung- Ying (Xu Yongying), etc., initiated a society to study the Three Principles of the People to support the National Revolutionary Army in the First Chinese Revolutionary Civil War and promoted the revolution in China.

Both of them had taught at universities after returning to China. HSIANG Che-chun had taught at Peking University, Beijing Jiaotong University, Beijing Hosei University, and National Central University successively before participating in the Tokyo Trial. MEI Ju-ao had taught at Shanxi University, Nankai University, Wuhan University, and Fudan University successively. After transferring to the judicial field, HSIANG Che-chun served successively as the Secretary of the Ministry of Justice and Ministry of Foreign Affairs, the President of District Court in Wu County, Suzhou City, the Chief Prosecutor of Shanghai First Special Zone District Court, the Secretary of Supreme Council of National Defense, the

Chief Prosecutor of Hunan and Guangdong Division of the High Court and the Chief Prosecutor of Shanghai High Court. While MEI Ju-ao devoted himself to teaching and legal research, he published more than twenty law papers and five academic monographs after returning to China from the Tokyo Trial. He had served as a legislator of the National Government of the Republic of China for a long time. He acted as the chairman of the Foreign Affairs Committee of the Legislative Yuan since 1934.

CHOU Fang (ZHOU Fang), HSIANG Che-chun's wife, was still in her rural hometown in Hunan Province when the Chinese delegation was organized. She wrote a book called *A Good Mentor and Good Husband* in her later years to recall HSIANG Che-chun's life, and the organization of the delegation was mentioned in it as well. "*I received a letter from Ming Si shortly before leaving my hometown, knowing that he had been sent by the government to the newly established International Military Tribunal for the Far East in Tokyo, Japan, to serve as the Chinese prosecutor to try the Japanese Class A war criminals who had invaded China. According to the structure of the court, each of the eleven allied countries should send one judge and one prosecutor. Ming Si was recommended to CHIANG Kai-shek by Mr. WANG Chung-hui* (WANG Chonghui)."[11]

The Ministry of Foreign Affairs sent a telegram to Ambassador WEI Tao-ming concerning the decision of the Chinese government on December 10th: "*We have designated HSIANG Che-chun and MEI Ju-ao as representatives of China at the International Military Tribunal for the Far East. HSIANG Che-chun is the chief prosecutor of the Shanghai High Court. MEI Ju-ao is a legislator and the acting chairman of the Foreign Affairs Committee of the Legislative Yuan. Please inform this the United States.*"[12]

Minister HSIEH Kuan-sheng (Xie Guansheng) of the Ministry of Justice and Administration wired HSIANG Che-chun the appointment on December 29:

> *Dear Che-chun, chief prosecutor of Shanghai High Court on North Zhejiang Road, we have designated Mr. MEI Ju-ao and you as representatives of China at the International Military Tribunal for the Far East in Japan. The United States had been informed that you would serve as the prosecutor and Mr. MEI the judge. You are urged to go to Japan to assist the U.S. Attorney General prepare everything as soon as possible. Please come to Chungking within a week for discussion.*[13]

Deputy Minister of Foreign Affairs KAN Nai-kuang wired MEI Ju-ao on the same day, informing him of the appointment:

*Dear Ju-ao, you have been designated as the representative of China at the International Military Tribunal for the Far East, and Director SUN Ko of the Executive Yuan has already approved it. Ambassador Wei wired us on the matter that was informed to the United States. Therefore, please do not refuse any more, and come to Chungking as soon as possible to discuss the matter with Director SUN.*[14]

Minister WANG Shih-chieh wired Ambassador WEI Tao-ming once again on January 3, 1946:

*HSIANG Che-chun will be the prosecutor, and MEI Ju-ao will be the judge. Mr. HSIANG will go to Japan immediately, and Mr. MEI will go when the tribunal is ready. Please inform the Department of State of the U.S. and Douglas MacArthur for their entry to be granted.*

The International Military Tribunal for the Far East was initially composed of nine allied countries. In the order they signed on the Japanese surrender instrument, they were the United States, China, Britain, Soviet Union, Australia, Canada, France, the Netherlands, and New Zealand. The Philippines and India were added at the request of the United States and Britain later. Every eleven Allies recommended one judge and one prosecutor. The list is as follows:

**Judges:**
President William Flood Webb (Australia)
John Patrick Higgins, Myron C. Cramer later (U.S.A.)
MEI Ju-ao (China)
Lord William Donald Patrick (Britain)
I. M. Zaryanov (Soviet Union)
Edward Stuart McDougall (Canada)
Henry Bernard (France)
Bernard Victor A. Roling (Netherlands)
Sir Erima Harvey Northcroft (New Zealand)
Radhabinod Pal (India)
Delfin J. Jaranilla (Philippines)

**Prosecutors:**
Chief Prosecutor: Joseph Berry Keenan (U.S.A.)
Associate Prosecutors:
HSIANG Che-chun (China)
Arthur Strettell Comyns Carr (Britain)
Sergei A. Golunsky (Soviet Union)
Sir Alan James Mansfield (Australia)
Henry Grattan Nolan (Canada)
Oneto (Robert L. Oneto) (France)
W. G. Frederick Borgerhoff-Mulder (Netherlands)
Ronald Henry Quilliam (New Zealand)
Panampilly Govinda Menon (India)
Pedro Lopez (Philippines)

## *A Team from China*

According to the International Tribunal, the prosecution should be carried out first, and then the penalty amount. After HSIANG Che-chun was designated as the prosecutor, the top priority was to find a secretary who was proficient in law and English. HSIANG Che-chun asked LIU Shih-fang (Liu Shifang), one of his classmates from Yale University, for help. LIU Shih-fang was a professor at the Law School of Soochow University, and he immediately recommended his student Henry CHIU (QIU Shaoheng).

Henry CHIU (1913–2009), a native of Wuxi, Jiangsu Province, was born in 1913. He was admitted to the Shanghai Conservatory of Music, founded by T.S.A.I. Yuen-pei (CAI Yuanpei) in 1931, and HO Lu-ting (He Luting) was one of his classmates. He was transferred to Soochow University a year and a half later and received his bachelor's degree in Chinese and law in 1935. During the Anti-Japanese War, he was invited by one of his friends Fu Lei to litigate with a Swiss businessman in the Swiss consular court and won the lawsuit with his profound knowledge of law and fluency in English.

Henry CHIU did not want to be an official, so he politely declined at first. Then LIU Shifang invited him to his home to have a heart-to-heart talk. He said to his beloved student: "*I know you well, and I am not recommending you to be an official. I just think that you are good at comparative jurisprudence. If you want to accomplish something, you shouldn't be confined to Shanghai. If you accept the offer, on the one hand, you can make some contributions to the country and the nation. On the other hand, the International Military Tribunal for the Far East is an unprecedented one with a group of world-class legal experts being there. How can you throw away this chance of a lifetime?*"[15] Henry CHIU was deeply moved by his mentor's words and finally took the responsibility of trying the culprits of the war on behalf of the country.

With the approval of the Ministry of Foreign Affairs, Henry CHIU was chosen by HSIANG Che-chun as the first secretary of the Chinese prosecutor. He became one of the assistant prosecutors of the International Military Tribunal for the Far East.

HSIANG Che-chun and Henry CHIU arrived in Tokyo on a plane provided by the U.S. Air Force on February 7. On February 9 HSIANG Che-chun sent a wire in English to Minister WANG Shih-chieh from Tokyo stating they had arrived in Tokyo on the 7th and had met with Prosecutor Joseph Berry Keenan on the 8th.[16]

Later, FANG Fu-shu (1914–1976), a graduate of Soochow University Law School, was added to the team by the Ministry of Foreign Affairs as a secretary of the Chinese judge. FANG F.S., a native of Beijing, was born in 1913. He graduated from Soochow University Law School in 1935. He often spoke up for his compatriots and gained a high reputation during his tenure as a representative lawyer of the Legal Department of the Municipal Council of Shanghai.

Judge MEI Ju-ao arrived in Tokyo on a U.S. military aircraft on March 20, 1946, and his Secretary FANG F.S. arrived on April 10th.

The top priority was to enlarge the team because Henry CHIU was the only assistant to the Chinese prosecutor. Although the Ministry of Foreign Affairs later assigned LUO Chi-i (Luo Jiyi 1896–1976), who was a graduate of Tsinghua University and the deputy consul of China in Yokohama at the time, as the judge's secretary, the prosecutor, and the judge should work separately according to the charter of the tribunal. Therefore, the Ministry of Foreign Affairs immediately designated LIU Tzu Chien (LIU Zijian), who graduated from the Department of Political Science of Yenching University as another secretary at HSIANG Che-chun's request.

LIU T.C. (1919–1993), a native of Guiyang, Guizhou Province, was born in 1919. He was admitted to Tsinghua University at first and then transferred to the Department of Political Science of Yenching University after the Japanese occupied Peiping and Tsinghua University, then later moved to Changsha. He was suspected of engaging in resistance and arrested for a while after the outbreak of the Pacific War. He was outstanding in academic performance and proficient in Japanese.

The Ministry of Foreign Affairs sent CHU Tsing-Ju (ZHU Qingru) to Tokyo as another secretary assigned to HSIANG Che-chun in June of the same year.

Translators were urgently needed because a large amount of evidence and testimony had to be translated from Chinese to English since the working languages of the tribunal were English and Japanese. With the consent of the Allied Headquarters, HSIANG Che-chun took the opportunity to collect evidence in China and go to Shanghai to recruit translators in April 1946. One of the candidates was KAW Vung-ping (GAO Wenbin 1922–2020), who graduated from Soochow University Law School in 1945. KAW Vung-ping was both excellent in character and study, especially in English. In his graduation album, one of his classmates said, "He is proficient in English. He could recite the whole book of *The Life of Samuel Johnson* after a few days' reading."

Such a brilliant student was hired immediately, of course. KAW Vung-ping mentioned this in his later years:

> *"I was honored to meet Mr. HSIANG just before the Tokyo Trial started sixty-three years ago. At that time, Mr. HSIANG, as the Chinese prosecutor in one of the eleven allied countries, was entrusted by the International Prosecution Section to recruit people who knew the law and were proficient in English as translators. I just graduated from Soochow University in July 1945, and my teacher, Professor LIU Shih-fang, recommended me for the job. I went to Huamao Apartment (now Jin Jiang Hotel) to participate in the interview one day in April 1946, and the chief interviewer was Mr. HSIANG Che-chun. Mr. HSIANG was very kind and scholarly. He extracted a paragraph from Shun Pao for me to translate into English at his request. He asked about my family and school and handed me a cup of coffee. I had an advantage because Soochow University Law School was the only one in China at that time to teach Anglo-American law systematically. I received a call a few days later from Mr. HSIANG, saying that I was hired."*[17]

A total of five translators were hired at that time and were all talents like KAW Vung-ping. The oldest was Chou Hsih-ching (Zhou Xiqing 1915–2004), formerly known as Chou Shih-cheng, a native of Ningxiang, Hunan Province, born in 1914. His father was CHOU Chen-lin (Zhou Zhenlin), a veteran of the Revolution of 1911 who graduated from the Management Department of Shanghai Jiao Tong University in 1936 and received a master's degree in economics from the University of Pennsylvania in 1938. He disclosed to the Chinese government the determination of the overseas students to fight to the end at the New York memorial on the first anniversary of the Lugouqiao Incident on July 7, 1938. Then he returned to China and devoted himself to the fight against Japan in August of the same year. He served as the deputy head of the group of Hunan Anti-Japanese War Committee, the secretary of the Changsha Administrative Office, the commissioner of the Hunan government, and the manager of *Guomin Daily* successively. In addition, he served as the mayor of Guidong County, Hanshou County, and Xiangxiang County successively after 1940, raising funds and soliciting food, as well as organizing teams to support the frontline. He also served as the commander of the self-defense regiment to cooperate with the official troops and contain the enemy until the victory of our Anti-Japanese War. With a desperate need for talent, HSIANG Che-chun hired him even though he was CHOU Fang's younger brother.

Another translator was CHANG Pei-chi (Zhang Peiji 1921–2021), a native of Fuzhou, Fujian Province, born in 1921. He graduated from the Department of English Literature at St. John's University in Shanghai in 1945. In the same year, he served as an English reporter for the *Shanghai Herald*, a special writer for the English version of *The China Critic,* and the deputy editor-in-chief of the *China Yearbook (English)*.

The other two were also talents who graduated from Soochow University. One was LIU Chi-sheng (Liu Jisheng 1920–?), Liu Shih-fang's nephew. He graduated from Soochow University Law School in Chungking in 1944.

CHENG Lu-ta (Zheng Luda 1916–1993), another translator, was a native of Shantou, Guangdong Province, born in 1918. He graduated from Soochow University Law School in Shanghai in 1945, and he was a classmate of KAW Vung-ping. One of his classmates praised him in the yearbook: "*He is bold, resolute, persevering, calm, organized, and proficient in English.*"

Henry CHIU resigned due to illness and returned to China in the early 1947s. With the approval of the Ministry of Foreign Affairs, KAW Vung-ping became HSIANG Che-chun's last secretary. He wrote about the hard work of the translation team in Tokyo in his later years:

*"We arrived in Tokyo by a military transport plane from Shanghai Jiangwan Airport on May 10 or so and began to translate Chinese testimony into English immediately. Our salary was paid by the International Prosecution Section (IPS). The translators were divided into 12 grades according to their competence. Among the five of us, Chou Hsih-ching was in grade 7, the highest. Chang Pei-chih was in grade 6, and Mr. Liu, Mr. Cheng, and I were in grade 5. The Tokyo Trial was arranged according to the sequence of the Japanese invasion. Their invasion of China was the earliest, from the Kwantung Army's assassination of CHANG Tso-lin (Huanggutun Incident) in 1928 to the September 18 Incident, the establishment of the Japanese puppet state Manchukuo in Northeast China, the Marco Polo Bridge Incident, the Nanking Massacre. Then the Japanese invaded Hong Kong and the Philippines and launched the Pacific War. Therefore, we were extremely busy translating from May to October. Our work was suspended in October, and the Allies stopped paying us. Then Mr. HSIANG introduced the other four translators to the Chinese Military Delegation to Japan and left me to work with him."*[18]

Jurists who were proficient in English and Japanese were especially required to provide evidence and debate in the trial. HSIANG Che-chun returned to China to hire consultants at the beginning of 1947 when Japanese aggression in non-Chinese areas was dealt with.

The chief consultant was NYI, Judson T.Y. (1906–2003), who had just returned from an inspection in Europe and the United States. NYI, Judson T.Y., Che-tsun (courtesy name), was born in Wujiang, Jiangsu Province, in 1906. He was determined to study law when he observed a court trial in the Shanghai concession in middle school and found out that because of extraterritoriality, foreign consuls and lawyers were very arrogant in China. Although he ranked first in the Middle School Attached to the University of Shanghai and went straight to the University for free in 1923, he transferred to Soochow University Law School, which was known for its comparative jurisprudence for two years later. In 1928, he earned a Bachelor of Law degree from Soochow University and a Bachelor of Liberal Studies degree from Chizhi University, the original Shanghai Foreign Language Institute. He went to Stanford University for further studies in the same year and obtained a Doctor of Law degree in 1929. After returning to China, he taught law at universities whilst working as a lawyer. He went to Europe and the United States to study law again from 1945 to 1946. He visited the Nuremberg Trial and observed the Western judicial system, trial procedures, and evidence collection. He gained a deeper understanding of the comparative study of Chinese and foreign laws. NYI, Judson T.Y. had been colleagues with HSIANG Che-chun at the Ministry of Justice and Administration and the Shanghai Special Administrative Region Court. Moreover, the Ministry of Justice and Administration recommended him as a candidate when the Chinese delegation was organized. In addition, LUO Chia-lun (LUO Jialun), a well-known scholar in the United States, wrote to the Ministry of Foreign Affairs to recommend him. NYI, Judson T.Y. wrote about it in his later years:

> *"HSIANG Che-chun returned to China for support and asked me to go, especially because I had just returned from an inspection of the judicial system in the United States and Britain. With me as the chief consultant, he decided to employ three more consultants after discussing with me. They were E Sen and KWEI Yu, both lawyers in Shanghai, and Professor WU Hsueh-yi from the National Central University in Nanking."*[19]

The other three consultants mentioned by NYI, Judson T.Y., were also elites with a thorough knowledge of both western and Chinese law systems.

AO Daniel S. (E Sen 1902–1970), Lu Kung (courtesy name), was born in Yangzhou, Jiangsu Province, in 1902. He graduated from Soochow University Law School in 1928 and received a doctor of laws degree from Lincoln Law School in 1929. After returning to China, he worked as a lawyer in Shanghai and concurrently as a professor at Soochow University Law School. He was appointed as the President of Soochow University Law School in 1944.

KWEI Yu (Qui Yu 1903–2002), Kung Chuo (courtesy name), was born in Ningbo, Zhejiang Province, in 1902. He graduated from Soochow University Law School in 1927. After being a lawyer and an English editor of The Commercial Press in Shanghai, he served as an editor of the Ministry of Justice and Administration, a judge of Shanghai No. 1 Special Zone District Court, and a judge of Shanghai and Jiangsu Second Branch of the High Court after 1930. He had translated and published the *English Translation of the Civil Procedure Law of the Republic of China*, participated in the editing of the sequel of *Ciyuan* (A Chinese dictionary), and published more than ten papers such as *Civil Law System and Common Law System, Quality and Quantity of Judicial Officers, Law Theory and Practice* and *The Legal View of the Handling of Japanese Property in China.*

WU Hsueh-i (WU Xueyi 1904–1966) was born in Nanchang, Jiangxi Province, in 1904. He graduated from the Law Department of Chaoyang University in 1926 and was awarded a scholarship to study in Japan due to his excellence. He obtained LLB from Kyoto Imperial University in 1931. After returning to China, he served as a professor at National Central University and Wuhan University and wrote and published many civil law books and textbooks. WU Hsueh-yi was an expert in Anglo-American law. He and MEI Ju-ao had assisted SOONG Tse-ven (Song Ziwen), President of the Executive Yuan, and WANG Shih-chieh, Minister of Foreign Affairs, participating in the signing of many international treaties and international negotiations. In February 1945, he was appointed as a legislator of the Legislative Yuan of the National Government of the Republic of China.

As a busy lawyer in Shanghai, FANG F.S., Judge MEI Ju-ao's first secretary, returned to China at the end of 1946. Then YANG Shou-lin (1912–1991), a native of Suzhou, Jiangsu Province, was hired as the secretary. Born in 1912, he graduated from Soochow University Law School in 1934 and was the director of the American Texaco Company.

In short, in the Tokyo Trial that lasted for nearly three years, the Chinese delegation had 17 members: Four were on the judge team. In addition to Judge MEI Ju-ao, there were three secretaries. They were FANG F.S., LUO Chi-I, and YANG Shou-Lin.

There were 13 members of the prosecutor team. In addition to Prosecutor HSIANG Che-chun, there were four secretaries: Henry CHIU, LIU T.C., CHU Tsing-Ju, and KAW Vung-ping (concurrently), and four consultants: NYI, Judson T.Y. (chief consultant), E Sen, KWEI Yu, and WU Hsueh-i, and five translators: CHOU Hsih-ching, CHANG Pei-chi, KAW Vung-ping, Cheng Lu-ta and LIU Chi-sheng.

## *An Arduous Course*

The Tokyo Trial lasted almost two years, from May 3, 1946, to April 16, 1948. When all the defendants were presumed innocent, the prosecutors argued and provided evidence, and then the defendants also submitted evidence to refute the prosecutors' claims.

The deliberation lasted six months, from May 1948 to November 12, and the panel of judges brought in their verdict based on the evidence from both the prosecutor and the defense.

The International Military Tribunal for the Far East lasted two and a half years with a total of 817 hearings and as many as 49,857 pages of proceedings, including pages with the same number and unmarked pages. Someone claimed that there were 818 hearings because a preparatory meeting was held on April 29, 1946, before the formal hearings. Compared with the Nuremberg Trial, which lasted from November 21, 1945, to October 1, 1946, which had a total of 403 court sessions and more than 17,000 pages of proceedings, the Tokyo Trial was arduous.

The English version of *Transcripts of the proceedings of the International Military Tribunal for the Far East*, the Chinese and English indexes[20], and the Chinese version of the Chinese part[21] have been jointly published by Shanghai Jiao Tong University Press and National Library of China Publishing House. Translation of the proceedings is in progress, and the first volume has already been published.[22]

## *References*


[1] Official Newspaper (Extra). August, 1945. Japanese Ministry of Economy Press.

[2] Cheng, Zhaoqi, Gong Zhiwei, and Zhao Yuhui. 2013. *Handbook of the Tokyo Trial Studies.* Shanghai Jiao Tong University Press, 251.

[3] Ibid., 252.

[4] *The People's Daily.* July 8, 1921.

[5] Cheng, Zhaoqi, Gong Zhiwei, and Zhao Yuhui. 2013. *Handbook of the Tokyo Trial Studies.* Shanghai Jiao Tong University Press, 249.

[6] Ibid., 251.

[7] Mei, Ju-ao, 2005. *International Military Tribunal for the Far East.* Law Press; People's Court Press, 132–150.

[8] Official Letter No. 34-1324 (1945). Ministry of Foreign Affairs of the National Government.

[9] Official Letter No. 34-503 (1945). Ministry of Foreign Affairs of the National Government.

[10] Official Letter No. 34-1693 (1945). Ministry of Foreign Affairs of the National Government.

[11] Xiang, Longwan. 2010. *The Tokyo Trial, Chinese Prosecutor Hsiang Che-chun.* Shanghai Jiao Tong University Press, 254.

[12] Official Letter No. 34-533 (1945). Ministry of Foreign Affairs of the National Government.

[13] Official Letter No. 34-541 (1945). Ministry of Foreign Affairs of the National Government.
[14] Official Letter No. 34-543 (1945). Ministry of Foreign Affairs of the National Government.
[15] Zheng, Shanlong. 2006. "Henry CHIU in the Tokyo Trial." *Forward Forum*, no. 10.
[16] Official Letter No. 35-320 (1945). Ministry of Foreign Affairs of the National Government.
[17] Xiang, Longwan. 2010. *The Tokyo Trial, Chinese Prosecutor Hsiang Che-chun (Xiang Zhejun)*. Shanghai Jiao Tong University Press, 1.
[18] Ibid., 1–2.
[19] NYI, Judson T.Y. 1999. *Me and the Law*. Law Press, 107.
[20] Tokyo Trial Literature Committee. 2013. *Transcripts of the Proceedings of the International Military Tribunal for the Far East (English version)*. National Library of China Publishing House; Shanghai Jiao Tong University Press.
[21] Cheng, Zhaoqi. 2016. *Transcripts of the Proceedings of the International Military Tribunal for the Far East: The China Related*. National Library of China Publishing House; Shanghai Jiao Tong University Press.
[22] Cheng, Zhaoqi, and Xiang Longwan. 2017. *Transcripts of the Proceedings of the International Military Tribunal for the Far East (Chinese version) (First Series)*. Shanghai Jiao Tong University Press.

CHAPTER 2

# A Setting Agenda

According to the Common Law, after the establishment of the Military Tribunal for the Far East, the prosecutors of all countries shall determine three aspects of the trial: What is the date the war crimes were first committed, and the date ended? What are the crimes? Who are the war criminals?

## *The Dates of Start and End of the Criminal Acts*

The first aspect is the starting date of the crimes of Japanese Class A War Criminals committed and the date ended.

The International Prosecution Section agreed on the date of the war ended because the Japanese government signed the instrument of surrender on September 2, 1945, which was, of course, the end day of their crimes. However, there were disagreements on the starting date.

Countries such as the United Kingdom, the United States, and Australia believed that the International Military Tribunal for the Far East was established to trial Japanese war criminals in World War II. It was the Japanese attack on Pearl Harbor that led to the Japanese invasion of China being part of WWII, and the United States, the United Kingdom, and China declared war on Japan after the Attack on Pearl Harbor. Therefore, December 7, 1941, the day the Japanese attacked Pearl Harbor, should be the starting date of the crimes. On the other hand, the Japanese believed that the war began the starting date should also be on December 7, 1941. The Chinese government disagreed.

The Japanese attack on Pearl Harbor and the subsequent operations against several Pacific countries were to end the protracted war in China as soon as possible. Japan's full invasion of China began with the Marco Polo Bridge Incident on July 7, 1937 – the aftermath of the Mukden Incident. On September 18, 1931, the Japanese army invaded and occupied Shenyang and began to annex China's northeastern region, which is the beginning of the Sino-Japanese War. The Ministry of Foreign Affairs of China sent a diplomatic note to the British government when the United Nations War Crimes Commission was established in 1943 in the United Kingdom: "*The war criminals should include all those who participated in the atrocities in Chinese territory since the Mukden Incident.*"[1] Representatives of China have been insisting on this in all their meetings at home and abroad.

In reviewing the history, the Japanese militarists plotted the Mukden Incident, the Huangkutun Incident, as early as June 4, 1928, killed CHANG Tso-lin, the chief executive of Northeast and Northern China at that time. This was an act of war. The war between China and Japan had already begun since then. Therefore, the International Prosecution Section recognized the Japanese war crimes starting from January 1, 1928. In addition, the *Pact of Paris,* signed by 63 countries, including China and Japan, also came into effect in 1928. Therefore, the International Prosecution Section determined that the Japanese war crimes started on January 1, 1928.

This starting date is very important. For 14 years, the Japanese fascists committed atrocious crimes in China from January 1, 1928, to December 7, 1941. They must be accounted for. Had it been limited to the time after the Attack on Pearl Harbor, many atrocities, including the Nanking Massacre, would have been accounted for, and the Japanese war criminals who committed unforgivable crimes would have gone unpunished. The Chinese people will not accept it.

However, George Yamaoka, the defendant HIROTA Koki's Japanese American lawyer, strongly opposed it.

He attacked the issue of the date on the morning of May 14, 1946:

> *If the acts alleged as war crimes in the Indictment occurred during times of peace between Japan and other countries involved, no war existed; there could be no war crimes in a legal sense...As to China, Japan was also at peace with the properly constituted government of that country during the entire period of the Indictment,*

*according to her contention; and, according to her contention, no state of belligerency ever existed between them... it must be admitted that even this government did not declare war against Japan until December 9, 1941. This also is a matter of public record of which this Tribunal must take judicial notice. The counts of the Indictment, therefore, that allege as war crimes acts of commission or omission perpetrated during the period January 1, 1928, to December 9, 1941, are not, in fact, or law under any construction, war crimes since they occurred during times of peace.*[2]

In the afternoon of the same day, Chinese prosecutor HSIANG Che-chun rebutted George Yamaoka in his first statement:

*Then, I would like to ask the permission of the Court to spend a few minutes on a few observations in answer to the motion brought about this morning with reference particularly to China, my country. The learned counsel for the defense said there was no war existing between China and Japan because Japan never declared war against China. Of course, it is a question as to what is the correct definition of war. But on September 18, 1931, Japan took warlike actions in China. killing thousands and thousands of people, soldiers as well as civilians. That was fourteen years ago. On July 7, 1937, Japan started a war at Marco Polo Bridge, killing hundreds in one night. Later, Japan sent her soldiers all over China, killing millions and millions of soldiers, children, and women, ending helpless civilians – noncombatants. I think those are facts known all over the world. If that were not war, what is a war – what is a war, I wonder? Since 1931 Japan sent her soldiers all over China, all over the provinces, without any provocations on the part of China. I submit that there was a war, whether Japan declared war against China or not, although China did not declare war against Japan until December 9, 1941. But there was a war; that was my submission.*[3]

TAKIKAWA Masajiro was the attorney for the defendant SHIMADA Shigetaro. In 1953, he published the monograph *To Trial the Tokyo Trial*, which completely denied the Tokyo Trial. However, he had to express his admiration for Prosecutor Hsiang Che-chun when he mentioned him: "*The Chinese prosecutor HSIANG Che-chun rebutted George Yamaoka's defense. He said in his impassioned statement that there had been a war between China and Japan since the Manchurian Incident. Prosecutor Hsiang is really a gallant Chinese man!*"[4]

Japan had two battles with the Soviet Union before the Attack on Pearl Harbor: the Changkufeng Battle from July to August 1938 and the Battle of Nomonhan from May to September 1939. Japan also had a few battles with Britain and France in their Asian colonies. Therefore, from 1931 to 1941, the main Japanese militarists were used to invade China, becoming the main eastern battlefield of the world's anti-fascist war. The Ministry of Education in China issued a document on January 3, 2017, requiring an examination of various textbooks at all levels: The War of Resistance Against Japanese Aggression started in 1931, that is, the "Fourteen Years of Resistance." It should be noted that this is completely consistent with the claims of the Chinese government and the International Military Tribunal for the Far East's timeline determination.

## *Three Major Accusations*

Second aspect: what are the crimes of Japanese Class A war criminals?

At first, the tribunal reviewed the relevant international treaties that had been signed before World War II. The following is a selection of several of them.

Keeping the peace and opposing the war:

Two peace conferences were held in The Hague in the Netherlands in 1899 and 1907, and attended by more than 40 countries, including China, Russia, the United States, the United Kingdom, France, and First Hague Convention, signed in and attended by more than 40 countries including China, Russia, the United States, the United Kingdom, France, and First Hague Convention, signed in 1907, reached an agreement for peaceful settlement of international disputes. Signed in 1907, they reached an agreement for a peaceful settlement.

The *Treaty of Versailles* was signed in France by 22 countries, including the United States, the United Kingdom, France, Italy, Japan, the Netherlands, Portugal, Germany, China, and Thailand, after the First World War on June 28, 1919.

The *Covenant of the League of Nations*, signed by 63 countries in 1920, stipulated that Japan had to disarm and respect other members' territorial integrity. All states were required to submit complaints about arbitration or judicial inquiry before going to war.

The *Nine-Power Treaty* was signed in Washington by China, the United States, the United Kingdom, Belgium, France, Italy, Japan, the Netherlands, and

Portugal on February 6, 1922; the purpose was to affirm the sovereignty and China territorial integrity Open Door Policy and preserve stability in the Far East.

The *Kellogg–Briand Pact* or *Pact of Paris* (Named by French foreign minister Aristide Briand, and the U.S. state of secretary, Frank Kellogg—noted by the author) was signed in Paris by 63 countries on August 27, 1928. The signatory states condemned the invasion and restated the principles set forth by First Hague Convention, which was to peacefully resolve international disputes and desert war as a country policy.

Counter-narcotics:

The *International Opium Convention* was signed by 46 countries at The Hague on January 23, 1912. The Convention stipulated that "*The contracting Powers shall use their best endeavors to control, or to cause to be controlled, all person's manufacturing, importing, selling, distributing, and exporting morphine, cocaine, and their respective salts, as well as the buildings in which these persons carry such an industry or trade.*"

A revised International Opium Convention, which is called *International Convention relating to Dangerous Drugs,* was signed in Geneva on February 19, 1925. It introduced a statistical control system to be supervised by a Permanent Central Opium Board, a body of the League of Nations.

An amending convention on narcotic drugs was signed in Geneva by 70 countries on July 13, 1931.

Humanitarianism under War:

The *1907 Hague Convention IV,* signed by 19 countries in The Hague, stated that prisoners of war should be treated humanely.

The *Convention relative to the Treatment of Prisoners of War* was signed in Geneva on July 27, 1927. This Convention emphasized that prisoners be treated humanely and protected, not to be abused, and no forced labor for officers and the wounded. The Geneva Convention relative to the Treatment of Prisoners of War specified the requirements to respect wounded soldiers, protect the medical staff, etc.

Japan is a signatory to most of these international treaties, which is also the basis for the Tokyo Trial.

Concerning the international treaties and the characteristics of the Second World War, and in accordance with the *International Military Tribunal for the Far East Charter*, the suspects were prosecuted on three charges, namely: A. crimes against peace, B. conventional war crimes, and C. crimes against humanity, which were similar to the Nuremberg Trial.

According to the *International Military Tribunal for the Far East Charter*, Crimes against Peace are the planning, preparation, initiation, or waging of a declared or undeclared war of aggression, or a war in violation of international law, treaties, agreements or assurances, or participation in a common plan or conspiracy for the accomplishment of any of the foregoing.[5] This is the most important crime in both the Nuremberg Trial and Tokyo Trial. The target was those who were primarily responsible for the aggressive policies and wars, that is, Class A war criminals.

What are Conventional Was Crimes? Conventional War Crimes are violations of the laws or customs of war. It includes killing civilians, raping women, burning, and plundering public and private property, torturing and killing prisoners, using illegal weapons, and so on. The above listed international treaties are principles and conventions mainly formed for "Conventional War Crimes."

Why establish "Crimes against Humanity" when "Conventional War Crimes" has included crimes against humanity? Conventional War Crimes may not comprise all crimes against humanity. It is restricted to the acts during the war when enemies fight each other. In particular, it does not involve large-scale crimes against humanity. For example, it does not apply to the holocaust committed by the Nizes when over six million of people were killed. Not only did Holocaust include the Jews in Poland, Hungry, and the Soviet Union, but also the Jews in Germany. Those crimes if out of the limits of "Conventional War Crimes."

According to these three crimes, especially the Crimes against Peace, those who planned and launched a war of aggression must be prosecuted as the criminals of Crimes against Peace.

## *Determining the List of War Criminals*

Third aspect: which Japanese Class A war criminals should be on trial?

Long before the Japanese surrender, WANG Shih-chieh, director of the Counselor's Office of the Military Commission of the Republic of China has proposed the establishment of the "Crime Investigation Committee" on July 16, 1943, and one of its missions was to determine a list of Japanese war criminals.

At one of the conferences held by the Allies on April 25, 1944, Mr. Wellington Koo (GU Weijun), The Ambassador of the Republic of China to the

United Kingdom, proposed to form a Far East and Pacific subcommittee. The subcommittee was actually established in Chungking on November 29, and its task was to collect evidence and provide a list of Japanese war criminals. China had proposed the most war criminals among the Allies.

However, ever since the preparation of the Nuremberg Trial and the Tokyo Trial began, there have always been some people questioning why those war criminals should be held responsible personally?

On May 14, 1946, the same day that George Yamaoka questioned the starting date, Major Ben Bruce Blackeney, the defendants UMEZU Yoshijiro and TOGO Shigenori's American lawyer, made a lengthy statement. His first argument was that "war is not a crime." He also quoted Hugo Grotius, the Dutch scholar who laid the foundation of international law, stated:

> *No academician, no writer of texts, not Grotius nor the League Covenant, no court administering municipal or public law, has ever breathed such a suggestion. Nor has it been asked whether such killings occur in a just or unjust war, in a legal or an illegal war, a war of defense, or a war of aggression.*

His second point was that:

> *War is the act of a nation, not of individuals. It is hardly necessary to do more than state the proposition. The entire body of international law assumes that war is the act of and brings into being relationships between states; no treaty, no convention touching on the subject of war, refers to individuals. International law, by definition, is applicable among nations and excludes individuals from its operation. If war were a crime (as we have just seen), it could be so only by virtue of treaties making it so. Yet, those treaties bind only those bodies politic, the nations by whom they were entered into, and no men of flesh and blood*[6]

These arguments are obviously untenable. A nation is, of course responsible for its war of aggression, but crimes against international law are committed by many "individuals." On the same day, Australian prosecutor Mansfield and British prosecutor Comyns Carr argued on behalf of the prosecution.

Mansfield quoted the argument of Lord Wright, a distinguished scholar of international law as

> *individuals may be penally liable for particular breaches of International Law is now generally accepted. Thus the violation of the principle that war, if unjust, is illegal and is not only a breach of the treaty on the part of the nation which violates it, carrying with it all the consequences which attend a treaty-breaking but is also a crime on the part of the individuals who are guilty as conspirators, principals or accessories of actively bringing it about, as much as a violation of the customary laws of war. Nations can only act by responsible instruments, that is, by persons. If a nation, in breach of a treaty, initiates aggressive war, the guilt of the responsible agents of the nation who bring this about, being able to do so because of their high position in the State, is a separate, independent, and different liability, both in its nature and penal consequences.*[7]

British prosecutor Comyns Carr quoted from Stowell's International Law in which he pointed out that laid down the proposition that it was "in 1919, the nation who won a war has the right to define the crimes of the defendants, who lost the war, to prosecute the Kaiser.[8]

Starting from the Mukden Incident, people like ITAGAKI Seishiro and DOIHARA Kenji played a very prominent role in the Japanese war of aggression against China. They didn't just obey orders but took the initiative to act than to report afterward so to make the crimes a fact.

Judge MEI Ju-ao made an analysis in his monograph on the Tokyo Trial written in his late years: "*The argument that international law did not stipulate the method of sanctions against individuals and therefore could not punish them is invalid. Over 300 years ago, Grotius, known as the founder of international law in the West, agreed that those who captured or tried a violator of international law had the right to execute him.*"[9]

Chapter 1 mentioned that the Allies arrested 118 Class A war crime suspects in four times 1945. At the same time, the International Prosecution Section sorted out the related documents of the Japanese government and the Allies and had a general knowledge of all the suspects' functions and crimes at the beginning of the spring of 1946.

The Nuremberg Trial had started at that time, and there were 24 Nazi defendants. In referencing that trial, the International Prosecution Office believed that the trials of the Japanese Class A war criminals could be conducted in three or four groups, with no more than 30 defendants each time. The question was how to determine the list of the first groups. After consulting the prosecutors, Chief of

Counsel Keenan finally determined 28 defendants from the lists provided by the Allies. In alphabetic order, the list is as follows:

> *ARAKI Sadao, DOIHARA Kenji, HASHIMOTO Kingoro, HATA Shunroku, HIRANUMA Kiichiro, HIROTA Koki, HOSHINO Naoki, ITAGAKI Seishiro, KAYA Okinori, KIDO Koichi, KIMURA Heitaro, KOISO Kuniaki, MATSUI Iwane, MATSUOKA Yosuke, MINAMI Jiro, MUTO Akira, NAGANO Osami, OKAWA Shumei, OSHIMA Hiroshi, OKA Takazumi, SATO Kenryo, SHIGEMITSU Mamoru, SHIMADA Shigetaro, SHIRATORI Toshio, SUZUKI Teiichi, TOGO Shigenori, TOJO Hideki, and UMEZU Yoshijiro.*

These 28 defendants can be divided into nine groups:

Four former Prime Ministers, namely TOJO Hideki, the initiator of the Pacific War; HIROTA Koki, an experienced diplomat; HIRANUMA Kiichiro and KOISO Kuniaki, two fascist officers.

Three former Ministers of Foreign Affairs: MATSUOKA Yosuke, SHIGEMITSU Mamoru, and TOGO Shigenori actively plotted the aggression.

Two diplomats, OSHIMA Hiroshi and SHIRATORI Toshio who actively colluded with the Axis powers to organize an anti-communist military alliance.

Four former Ministers of War: ARAKI Sadao, who actively advocated aggression; MINAMI Jiro, who was the commander of the Kwantung Army and the commander of the Tianjin Garrison; and HATA Shunroku, and ITAGAKI Seishiro, who commanded the Japanese invaders in China.

Four generals and officers in the army: special agent DOIHARA Kenji, chief culprit of the Nanking Massacre, MATSUI Iwane, MUTO Akira, and KIMURA Heitaro, who committed atrocities in China and Southeast Asia, SATO Kenryo, who was regarded as the chief apprentice by TOJO Hideki, and UMEZU Yoshijiro, one of the chief culprits of Japan's invasion of China.

Two former Ministers of the Navy: NAGANO Osami and SHIMADA Shigetaro, and one officer in the navy, OKAWA Shumei.

Three former ministers in charge of economy and finance: HOSHINO Naoki, KAYA Okinori, and SUZUKI Teiichi.

Two propagandists and instigators who frantically advocated fascism and aggressive policies: OSHIMA Hiroshi and HASHIMOTO Kingoro.

One nobleman who was the closest advisor to Emperor HIROHITO; was KIDO Koichi.

In short, these 28 defendants were all ambitious and notorious fascists who played a prominent role in the criminal activities of Japan's politics, military, diplomacy, and propaganda.

China has made a great contribution to the compilation of the list because most of them committed terrible crimes against the Chinese military and civilians.

After the establishment of the International Military Tribunal for the Far East, China provided the first batch of 18 war criminals, and these were:

ISOGAI Rensuke, MEZU oshijiro, DOIHARA Kenji, WACHI Takaji, SAKAI Takashi, HONJO Shigeru, ITAGAKI Seishiro, ABE Nobuyuki, HATA Shunroku, TOJO Hideki, TANI Hisao, HASHIMOTO Kingoro, TADA Hayao, KAGESA Sadaaki, HATA Kikosaburo, KOISO Kuniaki, MINAMI Jiro, and KITA Seiichi.

CHIANG Kai-shek handwrote the list in October 1945 and ranked the top 12, namely:

1. DOIHARA Kenji, 2. HONJO Shigeru, 3. TANI Hisao, 4. HASHIMOTO Kingoro, 5. ITAGAKI Seishiro, 6. ISOGAI Rensuke, 7. TOJO ideki, 8. WACHI Takaji, 9. KAGESA Sadaaki, 10. SAKAI Takashi, KITA Seiichi, and 12. HATA Shunroku.

CHIANG Kai-shek annotated: "*KITA Seiichi is no different from WACHI Takaji and KAGESA Sadaaki, who are serious offenders of aggression against China. His crimes should be identified and should be punished.*"[10]

When the Chinese Ministry of Foreign Affairs submitted the list of the 12 war criminals to the Allies Headquarters, the following information was added: "Of all the 12 war criminals China listed, with the exemption of those included in the IMTFE trial, the rest should be taken to China to be trialed."[11] In other words, even if some of the 12 war criminals were not included in the Tokyo Trial, they would be trialed by China.

On this list, seven war criminals were not included in the IMTFE due to various reasons. HONJO Shigeru deserved the harshest punishment as the Commander of the Kwantung Army, who invaded Northeast China directly. However, he committed suicide on November 20, 1945.

TANI Hisao, the No. 3 war criminal, was the driving force of the Nanking Massacre. The No. 10 war criminal, SAKAI Takashi, was not only responsible for Jinan Massacre but also the one who connived the Japanese army's burning, killing, rapping, and looting after they occupied Hong Kong. However, these two butchers were not included in the Class A war criminals list. After being brought to trial at the Nanking Military Tribunal for Class B and C war criminals and sentenced to death, they were executed by shooting in Yuhuatai, Nanking on April 26, 1947, and ended their shameful lives.

ISOGAI Rensuke, the No. 6 war criminal, who once served as Chief of Staff of the Kwangtung Army, Governor-General of Japanese-occupied Hong Kong, and Chief Executive of Taiwan, was put on trial in Nanking for war crimes on the bases of forcefully imposing Japanese localization, prohibiting English, changing local street names to Japanese during the occupation of Hong Kong, and was sentenced to life imprisonment.

WACHI Takaji, the No. 8 war criminal, KAGESA Sadaaki, the No. 9 war criminal, and KITA Seiichi, the No. 11 war criminal, identified by CHIANG Kai-shek, were all chief espionage agents of the notorious "*Orchid Espionage Agency*," "*Plum Espionage Agency*," Tianjin, and Huabei Espionage Agencies operated in China. They were not listed as Class A war criminals for being absent from the planning of the Japanese invasion of China, even though they committed many crimes.

Soon, the Ministry of Foreign Affairs of China prepared a second list of 22 war criminals. They were:

MINAMI Jiro, HIRANUMA Kiichiro, KONOYE Fumimaro, ABE Nobuyuki, YONAI Mitsumasa, KOISO Kuniaki, ARAKI Sadao, MATSUOKA Yosuke, TOGO Shigenori, UMEZU Yoshijiro, MATSUI Iwane, TERAUCHI Hisaichi, MUTAGUCHI Renya, YAMADA Otozo, AOKI Kazuo, NOBUMASA Suetsugu, TOSHIZO Nishio, SHIMADA Shigetaro, HACHIRO Arita, HIROTA Koki, MASAKAZU Kawabe and MASAYUKI Tani.

There were only 21 since KONOYE Fumimaro had committed suicide. Taking the list seriously, CHIANG Kai-shek telegraphed Minister WANG Shih-chieh on January 9, 1946, and said, "There are 21 war criminals on the second list because KONOYE Fumimaro has committed suicide. The Ministry of Foreign Affairs should notify the U.S. government and the Supreme Commander for the Allied Powers about it."[12] On the same day, China submitted the 21 war criminals to the International Prosecution Section.

Of the two criminal lists, 15 were from the lists provided by China, which accounted for 53.6% of the total 28 defendants in the Tokyo Trial. Among the remaining 13, many were also involved in wars and atrocities in aggression against China. For example, HOSHINO Naoki once served as the "Minister of Financial Affairs" and "Chief of General Affairs of the State Council" of the puppet state of Manchukuo. KAYA Okinori was responsible for Japan's budget in wartime after the Marco Polo Bridge Incident. MUTO Akira served as Vice Chief of Staff of the Japanese Central China Area Army during the Nanking Massacre. SHIGEMITSU Mamoru was blasted off the right leg by a Korean in Hongkou Park in Shanghai. OKAWA Shumei was a theorist who fanatically advocated militarism. He once advocated the independence of Manchuria to CHANG Hsueh-liang and conspired with ITAGAKI Seishiro and DOIHARA Kenji to instigate the Japanese annexation of Manchuria. Therefore, more than 70% were closely related to the Japanese invasion of China among the 28 defendants.

It should be noted that DOIHARA Kenji, who was responsible for espionage in China, had already returned to Japan upon the Japanese surrender. He initially was not included in the trial for lack of evidence, but thanks to the Chinese prosecutor's efforts, this notorious head of spies was brought to justice.

Arnold C. Brackman, an American reporter, witnessed almost the entire process of the Tokyo Trial. After the Trial, he spent "more than a quarter of a century and over 100,000 miles" writing the book, *The Other Nuremberg: The Untold Story of the Tokyo War Crimes Trials*, in which he made a comparison between the defendants in the Tokyo Trial and the Nuremberg Trial: "*Among the accused were nine civilians and nineteen professional military men. This was almost the opposite of Nuremberg, where seventeen of the twenty-two defendants were civilians. In Japan, the military leaders—in particular, the expansionists who dominated the army—had gained control over the government in the late twenties. In Germany, just a few years later, Hitler and his gang coopted the armed forces.*"[13]

## *Shall the Japanese Emperor be Prosecuted*

There was widespread controversy surrounding whether the Emperor of Japan should be on the list of war criminals. The arguments focused on whether the emperor is guilty? If guilty, should he be put on trial?

Firstly, is the emperor guilty? The international outcries for HIROHITO's trial were running very high at the end of the war. However, some believed that Japan's decision to launch and expand the war lay on the military; thus the Japanese Emperor HIROHITO, as just a symbol with no real power, should not be prosecuted as a war criminal. On September 27, 1945, less than a month after *The Japanese Instrument of Surrender*, HIROHITO requested to meet General

MacArthur. After the meeting, HIROHITO left the scene; HIROHITO later on indicated that "At that time, he and General MacArthur had reached a gentleman's agreement to keep the meeting a secret." However, MacArthur's expression and behaviors indicate that he represented this understanding. On January 25, 1946, six days after the promulgation of the *Charter of the International Military Tribunal for the Far East*, MacArthur wrote to Dwight D. Eisenhower, the U.S. Chief of Staff of the Army: "There is no clear evidence showing that the emperor's actions on different occasions in the past ten years were related to the political decisions of Japanese Empire."[14]

The point of *the Emperor had nothing to do with political decisions* is completely baseless. The Japanese Emperor's status is clearly stated in the 17 articles in Chapter One of the *Constitution of the Empire of Japan* proclaimed in 1889. For example,

> *Article 1. The Empire of Japan shall be reigned over and governed by a line of Emperors unbroken for ages eternal.*
> *Article 3. The Emperor is sacred and inviolable.*
> *Article 4. The Emperor is the head of the Empire, combining in Himself the rights of sovereignty, and exercises them, according to the provisions of the present Constitution.*
> *Article 11. The Emperor has the supreme command of the Army and Navy.*
> *Article 13. The Emperor declares war, makes peace, and concludes treaties.*

Throughout the course of the War, all the important decisions must be implemented only after Emperor's approval at the Imperial Conference. Therefore, the Emperor had indisputable legal responsibilities to the War.

A classified document, "*On the Japanese Emperor HIROHITO's Responsibility for the War of Aggression*"[15], was drafted by Lin Jianmin and issued by the Ministry of Foreign Affairs of China in April 1946. It clearly indicates the status of the emperor in the *Constitution of the Empire of Japan*. Then a number of imperial edicts issued by the emperor during the war are included as listed below:

Authorized the invasion of Manchuria, established and recognized Manchukuo on December 1, 1932; Signed the *Imperial Edict of Withdraw of the League of Nations* on March 27, 1933; Signed the *Confidential Agreement by Japan, Germany, and Italy* on November 25, 1936; Issued a decree about Japan's supreme s and its power on November 8, 1937; Proclaimed *National Mobilization Law* on April 1, 1938; Declared war on the United Kingdom and the United States on December

8, 1941; Issued an edict on March 6, 1942, to award the involved ones in its wars against other countries in East Asia, especially its invasion against China and its attack on Pearl Harbor.

The document concludes that "HIROHITO should bear the responsibilities for the war of aggression" on three accounts:

(1) The world peace was undermined.
(2) The charter of the League of Nations and international treaties were breached.
(3) The sovereignties, public and private property, human and material resources, people's health, lives, and national order of China and its allies were violated, especially those of China.

Countries like Australia and the Philippines also strongly demanded the punishment of the Japanese Emperor.

Shortly after he arrived in Tokyo; Judge MEI Ju-ao expressed his idea in his diary on April 8, 1946:

*Ming Si told me that the procurator from a certain country argued that the Emperor of Japan should be listed as a war criminal and indicted, which aroused a heated debate at the procurators' meeting today. The issue ended up getting tabled without being put to the vote for the time being. I told Ming Si that this was a political issue; from a legal perspective, I could not see why the Emperor was not responsible for Japan's war of aggression. This issue had also been discussed several times among the judges in our private conversations, and many of them shared my view.*[16]

It is not complicated to prove whether the emperor is guilty. The more important question is whether he should be on trial even if he is guilty? The U.S. government had already decided not to put the Emperor on the trail before the International Prosecution Section determined the list of the defendants and wrote the indictment. In the letter from MacArthur, indicated above, to Eisenhower, he pointed out that: "*The occupation plan must be changed drastically if the emperor is to be tried; the emperor's prosecution will inevitably cause great riots among the Japanese people because he is a symbol of the unity of the Japanese nationals. The entire country will collapse without its emperor.*"[17] The U.S. government adopted MacArthur's suggestion, and the Emperor escaped the trial.

In 1968, HSIANG Che-chun mentioned in his *Reminiscence Outline about the Tokyo Trial* that he suggested to Mr. Keenan twice that year to prosecute the emperor:

> *Emperor HIROHITO of Japan is the head of state with real power. He should be held responsible and prosecuted for Japan's invasion of so many countries in Asia and the Pacific region, especially China. In February and March 1946, I suggested twice to Chief of Counsel Joseph B. Keenan to investigate and prosecute him. Mr. Keenan agreed with me on the emperor's responsibility for the war, but not on his trial. The main reason is that the emperor's trial would surely cause turmoil and resistance among the Japanese people, making it more difficult for the Allied forces to rule over Japan. I agreed with him when we discussed it for the second time. Thus I have not insisted on the emperor's trial since then.*[18]

Many scholars believe the United States spared the Japanese Emperor because of the Cold War. *The Emperor's Monologue,* written by TERASAKI Hidenari, Liaison Officer to the Imperial Household, was published in Japan in 1991. when both the author and HIROHITO had already passed away. The material, gathering dust for so many years, was discovered by TERASAKI's daughter and published after being sorted out by experts. Both the author and HIROHITO had already passed away then. After studying this monologue, Chinese scholar Cheng Zhaoqi concluded in his book *For World Peace: The Tokyo Trial*: "*It is a misjudgment for the United States to believe that HIROHITO is not responsible for the war, Not to investigate the Emperor's responsibilities to the war is a fault in determining Japan's responsibility for the entire war.*"[19]

HIROHITO was the head of the Japanese Empire and symbolized an idol worshiped by the Japanese militarists. His escape from the Tokyo Trial has indeed left significant negative consequences. As a result, that has been responsible for the increase of militarism in Japan and the calls for the reversal of the Japanese war criminals' convictions. Even the ashes of war criminals sentenced to death, such as TOJO Hideki, are placed in Yasukuni Shrine for worship by the public. It is such a sharp contrast where Germany Hitler's fascism has long been despised and condemned after the Nuremberg Trial, and a memorial in Berlin condemns the slaughter of the Jews.

In his book *Nach Nürnberg und Tokio: 'Vergangenheitsbewältigung' in Japan und Westdeutschland 1945 bis 1968*, German scholar Manfred Kittel specifically compared Germany and Japan in historical introspection and political culture and wrote in the introduction:

> *"As far as Japan is concerned, war criminals in the Yasukuni Shrine in Tokyo are even memorialized in another way. A surviving American prisoner said it is like the German plan to build a cathedral to commemorate Hitler in the center of Berlin."*[20]

## *References*


[1] East Asia Division (1943) No.073-4. Establishment of the Enemy Crime Investigation Committee. Ministry of Foreign Affairs of the National Government.

[2] Cheng, Zhaoqi, and Xiang Longwan. 2017. *Transcripts of the Proceedings of the International Military Tribunal for the Far East (Chinese version).* Vol. 1. Shanghai Jiao Tong University Press, 100–101 (221–222 of the English court records).

[3] Xiang, Longwan. 2010. *The Tokyo Trial, Chinese Prosecutor Hsiang Che-chun.* Shanghai Jiao Tong University Press, 5–6 (272–274 of the English court records).

[4] TAKIKAWA. Masajiro. 2009. *To Try the Tokyo Trial,* Keibunsha Press.

[5] Cheng, Zhaoqi, and Xiang Longwan. 2017. *Transcripts of the Proceedings of the International Military Tribunal for the Far East (Chinese version).* Vol. 1. Shanghai Jiao Tong University Press, 250.

[6] Ibid., 93–97 (201–212 of the English court records).

[7] Ibid., 109 (245 of the English court records).

[8] Ibid., 110 (259 of the English court records).

[9] Mei, Ju-ao. 2005. *International Military Tribunal for the Far East.* Law Press; People's Court Press, 30.

[10] The Handling of War Criminals (October 1945). National Government Archives, 417.

[11] Official Letter No.35-745 (April 1946). Ministry of Foreign Affairs of the National Government.

[12] Official Letter No.35-1324 (January 1946). Ministry of Foreign Affairs of the National Government.

[13] Brackman, Arnold C. 2017. *The Other Nuremberg—The Untold Story of the Tokyo War Crimes Trials.* Translated by Mei Xiaokan and Yu Yanming. Shanghai Jiao Tong University Press, 75.

[14] Cheng, Zhaoqi. 2017. *The Tokyo Trial—for world peace.* Shanghai Jiao Tong University Press, 202.

[15] Confidential File: Setting up International Tribunal for the Trial of War Criminals in the Far East (1946). Ministry of Foreign Affairs of the National Government.

[16] MEI, Ju-ao. 2016. *My Personal Experience at the Tokyo Trial.* Edited by Mei Xiao'ao and Mei Xiaokan. Shanghai Jiao Tong University Press, 311.
[17] Cheng, Zhaoqi. 2017. *The Tokyo Trial—for World Peace.* Shanghai Jiao Tong University Press, 203.
[18] HSIANG, Che-chun. *An Outline of Memories about the Tokyo Trial* (collected by his family).
[19] Cheng, Zhaoqi. 2017. *The Tokyo Trial—for World Peace.* Shanghai Jiao Tong University Press, 201.
[20] Kittel, Manfred. 2014. *Nach Nürnberg und Tokio—"vergangenheitsbewältigung" in Japan und Westdeutschland 1945 bis 1968.* Translated by Lu Shu and Wang Weijiang. Shanghai Jiao Tong University Press, 1.

CHAPTER 3

# The Indictment

## *Evidence Collection*

The International Military Tribunal for the far East has to establish an indictment which is an important first step in trials by the Common Law. The case can be filed only after the plaintiff or prosecutor's Indictment is submitted and accepted by the court; then the corresponding trial procedures can begin. Therefore, the Indictment of the Tokyo Trial is a declaration of a legal war.

*The International Military Tribunal for the Far East*, a monograph was written by Justice MEI Ju-ao in his late years, briefly describes the preparatory work of the prosecution team for the formation of the *Indictment*:

> *In general, the preparatory work for the prosecution by the Tokyo Tribunal was divided into the following tasks: (a) interrogating the arrestees and obtaining their statements; (b) collecting documents that could be used as evidence from voluminous Japanese government records; (c) conducting field investigations, obtaining written testimonies of any witnesses, and making appointments with them to appear in court; (d) contacting the government officials and relevant organizations of the Allied Powers for the collection of documentary evidence; (e) selecting the defendants for the first trial; (f) drafting the indictment and its appendices. All these challenging tasks, especially because of the wide geographical range, historical coverage, complex types of crimes, and a large number of defendants involved in the case.*

There were two major obstacles for the prosecutors working on preparations. The first one was the lack of evidence. The war crimes listed in the *Indictment* must be based on detailed evidence. However, the prosecutors had no time to collect sufficient evidence because the tribunal was established in such a hurry.

As stated in Chapter 1, It was December 8, 1945, CHIANG Kai-shek approved HSIANG Che-chun and MEI Ju-ao to be Chinese representatives. Mr. HSIANG received a notice from Minister HSIEH Kuan-sheng of Justice and Administration on December 29 and arrived in Tokyo with Henry CHIU on February 7, 1946. It is indeed very difficult to fully prepare within such a short timeframe. MEI Ju-ao noticed HSIANG Che-chun's struggle after arriving in Tokyo on March 20, 1946. In his diary on April 8, He wrote: "Ming Si has been in agony these days because China could provide only a small amount of evidence for the trial even though the Japanese war of aggression against China lasted at least 15 years, we should have been able to provide many pieces of evidence."[2]

The second obstacle was the lack of time. The Headquarters of Allied Forces decided that the trial by the Far East Tribunal would start on May 3, 1946, thus asked the International Prosecution Section to formally submit the Indictment on April 29, 1946, which would be the Monday of the week of 28th. So that the judges could know the details in advance. The prosecutors had less than three months to prepare it.

Since the Japanese War of Aggression against China lasted the longest time, Chinese prosecutors carried a heavy workload in collecting evidence. The brutal; invasion created great carouse. The Chinese general public was not only lack of the means to collect evidence, but also lack of awareness of evidence preservation; Furthermore, the Japanese archives indicated that the Japanese government and the military enforced extremely strict public opinion blockade. Besides tight media censorship, all Japanese officers and soldiers were ordered not to disclose any information related to the atrocities and setbacks on the battlegrounds otherwise they would be punished by martial law. the Japanese Imperial General Headquarters repeatedly ordered the destruction of any related documents near Japan's surrender.

Faced with many difficulties, the Chinese prosecutor and his colleagues from the International Prosecution Section had been working hard to collect evidence through multiple channels. The first effort was to seek domestic assistance via telegrams.

HSIANG Che-chun sent telegrams several times within a week soon after he arrived in Tokyo. Here is a telegram that was sent on February 21.

*Ministry of Foreign Affairs in Chungking,*

*The International Prosecution Section of the International Military Tribunal for the Far East urgently requests the following details and evidence: (1) Japan's violation of the related treaties and agreements during the "September 18 Incident" in 1931 and the "Lugouqiao Incident" in 1937; (2) The atrocities committed by the Japanese army under the command of MATSUI Iwane and HATA Shunroku and other violations of international law during the war; (3) The details of opium production and trade, as well as the estimated number of losses of Chinese military and civilian lives and public and private property due to Japanese aggression. The information is urgently requested by the International Prosecution Section led by Joseph B. Keenan. Please send it as soon as possible.*

*Yours,*
*HSIANG Che-chun*[3]

According to the request, the Ministry of Foreign Affairs issued official letters in February 15 to many organizations such as the Military Order Department, Justice Administration Department, Military Administration Department, Internal Affairs Department, the Compensation Investigation Commission of the Executive Yuan, the Investigation and Statistics Bureau of KMT Central Executive Committee, Investigation and Statistics Bureau of the Nationalist Government Military Committee, and the Institute of International Studies, with the information "Please collect and send HSIANG Che-chun, the Prosecutor at the International Military Tribunal for the Far East with all the evidence on the atrocities committed by the Japanese army under the command of MATSUI Iwane and HATA Shunroku and the facts that Japanese policy to intoxicate the Chinese people by using opium.[4]

Besides the Chinese Mainland, the Japanese invaders also committed atrocities in other areas of the Asia-Pacific region were also included.

HSIANG Che-chun telegraphed Minister WANG Shih-chieh of Foreign Affairs on February 21 as follows:

*For the purpose of writing a judgment, the International Prosecution Section requests urgently the evidence and witnesses of the atrocities committed by the Japanese against the Chinese in Hong Kong, Singapore, Thailand, and other Pacific regions, especially those committed by the top Japanese military and political officials. Please send them to Tokyo.*

*Yours,*
*HSIANG Che-chun*[5]

Undoubtedly, the Ministry of Foreign Affairs and other departments swiftly responded to HSIANG Che-chun's request. For example, on February 25, 1946, the Ministry of Foreign Affairs asked LUO Chi-i, Judge MEI Ju-ao's secretary, to bring HSIANG Che-chun some written evidence on the atrocities committed by troops commanded by MATSUI Iwane and HATA Shunroku and other Japanese aggression acts. On February 28, 1946, Minister CHEN Cheng of the Military of War sent the *"Memorandum of Japanese Compensation for Chinese Military Losses in the War of Resistance against Japan."*

On April 6, 1946, the Ministry of Foreign Affairs sent to HSIANG Che-chun some of the Japanese crimes in China.

1. *"Summary of Japan's Wars Crimes against China,"* with the noteworthy ones selected in chronological order from the "*September 18 Incident*" to the "*Battle of Shanghai*":

(1) Japanese occupation of Jehol, Jilin, Heilongjiang, and Liaoning,
(2) Japan's establishment of Manchukuo,
(3) Japanese invasion of Songhu in 1932,
(4) Japanese invasion of Hebei Province and Chahar Province in 1933,
(5) Japanese instigation of a puppet organization in eastern Hebei,
(6) The Six Counties Incident in Chahar Province,
(7) The Japanese and Korean Smuggling in China,
(8) Japanese Aircraft's Illegal Flying in China,
(9) A large scale of Japanese espionage organization established in China,
(10) Japanese and Korean Ronin's Drug Trafficking in China,
(11) The Japanese fishing vessels' intruding into China's territorial waters for fishing,
(12) Japan's breach of the international telecommunications convention,

(13) Japanese warships' sailing illegally on the Yangtze River and other places,
(14) Harbourage of the Japanese puppet forces' attacking of Suiyuan Province in 1936,
(15) Japanese army's illegal exercises near Beijing, Tianjin, and Shanghai,
(16) Japanese' interfering in traffic in Tianjin Station and Fengtai Station,
(17) Japanese' illegal land acquisition,
(18) Japanese' unauthorized surveying, mapping, and photography,
(19) The Hebei Incident,
(20) The Lugouqiao Incident,
(21) The Japanese government's rejection of the Chinese government's proposal on withdrawing troops and resolving disputes peacefully,
(22) Japanese' increase of a large number of army, navy, and air forces in China,
(23) The Shanghai Hongqiao Incident.

2. One copy of "*The Japanese Army's Atrocities in China and Its Opium Policy.*"

3. Two copies of "*The Japanese Army and Its Puppet Forces' Drug Production and Trafficking in China.*"[6]

The Ministry of Foreign Affairs issued an official letter to the Ministry of Justice and Administration on March 4, 1946, regarding the collection of evidence on the crimes committed by the Japanese army against the personnel of Chinese embassies, consulates, and overseas Chinese.

*According to Prosecutor HSIANG Che-chun from the International Tribunal for the Far East in Tokyo, hard evidence of atrocities committed by the Japanese army, especially by the high-rank officers, against overseas Chinese in the Pacific region such as Hong Kong, Singapore, Haiphong, and Siam is urgently needed. Please telegraph their consulates to collect it and send the original copy to the Ministry of Foreign Affairs as soon as possible.*

The Ministry of Justice and Administration immediately issued an official letter to the relevant embassies and consulates.

*Consulate Generals in Hanoi, Manila, Yangon, Singapore, Batavia, and Embassy in Australia, Hong Kong Office of the Guangdong and Guangxi Special Commissioners Office, Secretary SUN Ping-chien* (Sun Bingqian) *of the delegation to Bangkok:*

> *Hard evidence on Japanese atrocities against overseas Chinese, especially the ones committed by high-rank officers are urgently needed. Please collect it immediately and send it to the Ministry of Foreign Affairs.*[7]

Chinese embassies, consulates, and overseas Chinese swiftly collected the evidence and forwarded it to the Chinese prosecutor through the Ministry of Foreign Affairs. For example, YUAN Tzu-chien (Yuan Zijian), the Chinese Consul General in Hanoi, sent telegrams twice to the Ministry of Foreign Affairs on the atrocities committed by the Japanese military police in Vietnam on March 20 and April 4, 1946.

SUN Ping-chien, the temporary secretary of China in Thailand, submitted the "Twelve Documents on Atrocities by the Japanese" on May 25, 1946.

The Chinese Consul General in Yangon sent telegrams to the Ministry of Foreign Affairs regarding the collection of evidence on Japanese atrocities against overseas Chinese on May 27, 1946.

On July 2, 1946, the Chinese Embassy in the United Kingdom forwarded a report from the British military officers and diplomats to HSIANG Che-chun on the crimes of Japanese troops in Hong Kong and Malaya.

Chinese Consul General in Manila sent to HSIANG Che-chun the evidence on the murder of YANG Kuang Sheng (YANG Guangsheng) through the Ministry of Foreign Affairs on July 23, 1946.[8]

Besides these two obstacles, language demonstrated a big challenge. All the written evidence was in many different languages. All eyewitnesses spoke different languages too. The defense lawyers often took advantage of the translation inaccuracies to intentionally create confusion. Particularly, all the Japanese government official documents were written in Japanese and yet few prosecutors had knowledge of Japanese. The court had to hire Japanese to assist. It was clear that the qualities of their translations and their royalties to the court were questionable which complicated the process and made the work process very inefficient.

HSIANG Che-chun had expressed his opinions in the court on translation several times. For example, CHIN Teh-chun, a prosecution witness from China, appeared in court on July 22, 1946, to testify and respond to inquiries from the American assistant prosecutor colonel Thomas H. Morrow, as well as cross-examinations from American defense lawyers Alfred W. Brooks and Franklin N. Warren. CHIN Teh-chun spoke Chinese. The Japanese-Chinese translator hired by the court translated Chinese into Japanese, then to be translated into English by a Japanese-English translator. Yet English questions had to go through the English-Japanese process. Not only was it inefficient, but the accuracy of the work was very questionable.

Alfred W. Brooks was frustrated and related this problem to the President, Sir William Webb, but Webb was helpless and there was not much he could do, but only say:

> *The Court is fully aware of all the matters stressed by Mr. Brooks and is keeping them in mind, and for these reasons, the Court thinks the translation should be from Chinese into English directly if we have the translators to it. We think there must be translators in Tokyo today who can do this. We think if you make an effort to find them then you will win this argument.*

At this moment, HSIANG Che-chun immediately spoke:

> *For the Chinese translation, I understand the court's position. As to the prosecution side, we have noticed this issue already. This should be the court's decision. Initially, we were advised that the Chinese members of the prosecution may not be the best candidate to provide translation services to the witness. This was exactly the reason that all the Chinese members and associates of the prosecution team did not request to be translators. We don't offer this kind of service. The court should decide this. Now that the court believes the members and assistants of the prosecution could do the translations, it becomes a different story. I understand this arrangement under the condition of a lack of Chinese translation resources.*[9]

Subsequently, the prosecution recommended FANG W.F.S., the secretary of the Chinese judge MEI Ju-ao, to be one of the translators. He was proficient in Chinese and English and could be impartial because he was not a prosecution member. Without any objection from the presiding judge and the defense, FANG W.F.S. took the job immediately and did an excellent job.

## *Evidence Collection in Homeland*

The second approach for the Chinese prosecutor to obtain evidence was to travel back to China to collect evidence on site.

Since the Japanese invasion of China lasted the longest time, the International Prosecution Section decided to send a group of prosecutors, including Joseph B. Keenan, David N. Sutton, Thomas H. Morrow, John J. Crowley, etc., to China to conduct on-site investigations. HSIANG Che-chun and his secretary Henry CHIU returned to China in mid-March 1946 to help the investigations in cities such as Shanghai, Peiping (now Beijing), and Chungking. Mr. HSIANG informed the Chinese Ministry of Foreign Affairs before their arrival to alert them to prepare the following notice:

*Prosecutor General Joseph B. Keenan of the International Military Tribunal for the Far East will lead a group of six prosecutors and lawyers to go to China and other countries and areas in the Pacific Region to investigate and collect evidence on Japanese atrocities and the breaches of international laws. My Secretary Henry CHIU and I will fly to Shanghai with them on a certain day. Please be noted.*

*Yours,*
*HSIANG Che-chun*[10]

After arriving in China with Mr. Keenan, HSIANG Che-chun sent telegrams almost daily regarding their schedules to the Ministry of Foreign Affairs[11].

Mr. HSANG telegraphed on March 21:

*Joseph B. Keenan, Prosecutor General of the International Military Tribunal for the Far East, will lead his group, including me, to fly from Shanghai to Peiping this afternoon. He plans to fly to Chungking on the 23rd to investigate. Please prepare relevant materials.*

In his telegram on March 23, he stated that:

*Joseph B. Keenan, Prosecutor General of the International Military Tribunal for the Far East, will lead his group, including me, to fly to Chungking this morning by a U.S. military plane.*

Another telegram sent on March 24 stated as:

*Joseph B. Keenan, Director of the International Prosecution Section and Prosecutor General of the International Military Tribunal for the Far East, arrived in Shanghai today on business. He plans to fly to Chungking in several days. He is a trusted friend of General Douglas MacArthur. We don't know if he has any other mission or not there. Please be noted. Any reply should be transferred to me through the Prosecutor's Office of the High Court.*

The Chinese government had been enthusiastically supporting the investigations. CHIANG Kai-shek issued a mandate to the President of the Executive Yuan SOONG Tzu-ven on March 8, the same day he learned that Mr. Keenan's was coming to China.

*The Prosecutor General Joseph B. Keenan of the International Military Tribunal for the Far East will lead a group of six prosecutors and lawyers to come to China and other countries and areas in the Pacific Region to investigate and collect evidence on Japanese atrocities and their breaches of international laws. They will fly to Shanghai with our prosecutor, HSIANG Che-chun, and his Secretary, Henry CHIU, on a certain day. Then Mr. Keenan and Mr. HSIANG will go back to Tokyo first, leaving Mr. CHIU and others to investigate further in China. Please inform all the departments and units, in addition to the Military Commission to prepare the evidence for Japanese atrocities in China.*

*Yours,*
*CHIANG Kai-shek*[12]

Mr. Keenan and his group were very grateful for the help from many departments of the Chinese government. After returning to Tokyo, U.S. Assistant Attorney David N. Sutton sent a telegram on April 23, 1946, to WANG Hua-cheng, an official of the Ministry of Foreign Affairs, to express their gratitude:

*Dear Mr. Wang,*
*On behalf of my colleagues from many countries, including Colonel Morrow, Mr. Henry CHIU, Mr. Crowley, and me, I would like to express my sincere thanks for your assistance in Chungking at the end of March or early April. Help from you and other Chinese officials has reduced our workload and made our work very enjoyable."*[13]

CHIANG Kai-shek met with Mr. Keenan in Chungking. HSIANG Che-chun recalled in his later years:

> *In late March 1946, more than ten judicial officers of IMTFE from various countries were received by CHIANG Kai-shek in Chungking. After contacting the Ministry of Foreign Affairs, I, together with Prosecutor General Joseph B. Keenan, who led a group of more than ten judicial officers of IMTFE from various countries, flew from Tokyo, Japan, to Shanghai, Beiping, Chungking, and Nanjing in late March 1946 to collect evidence of the crimes committed by Japanese aggression against China.*
>
> *On March 26, 1946 (maybe 25 or 27, the exact date is not clear because there is no record), I, together with Prosecutor General Joseph B. Keenan, who led a group of more than ten judicial officers of IMTFE were, received by CHIANG Kai-shek in Chungking. The meeting lasted about 45 minutes. Only four people had spoken at that time, namely, CHIANG Kai-shek, SOONG Mei-ling, Joseph B. Keenan, and Mr. CHIANG's secretary and translator.*
>
> *Mr. CHIANG expressed his gratitude to Mr. Keenan and the International Military Tribunal for the Far East for their hard work and hoped that the Japanese war criminals would be punished. Mr. Keenan thanked Mr. CHIANG for his help and promised to do his best to make Japanese war criminals receive their due punishment through the trial by nine countries together with the United States and China.*[14]

In a letter to HSIANG Che-chun dated October 29, 1947, Joseph B. Keenan recalled this meeting.

> *I am very grateful for your kindness that allowed me to receive the autographed photo of President CHIANG Kai-shek, which I will treasure forever. I especially appreciate that you thoughtfully arranged for me to meet with him in March last year. This is another example of your politeness since we first met."*[15]

As scheduled, Prosecutor General Joseph B. Keenan submitted *the Indictment* to the 11 judges headed by Sir William Webb on the afternoon of April 29, 1946.

## *The Tokyo Trial Proceeding*

The court session of the International Military Tribunal for the Far East officially opened on the morning of May 3, 1946.

*Shen Pao*, the most influential newspaper in China at that time, reported it in detail:

> *The trial of 28 major Japanese war criminals began this morning in the Tribunal War Ministry Building Court House. Nine judges appeared in court facing the war criminals, except for the judges from India and the Philippines who were absent at the time; on the left side were the Allied Powers and audience. At about ten o'clock, General CHU Shih-ming and General Robert Eichelberger came to sit as observers. On the right were people from the Allied Powers and Japanese journalists. The trial was scheduled to begin at 10:30, but ITAGAKI Seishiro and KIMURA Heitaro, who had just arrived at Atsugi Airport from Bangkok yet, had to be transferred to the court therefore there was a bit of delay. After an hour's waiting, the two seats were still empty. The court session proceeded without them. Led by KIDO Koichi, six Japanese war criminals entered the court and sat quietly in the dock. TOJO Hideki sat in the center of the first row, with DOIHARA Kenji, HATA Shunroku, HIROTA Koki, and MINAMI Jiro on the right HOSHINO Naoki, KAYA Okinori, and KIDO Koichi on the left, and the rest behind. Led by Chief of Counsel Joseph B. Keenan, prosecutors of the Allied Powers sat in the center of the Bench. After Captain Van Meter, the Court Marshal announced, "All rise, the Honorable Judges presiding!" While all were standing up, the judges took their seats under the nine national flags of the Allied Powers. MEI Ju Ao, the Chinese judge, sited next to Chief Judge.*
>
> *Reporters from the Allied Powers all started whispering after seeing Chinese judge MEI Ju-ao sitting next to the presiding judge. Then they were told that China should have their voice in all international events because 20 million Chinese were lost during the War of Resistance against Japan. After Chief Judge Webb announced the court was in session, Joseph Keenan introduced the prosecutors to the judges one by one. The first one he introduced was HSIANG Che-chun, Chief Prosecutor of Shanghai High Court, who acted on behalf of the Republic of China. Then this Chinese prosecutor caught everyone's attention, especially those Japanese war criminals.*

*In the opening statement, Webb said, "There has been no more important criminal trial in the history than today. Indeed, we are a court of ordinary men selected from the supreme courts of our respective nations. On the other hand, the accused before us were leaders of Japan in its heyday. The crimes alleged are crimes against the peace of the world, against the laws of war, against humanity, and conspiracy to commit those crimes. They are so multitudinous and of such magnitude that it was decided the appropriate forum would be a military tribunal of an international character.*

MEI Ju-ao recorded his feelings in his diary of that day:

*Today was the first day that the International Military Tribunal for the Far East started its performance and the first act of this historical drama in which I played a role as a guest performer ... Could you imagine half a year ago that we would feel pride and elation today? What was it like this day of last year, when Dushan county and Duyun county were under attack, and even people in Chungking were panic-stricken? I responded to him that the rise and fall of a nation were unpredictable, and all these changes seemed to us like a drama... And now I am truly playing a role in this drama, which is about to begin."*

Particularly, he made a vivid description of the dock.

*Behind the three large tables was the dock for the accused, which was a rectangular platform a few feet above the ground. All the twenty-six war criminals were sitting up straight in two rows. Under the strong light, the gleaming camera flash, and people's close attention on us, I had no time to match all those defendants' faces with their pictures, which were arranged according to their seating positions and provided to each of the judges. The only ones who caught my eyes were TOJO sitting in the middle and DOIHARA with a round face. Behind TOJO was OKAWA Shumei, who pretended to have a mental disorder and tried to commit harassment from time to time. The American military police wanted to stop him from doing so and sometimes had to hold him from behind. OKAWA submitted a written application to examine his mental and physical conditions. He was undoubtedly the one who acted most ridiculously and drew the greatest attention, while all the others managed to keep a stern face and look calm, especially TOJO, who sat still like a gypsum statue.*

*While I was unable to recognize those twenty-six war criminals one by one, an endless resentment and sorrow rose in my mind when facing this crowd. All these men were old hands in the invasion of China. They afflicted China for decades and butchered tens of millions of Chinese people. My resentment toward them reflects that of my fellow countrymen. The opportunity I can sit at the bench today to punish these culprits was built on the flesh and blood of millions and millions of my compatriots. I shall be vigilant! I shall be solemn!"*[16]

There is no doubt that all Chinese representatives shared his feelings.

HSIANG Che-chun also briefly described the Tribunal in his later years when he wrote back to HAN Shuzhi, President of the Shanghai High Court:

*About the trial of criminal offenders in various countries and the trial of Japanese war criminals at the International Military Tribunal for the Far East you talked about in your letter, here is what I know:*

*(1) The seats for judges, prosecutors, jurors, and clerks of general criminal cases in the West are fixed, and those for the defendant's attorney. It is known to the public, and there is no need to mark them.*

*(2) The number of seats for the audience is unknown.*

*(3) Eleven judges from the United States of America, the Republic of China, the United Kingdom of Great Britain and Northern Ireland, the Union of Soviet Socialist Republics, the Commonwealth of Australia, Canada, the Republic of France, the Kingdom of the Netherlands, New Zealand, India, and the Republic of the Philippines who tried Japanese war criminals at the International Military Tribunal for the Far East sat in one row. Eleven court clerks were sitting in the same direction in front of the judges. Prosecutors sat facing the judges and clerks. The prosecutor's lectern was where the prosecutor gave his statement or questioned the defendant. The 25 defendants sat in three rows, facing the judges to stand trial. Among the 28 defendants prosecuted, two died of illness during the trial, and one was excluded due to his mental illness.*

*(4) The International Military Tribunal for the Far East court took a large space. Except for the seats occupied by judges, prosecutors, clerks, interpreters, and defendants, there must be hundreds of seats upstairs and downstairs for the audience. The exact number is unknown.*

*(5) Eleven judges from eleven countries were in the Tokyo Trial. More than half, which was six, of them were needed to make a quorum.*

*(6) In fact, the president often attended the trial, but the Charter does not include any requirements for his attendance.*[17]

## *55 Counts of Indictment*

From the afternoon of May 3 to the morning of May 4, the Chief prosecutor, Keena requested Captain Van Meter, the Court Marshal, and Mr. Edward Dell, the Acting Court Clerk, to read the Indictment.

The preface of the Indictment indignantly pointed out that:

*In the years hereinafter referred to in this Indictment, the internal and foreign policies of Japan were dominated and directed by a criminal militaristic clique, and such policies were the cause of serious world troubles, aggressive wars, and great damage to the interests of peace-loving peoples, as well as the interests of the Japanese people themselves. The mind of the Japanese people was systematically poisoned with harmful ideas about the alleged racial superiority of Japan over other peoples of Asia and even of the whole world. Such parliamentary institutions as existed in Japan were used as implements for widespread aggression, and a system similar to those then established by Hitler and the Nazi party in Germany and by the Fascist party in Italy was introduced. Japan's economic and financial resources were, to a large extent, mobilized for war aims, to the detriment of the welfare of the Japanese people. A conspiracy between the defendants, joined in by the rulers of other aggressive countries, namely, Nazi Germany and Fascist Italy, was entered. The main object of this conspiracy was to secure the domination and exploitation by the aggressive States of the rest of the world, and to this end, to commit or encourage the commission of crimes against peace, war crimes, and crimes against humanity as defined in the Charter of this Tribunal, thus threatening and injuring the basic principles of liberty and respect for the human personality."*[18]

Although the statement is brief, it profoundly revealed the essence of the Japanese militarist criminal group and is still thought-provoking today.

There was a total of 55 counts of criminal acts in the Indictment. From a legal point of view, only if those acts were proved to be criminal acts could one not name them as criminals. Therefore, let's call them the count of the indictment, or "the Count" Some counts were brought against all defendants, and others were brought against some of the defendants. These 55 counts were further divided into three groups Crimes against Peace (count 1 to 36), Murder (count 37 to 52), and Conventional War Crimes and Crimes against Humanity (count 53 to 55).

The following is a summary description of these 55 counts.

In group one, Crimes against Peace, count 1 to 5 are crimes committed by the Japanese Class A war criminals in plotting, formulating, and executing common plans or conspiracies of invasions against Northeastern China, the whole of China, East Asia, the Pacific, and the Indian Oceans between 1928 and 1945. Count 6 to17 are crimes committed by Japanese Class A war criminals' planning and preparing a war of aggression against the Republic of China, the United States, United Kingdom of Great Britain and Northern Ireland, the Commonwealth of Australia, New Zealand, Canada, India, the Philippines, the Kingdom of the Netherlands, France, Thailand, and the Union of Soviet Socialist Republics. Count 18 to 36 are the crimes of aggression committed by Japanese war criminals against a certain country or region during a certain period. The following counts are about Japanese aggression against China.

> *COUNT 18: The Defendants, on or about September 18, 1931, initiated a war of aggression and a war in violation of international law, treaties, agreements, and assurances, against the Republic of China.*
>
> *COUNT 19: The Defendants, on or about July 7, 1937, initiated a war of aggression and a war in violation of international law, treaties, agreements, and assurances, against the Republic of China.*
>
> *COUNT 27: All the Defendants, between September 18, 1931, and September 2, 1945, waged a war of aggression violating international law, treaties, agreements, and assurances against the Republic of China.*
>
> *COUNT 28: All the Defendants, between July 7, 1937, and September 2, 1945, waged a war of aggression and a war in violation of international law, treaties, agreements, and assurances, against the Republic of China.*
>
> *COUNT 32: All the Defendants, between December 7, 1941, and September 2, 1945, waged a war of aggression and a war in violation of international law, treaties, agreements, and assurances, against the Republic of China and the Kingdom of the Netherlands.*

The dates identified in these counts unambiguously demonstrated that Japan had invaded China long before any country. While Japanese aggression against other countries and regions such as the United States (count 20 and 29), the Philippines (count 21 and 30), the British Commonwealth of Nations (count 22 and 31), and Thailand (count 24 and 34) were from December 7, 1941, to September 2, 1945, which was after the Attack on Pearl Harbor, thirteen years after the Huanggutun Incident, ten years after the September 18 Incident, and four years after the Lugouqiao Incident, Japanese aggression against the Union of Soviet Socialist Republics (count 25 and 35) and the Mongolian People's Republic (count 6 and 36) were during the summer of 1939 and against the Republic of France (count 23 and 33) on and after September 22, 1940. They happened years after Japanese aggression against China. This also shows that China had suffered the most and for the longest time.

Group two is Murder, this was included in Conventional War Crimes, but it was specifically listed in the Indictment to raise the attention of the tribunal and the people. There are sixteen counts in this group, among which six (count 45 to 50) were committed in China. The defendants were charged with attacking Nanjing, Guangzhou, Hankou, Changsha, Hengyang, Guilin, and Liuzhou and unlawfully killing and murdering large numbers of civilians and disarmed soldiers of the Republic of China.

On specific dates, the other ten counts in group two are about Japanese atrocities in other countries and regions. For example, count 39 is about the Japanese attack on Pearl Harbor on December 7, 1941. Count 40 to 43 are about the Japanese attack on the British Commonwealth of Nations at Kota Bahru, Hong Kong, the British Settlement in Shanghai, and the Philippines on December 8, 1941. Count 51 and 52 are charges against Japanese troops for attacking the territories of Mongolia and the Union of Soviet Socialist Republics in 1938 and 1939 and unlawfully killing and murdering certain members of their armed forces. While count 44 is a charge against all the Defendants who instituted as leaders, organizers, instigators, or accomplices in the formulation or execution of a common plan or conspiracy to procure and permit the extensive murders of prisoners of war and civilians between September 18, 1931, and September 2, 1945.

Group Three is Conventional War Crimes and Crimes against Humanity, which contains Counts 53, 54, and 55. Under these three counts, the defendants were charged with violations of the law and the international conventions and with the commitment of war crimes against many thousands of prisoners of war and civilians. It should be noted that each of these counts covers two sets of periods: "*between December 2, 1941, and September 2, 1945*" for the various countries of the

Asia-Pacific region, while "*in the period beginning from September 18, 1931*" for China.

These three groups of crimes included in the Indictment are slightly different from the three crimes in the Charter of the International Military Tribunal for the Far East mentioned in Chapter 2. This is because the Charter followed the precedent of the Nuremberg Trials. While the International Prosecution Section found that Japan in Tokyo Trial differed from the Nuremberg Trials in Germany. The Nazis began to carry out planned genocide of Jews, including Jews in Germany, before the war, which is unprecedented and cannot be described as Conventional War Crimes, so Crimes against Humanity were used. Although Japanese fascists did not kill their people, their crimes such as the Nanjing Massacre, Malayan Massacre, Bataan Death March, and Thai-Burma Death Railway could hardly be classified as Conventional War Crimes. Therefore, the International Military Tribunal for the Far East kept Crimes against Peace as the first group of crimes, outlined Murder as the second, and combined Conventional War Crimes and Crimes against Humanity as the third.

There are five appendices to the Indictment.

Appendix A The Histories of Japanese Invasions against China and Other Countries, which includes ten sections.

Section 1 is Japan's military aggression against Manchuria.

Section 2 is Japan's military aggression against other regions in China.

Section 3 is Japan's economic aggression against China and other countries and regions in East Asia.

Section 4 is Japan's use of corruption and coercive methods in China and other occupied territories.

Section 5 is Japan's preparation for conventional wars.

Section 6 is Japan's policy on aggression and propaganda.

Section 7 shows Japan, Germany, and Italy's collusion and aggression against French Indochina and Thailand.

Section 8 is Japan's aggression against the Soviet Union.

Section 9 is Japan's aggression against the United States, the Philippines, and the British Commonwealth of Nations countries.

Section 10 is Japan's aggression against the Netherlands and Portugal.

Each section briefly describes the facts of Japanese aggression in two to three hundred words, or six to seven hundred words.

*Appendix B* is 20 international treaties Japan had violated, including the ones noted in chapter II of this book.

*Appendix C* specifies 15 assurances of non-invasion, and non-escalation Japan made and was alleged to have broken.

*Appendix D* contains important extracts from international war treaties related to war behavior, and the promises observed by Japan.

*Appendix E* illustrates the official positions of the 28 defendants indited by the Indictment to define their personal responsibilities during the Japanese aggression.

These appendices are important references for the 55 counts. They reveal the arrogance, greed, and hypocrisy of Japanese militarists. In addition, they manifest that Japan had invaded China for the longest time, and Chinese soldiers and civilians had suffered the most.

Eleven signatories are signed on the Indictment, with Chief of Counsel Joseph B. Keenan the first and Chinese Prosecutor HSIANG Che-chun the second.

The Chinese prosecutor was one of the main drafters of the Indictment because Japan had invaded China for the longest time. As HSIANG Che-chun recalled in a conversation in his later years:

> *As a prosecutor, I participated in the prosecution of Japanese war criminals. A large number of witnesses and evidence indicated that the crimes of aggression committed by Japanese militarists against the Chinese people were numerous and reprehensible. The Indictment was submitted to the Tribunal on April 29, 1946. Among the 55 counts listed in it, 44 are related to Japanese aggression against China.*[19]

These 44 counts involve the Japanese atrocities in China and those against overseas Chinese and Chinese embassies and consuls in the Asia-Pacific region.

Due to a shortage of skilled staff for the Tribunal, HSIANG Che-chun drafted and typed the Indictment himself. The typewriter he used back then is now kept in the Shanghai Humanism Memorial Museum.

The fifty Counts were clarified against their defendants. Count 1-17, 27-32, 34, and 44 were against all defendants, and the other 30 counts charged 7 to 26 defendants. Among all defendants, the most accused were TOJO Hideki, DOIHARA Kenji, ITAGAKI Seishiro, and KIDO Koichi. They were charged in more than 50 counts. In addition, the Japanese military's crimes against the same country or region were carefully distinguished according to time the acts were committed. On the other hand, too many details would make the case unnecessarily complicated and increase proof liabilities. Therefore, the 55 counts were merged into 10 at the conviction.

*Count 1 All the Defendants participated as leaders, organizers, instigators, or accomplices in the institution or execution of a common plan or conspiracy to wage wars of aggression in violation of international law.*

*Count 27 All the Defendants waged an undeclared war of aggression against the Republic of China.*

*Count 29 All the Defendants waged a war of aggression against the United States of America.*

*Count 31 All the Defendants waged a war of aggression against the British Commonwealth of Nations (its colonies and protectorates in the Far East, South Asia, the Commonwealth of Australia, and New Zealand).*

*Count 32 All the Defendants waged a war of aggression against the Kingdom of the Netherlands (Holland East India).*

*Count 32 All the Defendants waged a war of aggression against the Republic of France (Colony of French Republic, Indochina).*

*Count 35&36 All the Defendants waged a war of aggression against the Union of Soviet Socialist Republics.*

*Count 54 Some Defendants ordered, authorized, and permitted the offenses that violated the laws of War.*

*Count 55 Some Defendants deliberately and recklessly disregarded their legal duty to secure prisoners of war and civilians.*

The 45 counts merged are also mentioned in the judgment of the Tribunal.

In short, the Indictment is an official denunciation of Japanese war criminals and Japanese fascists.

## *References*

[1] Mei, Ju-ao. 2005. *International Military Tribunal for the Far East.* Law Press; People's Court Press, 152.

[2] Cheng, Zhaoqi, and Xiang Longwan. 2017. *Transcripts of the Proceedings of the International Military Tribunal for the Far East (Chinese version).* Vol. 1. Shanghai Jiao Tong University Press, 311.

[3] Xiang, Longwan. 2014. *HSIANG Che-chun's Letters, Telegrams, and Statements at the Tokyo Trial.* Shanghai Jiao tong University Press, 5–6.
[4] Official Letter No. 35-158. Ministry of Foreign Affairs of the National Government.
[5] Xiang, Longwan. 2014. *HSIANG Che-chun's Letters, Telegrams, and Statements at the Tokyo Trial.* Shanghai Jiao Tong University Press, 8–9.
[6] Official Letter No. 35-181. Ministry of Foreign Affairs of the National Government.
[7] Official Letter No. 35-522. Ministry of Foreign Affairs of the National Government; Official Letter No. 538. Ministry of Justice and Administration.
[8] Cheng, Zhaoqi, and Xiang Longwan. 2017. *Transcripts of the Proceedings of the International Military Tribunal for the Far East (Chinese version).* Vol. 2. Shanghai Jiao Tong University Press, 419–420 (2303 of the English court records).
[9] Ibid.
[10] Xiang, Longwan. 2014. *HSIANG Che-chun's Letters, Telegrams, and Statements at the Tokyo Trial.* Shanghai Jiao tong University Press, 10.
[11] Ibid., 10–12.
[12] Official Letter No. 35-538. Ministry of Foreign Affairs of the National Government.
[13] Official Letter No. 35-*. Ministry of Foreign Affairs of the National Government.
[14] Xiang, Longwan. 2014. *HSIANG Che-chun's Letters, Telegrams, and Statements at the Tokyo Trial.* Shanghai Jiao tong University Press, 187.
[15] Ibid., 295.
[16] MEI, Ju-ao. 2016. *My Personal Experience at the Tokyo Trial.* Edited by Mei Xiao'ao and Mei Xiaokan. Shanghai Jiao Tong University Press, 348–350.
[17] Xiang, Longwan. 2014. *HSIANG Che-chun's Letters, Telegrams, and Statements at the Tokyo Trial.* Shanghai Jiao tong University Press, 188.
[18] Cheng, Zhaoqi, and Xiang Longwan. 2017. *Transcripts of the Proceedings of the International Military Tribunal for the Far East (Chinese version).* Vol. 1. Shanghai Jiao Tong University Press, 19–20 (27–28 of the English court records).
[19] Xiang, Longwan. 2014. *HSIANG Che-chun's Letters, Telegrams, and Statements at the Tokyo Trial.* Shanghai Jiao tong University Press, 189.

CHAPTER 4

# Hard Evidence

## *Chains of Solid Evidence*

On May 3, 1946, the trial officially began.

The prosecution first read the Indictment, including as many as 55 counts. However, the defendants were very arrogant after hearing it. On May 6, when the president asked each of the defendants whether they pleaded guilty, every one of them answered, "I plead not guilty." Several defendants even shouted arrogantly. Therefore, continuing to provide evidence was all in all to the prosecutors.

The entire prosecution can be divided into three stages. Firstly, the prosecution had filed the lawsuit from June 4, 1946, to February 23, 1947. Secondly, the defendant had filed a counterclaim from February 24, 1947, to January 12, 1948. The last stage was a court trial from January 12, 1948, to April 16, 1948. It can be said that the production of evidence had run through the entire prosecution.

In addition to collecting evidence through letters and telegrams and seeking evidence in China personally, the Chinese prosecution team had three new channels.

The first is to ask for evidence from the relevant departments through the Chinese military delegation to Japan. The Chinese military delegation to Japan can be traced back to the Cairo Conference in 1943. During the talks with CHIANG Kai-shek, Franklin D. Roosevelt promised that the United States would support China playing an important role in the post-war occupation of Japan. After Germany surrendered in May 1945, the occupation of Japan became the core issue of the Joint Chiefs of Staff of the United States; they estimated that at least 800,000 soldiers should be deployed to Japan. The Americans would not agree to send so many soldiers to Japan, a place far from their home.

Therefore, the newly elected U.S. President Harry S. Truman indicated from time to time that he hoped to have a joint occupation with Great Britain, China, and the Soviet Union. In the *Potsdam Declaration* issued on July 26, 1945, in the name of the heads of China, Great Britain, and the United States, Article 7 says that "points in Japanese territory to be designated by the Allies shall be occupied..."[1]

Following the surrender of the Japanese Empire, the Far Eastern Commission was founded in Washington by representatives of Australia, Canada, China, France, India, the Netherlands, New Zealand, the Philippines, the Soviet Union, Great Britain, and the United States. All representatives agreed that occupation should be the priority to disarmament of Japan, and the Allied forces, with a supreme commander appointed by the United States, would carry out the occupation of the main islands of Japan.

On March 13, 1946, the U.S. Department of State suggested to the Chinese government that China should send a small group of troops to Japan in advance. The government of China accepted this proposal, and a delegation with 12 experts and 4 soldiers led by Lieutenant General CHU Shih-ming arrived in Tokyo on April 1. The mission of General CHU was also mentioned in Justice MEI Ju-ao's diary on April 4.

> *Gen. CHU is China's chief representative to the Allied Council for Japan, meaning he is the top Chinese official stationed in Japan. In accordance with the Chinese presidential order, all the Chinese officials here, whether military or civilian, are under his supervision and control, with the only exception of the judge of the International Military Tribunal for the Far East. He is also the only counterpart to deal with Gen. MacArthur's GHQ and is in charge of all the work concerning China's military, political, economic, and cultural affairs in Japan. Needless to say, he has an arduous job and a great task. The team that he brought the day before has less than twenty members, but it is said that there will be two more groups joining him within this month."*[2]

CHU Shih-ming (ZHU Shimiiiig), Ji Guang (courtesy name), and Gong Liang (literary name) was born in Xiangxiang, Hunan Province, in 1898. He was also admitted to Tsinghua School, the Study-in-American Prep School, then studied at the Massachusetts Institute of Technology and Virginia Military Institute, and then received a Ph.D. from Columbia University. After returning from the United States in 1926, he held many important positions such as personal assistant for CHIANG Kai-shek, Chief Education Officer of the Transportation Technical School of the Military Affairs Commission of National Government, Chief of the Staff of the Military Affairs Commission, Director of the Second National Defense Department, Military Attaché of the Embassy in the Soviet Union, Director of Department of Information, Ministry of Foreign Affairs and Military Attaché Washington, etc.

CHU Pin-yan (ZHU Binyuan), CHU Shih-ming's elder brother, was admitted to Tsinghua School in the same year as HSIANG Che-chun. He got his bachelor's degree in economics from Wesleyan University and master's degree from Columbia University. After returning to China, he founded the Department of Economics of Tsinghua University and served as the first head of the department. Later, he served as secretary of economist Ma Yinchu and manager of Jincheng Bank. CHU Shih-ming also treated HSIANG Che-chun as his elder brother, and he sent telegrams back to China several times to help Mr. HSIANG collect evidence. For example, he sent two consecutive telegrams to the Ministry of Foreign Affairs on May 22, 1946.

*Nanking Ministry of Foreign Affairs,*

*The Prosecutor Office of the International Military Tribunal for the Far East needs evidence about Japan's throwing in more troops to the northeast and north China via South Korea before the Lugouqiao* (Marco Polo Bridge) *Incident to prove that Japan had been preparing for the war for a long time. Moreover, evidence of China's handling of Japanese prisoners of war in accordance with the Geneva Convention Relative to the Treatment of Prisoners of War is also needed. Please send it to Judge MEI Ju-ao or LI Yun-li from the Ministry of Military Command and ask them to take it to Tokyo. Commissioner LIN Ding-ping will organize them to make them available.*

*Yours,*
*CHU Shih-ming*

*Nanking Ministry of Foreign Affairs,*

*Please inform the Ministry of Military Command and Ministry of Justice and Administration that according to prosecutor HSIANG Che-chun, the 28 major Japanese war criminals have already been prosecuted by the prosecutors of all allied countries at the International Military Tribunal for the Far East. The following information is needed urgently. A. Evidence and related materials of the atrocities committed by DOIHARA Kenji, HASHIMOTO Kingoro, HATA Shunroku, ITAGAKI Seishiro, and MATSUI Iwane in China; B. Evidence and related materials of Japanese atrocities in Canton, Wuhan, Changsha, Hengyang, Kweilin, and Liuchow when they fell. Please collect them as soon as possible and telegraph us the important ones first.*

*Yours,*
*CHU Shih-ming*[3]

Moreover, CHU Shih-ming promptly gave HSIANG Che-chun the evidence sent from China. For example, on June 8, 1946, the Ministry of Foreign Affairs sent him telegrams of the indictment of 30 suspects, namely, DOIHARA Kenji, the transcripts of HASHIMOTO Kingoro's crimes, and the evidence of Japanese atrocities in Kuangtung, Kuanghsi, Hunan, and Hubei Province and asked him to give them to Mr. HSIANG.

The second channel is to seek evidence from Japanese archives and their media reports during the war. The Chinese prosecution team spent much time looking through the archives of the Japanese Ministry of War and collecting and analyzing their media reports as the Japanese army had been preventing the release of information during the war and destroyed evidence of their crimes before surrender. The chief consultant of NYI, Judson T.Y., mentioned it in his work.

*After much consideration, the Chinese prosecution team decided to seek help from the Chinese military delegation to Japan to access the sealed archives of the former Japanese Army Ministry to look for evidence of the crimes of DOIHARA Kenji and ITAGAKI Seishiro during the Japanese war of aggression against China. However, it was not easy to find hard evidence as so many files were there. Fortunately, there are similarities between Chinese and Japanese characters, and it was not difficult to distinguish the category and title of those documents. In addition, LIU T.C. and*

*WU Hsueh-yi in the Chinese prosecution team are proficient in Japanese. After working day and night for many days, many valuable documents were found, and everyone was pleased to make use of indigenous materials.*[4]

As for this, Secretary KAW V.P. mentioned another example.

*I was furious when I read news in the Nichi Nichi Shimbun (predecessor of Mainichi Shimbun) about two Japanese officers, MUKAI Toshiaki and NODA Takeshi, using sabers to participate in a "killing competition." It said that one killed 105 people and the other 106 people, and the photo of these two beasts holding sabers in their hands was even published. At that time, the Nanking War Crimes Tribunal tried the Japanese Class B war criminals of aggression against China. The President SHIH Mei-yu (SHI Meiyu), who had been a student of Mr. HSIANG, and Mr. NYI, Judson T.Y., were good friends and colleagues in the Shanghai International Settlement Court. I made three copies of the newspaper, one for our office and two for SHI Mei-yu through Mr. NYI; Mr. Shi thought it was indeed strong evidence and immediately sent it to the Headquarters as an official document through the Chinese Ministry of National Defense. After several months of investigation, detectives from the Headquarters finally arrested these two Japanese second lieutenants who had already retired and set up stalls in the streets of Saitama Prefecture. Then these two murderers were brought to Nanking for trial by a regular plane of the Chinese military delegation to Japan. In the end, together with TANI Hisao, they were executed by shooting at Yuhuatai in Nanking.*[5]

The third channel was the interrogation of the arrested suspects. As mentioned in Chapter 1, 118 suspects were arrested in four batches and detained in the Sugamo Prison in Tokyo. They had been interrogated by officials of the International Prosecution Section headed by Chief of Counsel Joseph B. Keenan during the latter part of 1945. The Chinese prosecution team participated in the interrogation and checked and analyzed the related documents. Secretary LIU T.C., who was proficient in Japanese, played a major role in this.

For example, on June 30, 1946, he issued a memorandum to U.S. Assistant Attorneys David N. Sutton and Frank S. Tavenner Jr. with new evidence about AIKAWA Gisuke and KUHARA Fusanosuke after he checked the related documents. On August 9, 1946, he studied the evidence IPS No. 1005-22 and concluded that it revealed DOIHARA Kenji's secret activities in China since

1937. On May 9, 1947, he checked the documentary evidence labeled as Doc. No. 674 confirmed that the Japanese five ministers' conference in 1938 determined their policy of further aggression against China.

The trial began on May 3, 1946, and ended on April 16, 1948, a total of 418 days. There were approximately 199 days of a trial involving Japanese aggression against China, which accounts for 48%. Additionally, the Japanese army committed many atrocities against overseas Chinese and members of the Chinese embassies and consulates in other areas of the Asia-Pacific region. This shows that China had suffered the longest aggression and made the greatest sacrifices. Imagine the Chinese prosecution team had experienced a long and hard time.

The evidence found by the prosecution team through various channels played an important role in the trial. Here are two cases.

## *DOIHARA Kenji and PU Yi*

The first case shows the Japanese crime of intimidating PU Yi to travel to Northeast China to establish Manchukuo.

For the Japanese to invade Manchuria, DOIHARA Kenji made a special trip to Tientsin after Manchurian Incident to coerce PU Yi to go to Northeast China. To cover up their conspiracy, the Japanese made up some stories, claiming that "the Kwantung Army never wanted to invade Manchuria," "the Manchurian demanded the establishment of their new country," and "PU Yi attempted to become an emperor again." These claims were also their defenses in the Tokyo Trial.

As for PU Yi, his life is legendary. He was the last emperor of China as the eleventh and final Qing Dynasty ruler, becoming Emperor Hsuan Tung at age two in 1908, but forced to abdicate on February 12, 1912, due to the Xinhai Revolution. He was briefly restored to the throne as Qing emperor by the loyalist Genera CHANG Hsun (Zhang Xun) from July 1 to July 12, 1917. In 1924, with the support of SUN Yat-sen (SUN Zhongshan), he was expelled from the palace by General FENG Yu-hsiang (FENG Yuxiang) but found refuge in Tientsin, where he began to court the Japanese who had long desired control of China. In his book *From Emperor to Citizen,* written in his later years, he said repeatedly that not only himself but many of his loyalists, such CHENG Hsiao-hsu (Zheng Xiaoxu), were ambitious to restore him to the throne.

> *Thinking of the YANGXIN Hall and QIANQING Palace, which I have just left, and of my throne and all the bright yellow things, the desire for revenge and restoration has come to my mind... My only interest is restoration. In the words of people from the Forbidden City, it is also called "recovering the legacy." In the words of the elders and the old ministers, this is "recovering the old things" and "returning the government to the Qing Dynasty"... It can be said that from the promulgation of the abdication edict to the establishment of Manchukuo, my desire to restore to the throne had never stopped for a day.*[6]

However, the collapse of the Qing Dynasty made him frightened. His loyalists CHENG Hsiao-hsu and CHEN Pao-chen (Chen Baochen), had different attitudes towards the Japanese, so he did not dare to believe in the Japanese completely. Therefore, he had mixed emotional reactions when he met DOIHARA Kenji for the first time in Tientsin, and when he learned that the Japanese wanted him to go to Northeast China to be a puppet emperor, he refused it at first.

On August 27, 1946, HSIANG Che-chun's statement in court was "*on the subject of Japanese abduction of the dethroned Emperor Hsuen Tung to head independent movement in Manchuria – a movement the establishment of which Japanese were planning and engineering.*" He read four telegrams, including three from KUWASHIMA Kazue, Consul General at Tientsin to SHIDEHARA Kijuro, Foreign Minister of Japan, and one from the MURAI Kuramatsu, Japanese Consul at Shanghai to SHIDEHARA. These telegrams were marked by the court as evidence and numbered, becoming powerful weapons for the Chinese prosecutor.[7]

The first telegram from KUWASHIMA Kazue was sent on November 1, 1931. In late October 1931, LIU En-ko (LIU Enge) and CHIN Ting-hsun (JIN Dingxun), the so-called "People's Representatives of Northeast China" who actively planned the establishment of Manchukuo, sneaked into Tientsin from Northeast China to have a secret conference with the Japanese, and then left hurriedly. This telegram shows the result of their meeting.

> *(1) First to send telegrams for attacking HSUEH-LIANG.*
> *(2) To withdraw from the Nanking Government for the time being and try to restore the Five Races Republic Government, which will be law-governed.*

*(3) To appoint an elder statesman for the head of the Central Government who has rendered great services to the country and enjoys explicit confidence at home and abroad and put the Government under his charge. (This points to TUAN Chi-jui (DUAN Qirui).*

*(4) During the transition period, to place the administration of the Northeastern districts in the hands of the organ, as shown in telegram No. 458. The representatives, to add for your information, appear to intend to carry out these plans with the consent of the Japanese Inspector-Generals, such as the Commander HONJO. (Please do not publish for the time being.)*

This telegram was marked as *Exhibit Number 287*.

MURAI's telegram was sent on November 2, 1931. DOIHARA Kenji went to Tientsin secretly due to PU Yi's hesitation towards being a puppet and the growing public pressure in China. This telegram from MURAI shows the situation and DOIHARA's activities at the time.

*The Chinese newspaper of the 2nd instant published a telegram from Tientsin to the effect that the Japanese were stirring up agitation for the independence of the Three Eastern Provinces, that Prince Kung had already given his complete acceptance, but Emperor Hsuen Tung had refused, so Col. DOIHARA had to come to Tientsin secretly. The newspaper said he is now secretly planning to take various steps to take Emperor Hsuen Tung to Mukden, but since Emperor Hsuen Tung still refused, the Japanese were threatening him.*

This telegram was marked as *Exhibit Number 288*.

The second telegram from KUWASHIMA was also sent on November 2, 1931, and was marked as "*Exhibit Number 289*." In this telegram, KUWASHIMA analyzed the situation and made plans to lure PU Yi into Northeast China.

*(1) As the unity between CHIANG Hsueh-liang's (ZHANG Xueliang) and CHIANG Kai-shek was very strong recently, the chances of CHIANG Sue-liang's downfall became next to impossible. The present Manchuria Regional Government, except Mr. HSI-ciia (Xi Qia), would conspire with the old government in deference to it, so there was absolutely no prospect of any natural development of events expected by our government.*

(2) *In order to pretend that Japan had nothing to do with the abduction of the emperor, it would be needed to land him ashore at Yin-Kow, but if time was wasted, this port would be frozen.*
(3) *Taking advantage of the arrival at Tientsin of Ching-Liang from Mukden, we can propagate as if he had come, to receive here the emperor.*
(4) *Here we can get chartered and use a Chinese ship.*
(5) *The fact that the Chinese population in Manchuria is not talking much about this matter is due to their anxiety about the emperor's resolution and their discretion toward Japan. So, if the emperor is resolved to go to Manchuria at the risk of his life, and its method can be provided, it will be possible to make it appear like a Chinese movement, by enhancing Chinese public opinion and making public the statement to welcome the emperor.*

The third telegram from KUWASHIMA was sent on November 3, 1931, and was marked as "*Exhibit Number 290.*" In this telegram, in response to the opposition in the Japanese government, KUWASHIMA offered his method. "*DOIHARA told the staff of the Consulate that the Manchurian state of affairs was brought to the present condition solely by the activities of the military authorities there and that in case that the enthronement of the emperor becomes indispensable in order to save the situation, it would be outrageous for the present government to take the attitude of preventing it. If it should prove true, the Kwantung Army might separate from the government.*" This telegram also shows that the commander of the Kwantung Army, HONJO Shigeru indulged DOIHARA's conspiracy. "*Again, when Commander HONJO was requested by DOIHARA and others to get the understanding of the Consul-General, he simply gave them advice not to act in a hurry.*"

The court session continued onto August 28, 1946, and British prosecutor Comyns Carr, U.S. assistant prosecutor David N. Sutton and Indian prosecutor Menon provided more evidence on the matter.[8]

*Exhibit No. 291* is the telegram sent on November 3, 1931, from KUWASHIMA to SHIDEHARA.

*Exhibit No. 292* is the telegram sent on November 4, 1931, from KUWASHIMA to SHIDEHARA.

*Exhibit No. 293* is the telegram sent on some day in November 1931 from KUWASHIMA to SHIDEHARA.

*Exhibit No.294* is the telegram sent on November 13, 1931, from ARAKAWA, Consul-General at Yinkow to SHIDEHARA.

*Exhibit No.295* is the telegram sent on the same day from KUWASHIMA to SHIDEHARA.

*Exhibit No.296* is the second telegram sent on the same day from KUWASHIMA to SHIDEHARA.

*Exhibit No.297* is the telegram sent on the same day from Consul-General HAYASHI in Mukden to SHIDEHARA.

*Exhibit No.298* is the telegram sent on the same day from Liaoyang Deputy Consul YAMAZAKI to SHIDEHARA.

*Exhibit No.299* is the telegram relates to the instructions given by the War Minister to the Kwantung Army about the future of Pu Yi and the establishment of the Manchukuo Government.

*Exhibit No.300* is the telegram sent on November 17, 1931, from KUWASHIMA to SHIDEHARA.

*Exhibit No.301* is the telegram sent on November 22, 1931, from TSUKAMOTO, Governor-General of the Kwantung Army to SHIDEHARA.

*Exhibit No.302* is the telegram sent on the same day from ARAKAWA to SHIDEHARA.

*Exhibit No.303* is the telegram sent on November 26, 1931, from Consul YANO at Peiping to SHIDEHARA.

*Exhibit No.304* is the telegram sent on November 27, 1931, from KUWASHIMA to SHIDEHARA.

*Exhibit No.305* is the telegram sent on December 6, 1931, from Acting Consul General MORISHIMA at Mukden to SHIDEHARA.

These telegrams will not be elaborated on here. However, such a large number of telegrams in a short time and the many diplomatic officials involved are enough to show that the establishment of Manchukuo was not what PU Yi wanted at first, let alone the wishes of the Chinese people. They prove that the defendants were undoubtedly guilty.

## *KAGESA Sadaaki and WANG Ching-wei*

The second case here reveals the crimes committed by the Japanese and WANG Ching-wei (WANG Jingwei), another Japanese puppet in China.

WANG Ching-wei, born as WANG Chao-ming in Sanshui, Kuangtung Province, but of Chechiang origin, widely known by his pen name "Ching-wei," was a legendary Chinese politician. He joined the Tung Meng Hui (a Chinese revolutionary league led by Dr. SUN Yat-sen—Author notes) in 1905 and was jailed for plotting an assassination of the regent, Prince ZAI Feng, and readily admitted his guilt at trial. He remained in jail from 1910 until the Wuchang Uprising the following year and became a national hero upon his release. In the early 1920s, he held several posts in SUN Yat-sen's Revolutionary Government in Canton. He was the only SUN's inner circle member to accompany him on trips outside of Kuomintang. He is believed to have drafted SUN's will during the short period before SUN's death, in the winter of 1925.

He was pessimistic about China's chances in the war against Japan after Japan invaded Northeast China and went all out to make peace. The *Shanghai Truce Agreement* signed in May 1932, and the *HO-Umezu Agreement* signed in 1935 were both approved when he was the President of the Executive Yuan.

WANG Ching-wei held several high posts in the government after the Marco Polo Bridge Incident in 1937, and his power was only under CHIANG Kai-shek. However, even though he wanted to replace CHIANG Kai-shek, he was afraid of the Japanese militarists. He was so indecisive that he gradually became a traitor. In 1938, the Japanese Cabinet issued the *Konoe Statement* three times, proposing three principles of the so-called "Sino-Japanese good-neighborly and friendly cooperation and joint anti-communists," attempting to lure the Kuomintang government into surrender. CHIANG Kai-shek flatly refused the proposition, while WANG Ching-wei was determined to be a traitor. He asked his loyalists, namely CHOU Fu-hai (ZHOU Fohai), KAO Tsung-wu (GAO Chongwu), and MEI Szu-ping (MEI Siping), to have a secret conference in Shanghai with KAGESA Sadaaki and IMAI Takeo and sign a convention to agree on anti-communist recognition of the Manchukuo and Japanese priority to develop Chinese resources. In late 1938, Wang left Chungking for Hanoi, where he stayed for three months and announced his support for a negotiated settlement with the Japanese. On March 20, 1940, under the support of the Japanese, he became the head of state of what came to be known as the WANG Ching-wei

Regime (formally"the Reorganized National Government of the Republic of China"), which was based in Nanking and served as the President of the Executive Yuan and Chairman of the National Government. Then he brutally suppressed the people in the occupied areas and organized the puppet army to cooperate with the Japanese army to wipe out the anti-Japanese soldiers and civilians in China. However, as a puppet president, he was constantly under the surveillance of the Japanese military police. As the Chinese people's War of Resistance against Japan and the anti-fascist wars in the world were progressing, WANG Ching-wei was beset with difficulties both at home and abroad and was mentally and physically exhausted. He died in Nagoya on November 10, 1944, less than a year before Japan's surrender to the Allies, thus avoiding a trial for treason.

In the Tokyo Trial, the defense did everything possible to deny the Japanese conspiracy to establish the puppet regime of the WANG Ching-wei Regime. On April 22, 1947, Aristides G. Lazarus, the American lawyer of the defendant HATA Shunroku, argued in court that:

> *The evidence will show that at the time of the conflict between China and Japan, such autonomous bodies came into existence. As the incident progressed, they grew, joined together, grew in size, and supplanted the former government. As these bodies maintained peace and order, Japan naturally supported them to preserve stability in the occupied areas. These were not puppet governments as charged, but independent, as proved by the China-Japan treaty previously alluded to. ... As the evidence will show, WANG Ching-wei escaped from Chungking and sought to conclude speedy peace with Japan. It was natural that Japan, desiring peace with China, should support him. ... Japan recognized the Wang Ching-wei regime as the legitimate government of China and as the best means of effecting an early peace with China. Again, the treaty between Japan and China shows that the new government was not considered a puppet government. The evidence will sustain the defense contention that the accused did not enter into any conspiracy, did not plan and initiate a war of aggression against China, did not use opium to debauch its people and to raise funds for war, nor did they foist upon China a puppet government by supporting WANG Ching-wei.*[9]

Mr. Lazarus said the puppet regimes, including the WANG Ching-wei Regime, all came into existence naturally, and Japan supported them for peace and order.

The best defense against lies is evidence. On June 11, 1947, HSIANG Che-chun read eleven (11) telegrams from KAGESA Sadaaki to the Chief of General Affairs Section on how the Japanese secret service escorted the defected WANG Ching-wei from Hanoi to Shanghai and from Shanghai to Tokyo. The court marked them as evidence for the prosecution, although they were confidential diplomatic telegrams and codes were used for many names and places such as "KAGESA," "WANG Ching-wei," and "Shanghai."

For example, KAGESA Telegram No. 1 was sent on April 19, 1939, marked as Exhibit No. 2721, Exhibit B: "*From KAWAMURA (T. N. Code Term for KAGESA) to SHIRAISHI, Finished commercial dealings. Everything is favorable.*"

Then on April 20, KAGESA sent three secret telegrams one after another.

KAGESA Telegram No. 2, which was marked as Exhibit No. 2721, Exhibit C-1, shows their detailed plan.

> *(1) I visited Wang in his hide-out on the 18th with INUKAI and YANO and had about a three-hour talk with them. They said that, as they were already well informed of the details through "KO," they would prefer to discuss the main problems at once. They showed us their firm determination (the results, they trusted Providence, and our absolute goodwill, which they fully appreciated). They informed us of their desire to remove, as soon as possible, to a place safe and convenient for the development of their activities. They considered this to be a prerequisite condition.*
>
> *Thus, after various considerations, it was decided that the French authorities should be entirely responsible for the protection, etc., regarding the escape; that a French steamship should be chartered to carry him safely to a hide-out in the French Concession in Shanghai; that Japan should previously prepare two or three hide-outs in the International Settlement; and that the Japanese policemen from the Shanghai Municipal Council should be placed around them to keep guard.*
>
> *In this connection, I shall request the authorities of the Foreign Ministry to send appropriate instructions to Shanghai to prepare suitable hide-outs in the International Settlement immediately and to take necessary measures for the protection. (Regarding protection, it is believed advisable to secretly contact Vice-Inspector General AKAGI and have Japanese policemen guard him after his arrival.)*
>
> *Furthermore, Wang desires that you take proper measures so that he may pass the quarantine procedure incognito.*

*(2) ITO, here at present, shall be sent immediately to Shanghai. IWAI shall establish connection with SEIKI and participate in the preparations mentioned in the preceding paragraph.*

*(3) The "Hokko Maru" shall sail directly to Shanghai while secretly escorting Wang's steamer. INUKAI, KAGESA, YANO, OSUZU, and others shall be on board the ship. You are requested to make YAMASHITA (T. N. Steamship Co.) understand.*

*(4) Von Forenhoben/Phonetic/(730 tons) has been decided to be the French steamer mentioned above. The time of departure from French Indo-China and the time of arrival in Shanghai have not yet been fixed so you shall be informed later.*

KAGESA Telegram No. 3, marked as Exhibit No. 2721, Exhibit C-2, shows more details about the plan.

*1. The hide-out in the French Concession mentioned in the previous telegram is temporary. We intend to remove them to hideouts in the International Settlement as soon as possible. Regarding the preparation of houses in three places requested in the previous telegram, he desires that you make the following considerations.*

*A. All the windows of the houses shall be covered tightly with bullet-proof sheets of iron (the upper half to be made so that they can be folded down at any time)*

*B. Small peeping windows shall be made in these iron sheets, the outside of which shall be covered with screens.*

*C. Iron grilles that can be opened and closed shall be installed in various places in the houses.*

*D. It would be suitable if one of the houses were provided in the Hongkew district and two in the south of the Soochow Creek district (one near the extension).*

Then KAGESA Telegram No. 4, marked as Exhibit No. 2721, Exhibit C-3, shows that he revised the plan.

*1. As a result of further work, the following corrections shall be made in KAGESA telegram No.2, so you are requested to take measures for previous preparations. (Decision shall be made after deliberation with French authorities here.)*

*A. When the French Steamship arrives in Shanghai (scheduled for the end of this month), the Japanese authorities and Wang's comrades shall be in charge of the method of disembarkation and transportation of passengers who later boarded the ship.*

*B. If possible, it would be convenient if he could be taken directly to the hide-out mentioned in the previous telegram and not to the French Concession in Shanghai.*

*2. As ITO and Sergeant-Major KAWASHIMI will be sent to Shanghai first, the Army is requested to let the Japanese Agency in Shanghai deliberate with these two persons."*

Additionally, KAGESA sent a secret telegram to Foreign Minister ARITA on April 24. It was marked as Exhibit No. 2721, Exhibit D.

*From KAWAMURA, the negotiation is completed, and plans for loading the cargo (T. N. Code Term for WANG Ching-wei) have already been arranged. Moreover, as the situation does not permit any change in the plans, we wish to carry it out according to the fixed schedule. In this connection, you are requested to demand an immediate completion of preparations for at least one of the warehouses in Osaka (T. N. Code Term for Shanghai); and you are also requested to take charge of preparations for its unloading. May 6 has been decided for the arrival of the cargo in Osaka."*

On April 29, 1939, KAGESA sent two secret telegrams to the Eighth Section, Army Department, Imperial Headquarters, which was marked as Exhibit No. 2721, Exhibit E-1:

*I have been successful in establishing a liaison with Wang. Accordingly, the course of our ship (Note: the Hokko-Maru of the Yamashita Shipping Co.) has been changed from Takao to Keelung. (Will arrive there at 8:00 p.m. the 30th) Further destination will be decided later. I hope YAMAMOTO, who is currently at Taihoku, will also change his destination and go to Keelung.* And Exhibit No. 2721, Exhibit E-2:

*It seems that Wang is near Hong Kong, although not quite certain. I have successfully established a liaison with him and have been informed of his safety. (At 1:00 p.m. 28th). Please communicate this to all concerned authorities.*

On April 30, KAGESA forwarded a telegram from Major HARUKI to Colonel USUI, which was marked as Exhibit No. 2721, Exhibit E-3:

*Preparations for landing and guard of the residence will be completed with the help of the officials concerned by the evening of the 4th, at the latest, and it is going on satisfactorily with utmost secrecy. It will be very convenient for me if I am informed of the approximate time of arrival off Woosung since I hope to establish a liaison directly with KAWAMURA (T. N. Code Term for KAGESA) before landing.*

And on May 3, KAGESA sent a telegram to the Chief of the 2nd Department to elaborate the plan to take WANG Ching-wei to Shanghai from Hanoi, which was marked as Exhibit No. 2721, Exhibit F.

1. *Wang and his suite will arrive at the 'Pilot Station,' Shanghai Port, at 10.00 a.m. on the 6th, in accordance with the pre-arranged plan which I have notified you recently.*
2. *Wang is naturally anticipating, after he arrives in Shanghai, a battle of telegrams with Chiang and terroristic opposition. Accordingly, he wishes to set himself up as soon as possible at the place most convenient for his various activities.*
3. *Therefore, when Wang and suit arrive in Shanghai, they shall stay for the time being in a house prepared in Shanghai. We have to rely upon the Japanese Navy or Army or some other well-organized power for guard and protection.*
4. *It is reported that Japanese terrorists have been sent from Tokyo to Shanghai for the above purpose. But, considering the bitter experiences in the past, I wish you would stop the plan. It may seem a good plan to wait in some place outside Shanghai until the preparation for guard and protection by Ting Me-tsun is finished, but I don't believe it will be completed within two or three months, in view of the general situation.*
5. *Wang intends to call together all his followers (about 30 people) to decide the future negotiation plan. Considering the situation in Shanghai, Wang is also contemplating hiring a Japanese ship and, leaving China for about a month, holding a conference on board the ship while cruising around Singapore, Manila, etc.*
6. *According to my (KAGESA's) opinion, the Japanese ship available at present cannot accommodate so many people as thirty, and it is necessary to prepare another ship. Therefore, I ask the General Staff Headquarters to study the matter.*

On May 23, KAGESA sent a secret telegram to the Chief of General Affairs Section through the DOIHARA Agency, marked Exhibit No. 2721, Exhibit G.

1. *Mr. WANG Ching-wei will dispatch messengers to Peking and Nanking before long with his confidential letters to the Provisional and Renovation Governments and Wu Pei-fu, explaining the reasons for his action and requesting their cooperation.*
2. *The above is aimed at dispelling the misunderstandings based on the various rumors, particularly the rumor that (Wang's movement) was a camouflaged trick on the part of the Chiang Regime. It will also make clear that Japan would not initiate political negotiations prematurely.*
3. *Wang realizes that a friendly relationship with Wu would greatly influence his scheme's future. Wang decided to work on his unpreparedness (original) note in pencil.*

On May 30, KAGESA sent another secret telegram, instructing the Chief of the 2nd Department to escort WANG Ching-wei to Japan from Shanghai secretly. It was marked as Exhibit No. 2721, Exhibit H.

1. *WANG and his suite of 13 will fly on the 31st at 9:00 a.m. if weather permits. They will rest at Omura on their way and then fly directly to Tokyo.*
2. *The Navy informed us that their landing place shall be Yokusuka.*
3. *KAGESA, ICKIDA, INUKAI, and SUGA of the Navy will accompany them.*

*(Note: Telephoned by the General Staff: 1. They will land at Omura at 1:00 p.m., 31st; 2. They will leave Omura at 2:00 p.m. and reach Tokyo at about 6:00 p.m.)*

These telegrams[10] fully exposed the Japanese conspiracies and details, including the ship they took, the hide-out, the stories they made up, and the excuses they used. The defense couldn't deny any of these facts.

## *Evidence in Black and White*

In an official letter to the Ministry of Foreign Affairs on January 24, 1948, HSIANG Che-chun said that from the beginning of the trial in May 1946 to the end of 1947, "3,686 pieces of evidence were received, of which 2,391 were provided by the prosecution. As far as the Japanese atrocities in China were concerned, 99 pieces of evidence have been collected by the prosecution in China and submitted to the court... not to mention over 30 pieces of evidence that Chief Counsel NYI, Judson T.Y., and I provided during the defense that was not included."[11]

In another official letter on October 20, 1948, Mr. HSIANG elaborated the court records.

> *The International Military Tribunal for the Far East had been trying the Japanese war criminals such as TOJO Hideki from April 29, 1946, to April 16, 1948. Here is a list of the court records.*
>
> 1. *48,412 pages of trial transcripts in 226 volumes from the beginning to the end.*
> 2. *Excerpts from the trial transcripts of the International Military Tribunal for the Far East.*
> 3. *The argument collection of the International Prosecution Section.*
> 4. *The defense collection of the International Prosecution Section.*
> 5. *A total of 3,915 pieces of evidence were marked by the International Military Tribunal for the Far East, of which 2,282 were from the Prosecution, and 1,633 from the defendant.*
> 6. *The index for the above-mentioned materials.*[12]

Black and white evidence from 70 years ago reveals the truth, and no one can deny it!

## *References*

[1] Cheng, Zhaoqi, Gong Zhiwei, and Zhao Yuhui. 2013. *Handbook of the Tokyo Trial Studies.* Shanghai Jiao Tong University Press, 251.

[2] MEI, Ju-ao. 2016. *My Personal Experience at the Tokyo Trial.* Edited by Mei Xiao'ao anf Mei Xiaokan. Shanghai Jiao Tong University Press, 302.

[3] Official Letter No.35-1240. Ministry of Foreign Affairs of the National Government.

[4] NI, Zhengyu. 1999. *Me and the Law.* Law Press, 114.

[5] Xiang, Longwan. 2010. *The Tokyo Trial, Chinese Prosecutor Hsiang Che-chun.* Shanghai Jiao Tong University Press, 3–4.

[6] PU, Yi. 2007. *From Emperor to Citizen.* Qunzhong Press, 98, 190.

[7] Xiang, Longwan. 2014. *HSIANG Che-chun's Letters, Telegrams and Statements at the Tokyo Trial.* Shanghai Jiao Tong University Press, 90–93 (4360–4369 of the English court records).

[8] Cheng, Zhaoqi, and Xiang Longwan. 2017. *Transcripts of the Proceedings of the International Military Tribunal for the Far East (Chinese version).* Vol. 4. Shanghai Jiao Tong University Press, 272–284 (4373–4405 of the English court records).

[9] Tokyo Trial Literature Committee. 2013. *Transcripts of the Proceedings of the International Military Tribunal for the Far East (English version).* National Library of China Publishing House; Shanghai Jiao Tong University Press, 523–528 (20504–20506 of the English court records).

[10] Xiang, Longwan. 2014. *HSIANG Che-chun's Letters, Telegrams and Statements at the Tokyo Trial.* Shanghai Jiao Tong University Press, 103–109.

[11] Ibid., 54–55.

[12] Ibid., 71–72.

CHAPTER 5

# The Truth of the Mukden Incident

## *The Assassination in Huanggutun*

*The Indictment* divides Japan's invasion of China into two stages: first, invasion of Manchuria, that is, invasion of Northeast China. Second, invasion of the whole China. The fifth chapter of the *Judgment*, Japanese Aggression against China, points out clearly:

> *The war that Japan waged against China, and the Japanese leaders falsely described as the China Incident or China Affair, began on the night of September 18, 1931, and ended with the surrender of Japan in Tokyo Bay on September 2, 1945. The first phase of this war consisted of Japan's invasion, occupation, and consolidation of that part of China known as Manchuria and of the Province of Jehol. The second phase of this war began on July 7, 1937, when the Japanese troops attacked the walled city of Wanping near Peiping following the Marco Polo Bridge Incident and consisted of successive advances.*[1]

This chapter will focus on the court's trial of Japan's invasion of Manchuria in the prosecuting stage.

Although Japan's invasion of Manchuria was the first stage of its invasion of China, the trial of related war suspects ran through the whole prosecution stage. During the first stage, evidence was presented by the prosecution, which lasted eight days in succession from July 1 to July 10, 1946, except for Sundays. In the second stage, the defense presented evidence, which lasted for 12 consecutive days except for Sundays. In addition, the individual statements and summations also included Japan's aggression against Northeast China.

The September 18 incident, the Mukden Incident, signified Japan's invasion of Manchuria. It was an arduous task for Chinese prosecutors and their counterparts around the world to expose the facts of the Mukden Incident and its closely related Huanggutun Incident. It was also an important contribution of them to the trials.

The Huanggutun Incident did not happen by accident. Because of the fertile land and abundant produce in the northeastern area, Japan had coveted Northeast China for a long time, which is only one river away from Japan-occupied Korea. As early as 1904, after the victory in the Russo-Japanese War, Japan set up the Kanto Governor's Office in Northeast China, consulates in Mukden, Harbin, Chilin, Tumen River, and the Kwantung Army, with its headquarters in Port Arthur. In 1906, Japan established an economic entity which is the South Manchurian Railway Company, Limited and the shareholders of the company were exclusive to the Japanese government or Japanese nationals. The company's charter even stipulated that the Japanese commander had the right to issue orders to the company. In fact, South Manchurian Railway Company had been an organ of the Japanese government since its establishment, which was just a cover-up. The department with the largest number of staff was the Department of Investigation, which was as big as 5000. They visited all Northeast China and North China, whose main duty was to collect Chinese intelligence. At present, Dalian Library still keeps over 40,000 volumes of archives that were too late to be taken away or destroyed by Japan before and after its surrender. For example, the Survey of Coal Mines in North China describes in detail the distribution and reserves of coal mines in Northeast China. This information was obviously used for Japan's future aggression.

Japan's ambitions and measures against China aroused not only the Chinese people's resentment but also the vigilance of Western powers. On February 6, 1922, China, the United States, Britain, France, Italy, the Netherlands, Belgium, Portugal, and Japan signed the Nine Power Treaty in Washington, which stipulated: To respect the sovereignty, the independence, and the territorial and administrative integrity of China; to provide the full and most unembarrassed opportunity to China to develop and maintain for herself an effective and stable government; to establish and safeguard the principle of equal industrial and commercial opportunities of all countries throughout China; not to support natives to set up exclusive spheres of influence in designated areas of China.

Although Japan was one of the signatories, it never intended to abide by it. In March 1927, shortly after Emperor Hirohito succeeded to the throne, the worldwide financial crisis brought economic chaos. Factories stagnated, and enterprises closed down. In April of the same year, TANAKA Giichi, a military commander and ambitious politician, formed the cabinet. The strategic policy of invading China formulated by TANAKA's cabinet was against the spirit of the Nine Power Treaty. Pursuing an active intervention policy towards China, it regarded Northeast China as the lifeblood of Japan and tried to carve it from China as soon as possible and occupy it.

In order to find agents in Northeast China, their first target was CHANG Tso-lin, a warlord in Northeast China. CHANG Tso-lin was once a bandit known as the King of Northeast China and was the head of the Fengtian Army. In 1922, after defeat in the first Zhili–Fengtian War, he declared the independence of Northeast China. In 1924, during the Second Zhili–Fengtian War, he entered Peking as Grand Marshal, exercised sovereignty on behalf of the Beiyang government of China, and became the country's supreme ruler. TANAKA's Cabinet wanted CHANG Tso-lin to become the agent for the Japanese invasion of China. In March 1928, DOIHARA Kenji, the head of the intelligence agent and China hand, became the adviser to CHANG Tso-lin.

In the spring of 1928, the Northern Expeditionary Army led by CHIANG Kai-shek approached Shantung. On April 5, CHIANG Kai-shek took a mass pledge in Hsuchou and launched the Second Northern Expedition against the northern warlords headed by CHANG Tso-lin. At that time, CHANG Tsung Chang (ZHANG Zong-chang), the governor of Shantung, was a subordinate of CHANG Tso-lin, known as Dogmeat General. In the name of protecting Japanese nationals, Japan sent troops to Tsinan, Tsingtao, and Chiao-Chi Railway, ready to stop the National Revolutionary Army by force. On May 1, the Northern Expeditionary Army entered Tsinan. On May 3, with the excuse that CHANG Tsung-chang invited them, the Japanese army invaded the Shantung Foreign Office set up by the Chinese government. At that time, the head of the office was TSAI Kung-shi (Cai Gongshi), whose ears and nose were cut off by the Japanese before he and all the other staff were killed. After that, the Japanese attacked the base of the National Revolutionary Army in Tsinan, and the city was burned and slaughtered wantonly. In this atrocity, more than 17,000 Chinese were burned and killed, over 2,000 were injured, and more than 5,000 were captured; this was known as Tsinan Massacre in history. CHIANG Kai-shek referred to it as a national shame, he had the habit of keeping a diary, and wherever he referred to Japan in his diary, he would use "*Japanese pirates*" to show his hatred for Japan.

Though under great pressure, CHANG Tso-lin did not want to be the puppet emperor of the Japanese. He expressed disgust at Japan's various privileges in China and repeatedly refused to sign unequal treaties with Japan. CHANG Tso-lin's attitude aroused strong dissatisfaction from the Kwantung Army. Thus, a group of radical young officers decided to assassinate CHANG Tso-lin since they regarded him as an obstacle to the Japanese occupation of Manchuria. When CHANG Tso-lin was in Peking, the Japanese tried every means to urge him to return to the Northeast provinces of China. At this time, the new faction in the Fengtian Army, including his son CHANG Hseuh-liang, also advised CHANG Tso-lin to leave Peking to facilitate a compromise with CHIANG Kai-shek.

On the evening of June 3, 1928, CHANG Tso-lin took a train at Peking Station, and at 5:23 a.m. of June 4, just as the train arrived at Huanggutun, which was at the intersection of Peking- Mukden Railway and the South Manchurian Railway, there was a loud noise from the blasting of the granite pier. The rails and bridges blew up, and debris was thrown into the air, leaving only one chassis of the train. Zhang was thrown from the train and seriously wounded. When he was sent to an official residence in Mukden, the military doctor failed to save his life. He died at about 9:30 a.m. in the morning. His last words were to ask CHANG Hseuh-liang to return to Mukden quickly. Shortly after the bombing, the Japanese successively plotted the derailment of the Fengtian Army's train and the Mukden bomb case in an attempt to cause chaos. On June 16, more than 18,000 Japanese soldiers maneuvered their way into the south of Mukden, singing the song South Manchuria was Japanese hometown that exposed their plot to occupy Northeast China.

### *Two Key Witnesses*

Although it is evident that the Japanese plotted the Huanggutun Incident, they refused to admit it. They even spread the rumor that CHANG Tso-lin was assassinated by his Chinese political rivals. Since the Tokyo Trial started with the Huanggutun Incident, it was the duty-bound task of the IPS, especially the Chinese prosecutors, to trace the chief culprit.

After careful investigation by the prosecution, two key witnesses testified in court, revealing the Huanggutun Incident's detailed facts.

The first witness was OKADA Keisuke, Navy Minister of TANAKA's cabinet. On the afternoon of July 2, 1946, he appeared in court for the first time. In the Affidavit, he expounded the causes and results of the Huanggutun Incident:

> *In 1928, when the armies of CHANG Tso-lin suffered defeat at the hands of the Kuomintang Army, TANAKA again advised him to withdraw his armies into Manchuria before it was too late. The Marshal was obliged to take this advice on this occasion because of his embarrassing military position. By this time, the Japanese army in Manchuria, with headquarters in Mukden under General HONJO, had become dissatisfied with the policy of the TANAKA Cabinet to collaborate and negotiate with CHANG Tso-lin concerning Japan's interests in Manchuria. They did not want to wait on negotiations and were impatient to employ force to occupy Manchuria. A clique or group of officers in this army, which had completely isolated General HONJO and shut him off from communication with the affairs of the army, planned and plotted the murder of CHANG Tso-lin upon his return to Manchuria. They arranged on June 4, 1928, that the train on which CHANG Tso-lin from Peiping to Mukden should be wrecked by explosives placed on the track just outside Mukden. CHANG Tso-lin was killed in this wreck as planned.*[2]

The second witness was TANAKA Ryukichi, a former senior adviser of the Kwantung Army. On the morning of July 5, 1946, TANAKA revealed in court the details of the plot and assassination of CHANG Tso-lin, which was carried out by the Japanese army. The important point to note is that there was an insider report of the assassination of CHANG Tso-lin, which was written by Major General Feng, the commander of the Kempei unit, under the order of the War Minister. In January 1942, as the director of the Military Service Bureau, TANAKA Ryukichi found this report. In court, TANAKA retold the main content of the report: The assassination of CHANG Tso-lin was carried out by Colonel KAWAMOTO Daisaku, which was depicted in the report: *"As a result, on June 3, 1928, the train which departed from Peiping was blown up at the crossing of a South Manchurian Railway and the Peiping-Mukden Railway, and as a result, CHANG Tso-lin died.*

*This dynamiting was carried out by officers—by part of the officers and noncommissioned officers of the 20th Engineer Regiment which had come to Mukden from Korea."*

The following are the questions and answers between Henry A. Sackett, an American assistant prosecutor, and TANAKA.

> *Q (Sackett): Did the report indicate the number of people involved in the incident?*
>
> *A (TANAKA): Yes.*
>
> *Q (Sackett): How many did it disclose?*
>
> *A (TANAKA): Colonel KAWAMOTO and ten some odd others.*
>
> *Q (Sackett): Do you know Colonel KAWAMOTO personally?*
>
> *A (TANAKA): Yes, very intimately.*
>
> *Q (Sackett): Did you ever talk to him about the killing of MarshalCHANG Tso-lin?*
>
> *A (TANAKA): Yes.*
>
> *Q (Sackett): What did he personally tell you with reference to the killing of Marshal CHANG Tso-lin when you talked to him??*
>
> *A (TANAKA): Colonel KAWAMOTO told me thusly: that if the urgent mustering up of the Kwantung Army had been carried out, then the Manchurian Incident would have been carried out then and the State of Manchukuo would have been created then. The explosive used at that time belonged to the Engineer's Regiment No. 200, square dynamite 200.*

TANAKA also revealed the fact that another person, Captain OZAKI, participated in the Huanggutun Incident. He said, "*Captain OZAKI's purpose was to follow the orders given by Colonel KAWAMOTO to muster the forces then in Mukden to open fire against the train carrying CHANG Tso-lin.*"[3]

In the face of such powerful evidence, the counsel for the defense failed to cross examine. When Japan surrendered, KAWAMOTO Daisaku was arrested in Shanxi. In 1953, he died of illness in the War Criminals Administration where he also confessed his participation in plotting and implementing the assassination of CHANG Tso-lin.

The Japanese rightists have always tried to deny the Tokyo Trial, but no one dares to challenge the Huanggutun Incident, an ironclad case committed by Japanese radicals.

From the testimonies and confessions of OKADA, TANAKA, KAWAMOTO, and many other parties, it was obvious that the Huanggutun Incident was first plotted by a small clique or a group of people in the Army. Historical records showed that the Japanese government then did not approve of assassination, and Prime Minister TANAKA Giichi even wanted to punish the Army general who was held accountable for the murder. However, with the support of the War Minister, General Staff Headquarters resisted the proposal successfully. OKADA made this point very clear:

> *Therefore, in order to prevent civil war in southern Manchuria, the aforesaid Chang Tso Lin started for Mukden and, on the way, was killed by the blowing up of a railway bridge. When this reached the Cabinet, the aforesaid Premier TANAKA was very angry and said that if the Army takes such measures as that, we will never be able to develop our plan; the aforesaid Premier TANAKA said further that the responsible people must be severely punished to prevent such incidents again on the continent.... the aforesaid Premier TANAKA reached an agreement to proceed immediately to the Imperial Palace and make a report to the Emperor on this matter. Following this conference with the Emperor, the aforesaid Premier TANAKA returned from the Palace to the Cabinet and instructed the War Minister to go ahead and proceed with the punishment of the persons responsible for the killing of CHANG Tso-lin. The aforesaid General Shirakawa returned to the office of the War Ministry and was unable to obtain the desired action in connection with the punishment of the persons responsible for the aforementioned murder... As the Prime Minister, General TANAKA could not report to the Emperor that the culprits had been punished as the Throne desired, he resigned with his Cabinet. The Kwantung Army proved by this event that it was more powerful than the Japanese Government in Tokyo and that its influence extended even into the General Staff.*[4]

After that, Japanese military forces became increasingly arrogant; being grossly insubordinate was a distinctive feature of Japanese politics.

On February 11, 1948, when HSIANG made the summation on behalf of the prosecution, he pointed out: *We cannot escape the conclusion that all the activity during the period from the murder of CHANG Tso-lin until the Mukden Incident was all part of one conspiracy.*[5]

This small clique became more and more influential, including core members such as Captain ITAGAKI Seishiro, Captain DOIHARA Kenji, Colonel

ISHIHARA Kanji, Colonel HASHIMOTO Kingoro, Colonel HASHIMOTO Tadashi, and Japanese nationalist OKAWA Syumei. At that time, they were mostly middle-rank officials and agitators of militarism. These people planned and launched the Mukden Incident, that is, the September 18 Incident, after the Huanggutun Incident.

## *The Full Story of the Mukden Incident*

Before the Mukden Incident, there was a flashpoint, the NAKAMURA Incident.

At the beginning of 1931, the Army General Staff of the Japanese Empire sent NAKAMURA Shintaro, captain of the Intelligence Section, sneaking into Northeast China in plain clothes to collect intelligence and prepare for invading China. After arriving in China, NAKAMURA went around spying on the military situation together with NOBUTARO Isugi, a retired Japanese army sergeant. In the early morning of June 25, the party members were found by the sentries of the Third Regiment of the Chinese Army affiliated with Manchurian warlord Chang Hseuh-liang; company commander NING Wen-lung (NING Wenlong) immediately led a class of soldiers to investigate. It was soon found out that among the four people, there were two Japanese, one Mongolian, and one Russian interpreter.

These two Japanese are NAKAMURA Shintaro and NOBUTARO Isugi. NAKAMURA Shintaro claimed to be a Japanese agronomist went to Northeast China to conduct soil research. NING Wen-lung, with the intuition of a military man, perceived that NAKAMURA was not like an agronomist but a well-trained Japanese soldier. In order to figure out the truth, Ning Wen-lung ordered his men to bring the four men back to the regimental headquarters. When KUAN Yu-heng, commander of the regiment, inspected the seized items, he found that two of the three booklets recorded the population, products, and military and civilian distribution in the area. What was even more surprising was that the third one accurately recorded the distribution of troops, the types, and calibers of guns, the number of army, the names and positions of generals, the places where troops were stationed, the capacity and firmness of barracks in Xing'an Settlement Area, etc. The handwriting sketched in pencil was clearly left on the military map. These objects were undoubtedly hard evidence that NAKAMURA Shintaro was engaged in military espionage in China.

On the morning of June 26, KUAN Yu-heng interrogated NAKAMURA Shintaro in the regimental headquarters and sharply questioned why he was carrying weapons and military maps. Why did he record military intelligence? The cunning NAKAMURA refused to answer any questions with the excuse that he could not speak Chinese in an attempt to cover up his crimes of military espionage. When interrogating NOBUTARO Isugi and the other two, KUAN Yu-heng quickly got evidence of their espionage, so Yentaro had to confess that they were Japanese soldiers and NAKAMURA was a captain. What to do with these spies? If they were released, it would be tantamount to releasing the tiger to the mountain, and this military intelligence would bring endless harm. If they were not released, and once the news was leaked, the consequences would be equally unimaginable because Japan enjoyed extra-territorial rights in Northeast China. As the matter was *criticle*, KUAN Yu-heng immediately held a meeting discussing with other officers. TUNG Ping-yu (Dong Pingyu), assistant Regimental Commander proposed affirmatively that according to international law, foreign military spies could be sentenced to death. At present, the only way was to execute them in secret. His argument was quite reasonable, and all the officers reached a consensus. In order to get NAKAMURA's oral confession, KUAN Yu-heng arraigned him again, only to find that NAKAMURA was even more insubordinate, and he was dying to fight with Chinese officers. In the early morning of June 27, they were secretly executed.

CHANG Hseuh-liang immediately sent a secret telegram from Peking to KUAN Yu-heng, demanding that strict confidentiality should be kept in the troops after he was informed of the matter, but unfortunately, the secret was leaked.

As a result, the Japanese stirred up public opinion and constantly declared that there was no solution to the Manchurian issue except by force. In July, DOIHARA Kenji was dispatched by the Army Chief of Staff to investigate the death of NAKAMURA, but the purpose was to take over the Special Service Organ of the Kwantung Army.

At that time, the Japanese government wanted to localize the matter. On August 17, Foreign Minister SHIDEHARA Kijuro asked HAYASHI Kujiro, Japanese Consul General in Mukden, to investigate to quell the incident as much as possible. After that, SHIGEMITSU Mamoru, Japanese Minister to China, held talks with SOONG Tse-ven, Chinese Finance Minister, and both sides agreed to meet in Mukden on September 20, inviting CHANG Hseuh-liang and YASUYA Uchida, President of South Manchurian Railway Company, to negotiate and resolve the major disagreement between CHANG Hseuh-liang and Japan. On the afternoon of September 18th, JUNG Chen (RONG Zhen), Chief of Staff of the Commander-in-Chief's Office of the Northeast Border Defense Army, told Consul General SHIDEHARA Kijuro that KUAN Yu-heng, Commander of the Tunken Army, was responsible for the execution of NAKAMURA and decided to try him by a military court.

These measures by the Japanese government were obviously quite the opposite of the schemes of Japanese radical militarists. After Consul General HAYASHI released the report from the investigation, DOIHARA immediately visited MINAMI Jiro, the newly appointed War Minister, expressing strong dissatisfaction and won MINAMI's support. With the support of the Kwantung Army and the Army Headquarters, these radical militarists finally attacked the Chinese troops stationed at The North Barracks on the outskirts of Mukden at midnight on September 18. They created the Mukden Incident, which shocked the world and was called National Shame by the Chinese.

The course of the Mukden Incident was as follows: According to ITAGAKI's plan, Lieutenant IMADA Shintaro, assistant of SHIBAYAMA Kaneshiro, Chang Hseuh-liang's military adviser, took the command. In the name of patrol duty, the independent Garrison stationed in the northern suburb of Mukden exploded the Liutiaohu Railway track 800 meters away from the North Barracks. After hearing the explosion, IMADA Shintaro led a troop of KAWAMOTO Suemori and attacked the North Barracks. Losing no time, ITAGAKI ordered the 29 infantry regiment to attack Mukden City in the name of the commander of the Kwantung Army. At 11:30 p.m., the Japanese army occupied the northwest gate of The North Barracks. At the same time, HASHIMOTO Tadashi blamed the victim. At 11:46 p.m. and 0:28 a.m. on the 19th, he sent two telegrams to the Kwantung Army Headquarters in Port Arthur in the name of DOIHARA, falsely reporting that the Chinese army had destroyed the railway and attacked the Japanese army, leaving the Japanese army in a bitter battle. After receiving the telegram, Commander HONJO of Kwantung Army, General Staff MIYAKE Mitsuji, and Senior Staff Officer ISHIHARA Kanji urgently discussed countermeasures, agreeing that this was an excellent time to use force.

HONJO immediately decided to quickly concentrate the main force in Mukden to occupy the whole northeast of China with a preemptive strike. At 1:00 a.m. on the 19th, the 29th infantry regiment of the Japanese army attacked Mukden City in three directions. Kwantung Army Headquarters hasted to Mukden under the command of HONJO SHISERU. The Japanese army captured the North Barracks at 5:30 a.m. and Mukden at 6:30 a.m. In the meantime, the Japanese army raided the Chinese defenders along the South Manchurian Railway and captured Anton (now Dandong) at 5:30 a.m. on the 19th, and Nanling at 5:30 p.m. Changchun was captured at 10:00 p.m. on 21st, Japan captured Kirin, the capital of Kirin Province. Thus, the Japanese army occupied the major cities in Liaoning and Kirin provinces, in other words, the areas along the railway.

In the Tokyo Trial, Mukden Incident is an important case; regarding this, the Japanese can be said to call black, white, and full of lies. During the Tokyo Trial, the prosecution and the defense submitted many exhibits.

The main witnesses of the prosecution are OKADA Keisuke and TANAKA Ryukichi. TANAKA, in particular, testified in court for four days from July 5 to July 9, 1946.

The stage of presenting exhibits by the defense from March 18 to April 22, 1947, lasted for 12 days in succession except on weekends. Over a dozen witnesses for the defense testified in court for the Mukden Incident. Among them are YAMAGUCHI Juji, head of the South Manchurian Railway Company, Major General KATAKURA Tadashi, Staff Officer of the Kwantung Army, Major General HIRATA Yukihiro, Major General TAKEDA Hisashi, Major ENDO Sabur, KANAI Shoji, executive member of Flood Relief Committee, Honji Kazuo, the eldest son of HONJO SHISERU, KAWAMURA Kyoichi, Secretary of HONJO, SHISERU, Lieutenant Colonel KAWABE Torashiro general Staff, Captain SHIMAMOTO Masaichi, the Commander of the Japanese army in the attack of The North Barracks, OYAMA Ayao, the judge advocate of Kwantung Army, WACHI Takaji, official in the section of Chinese affairs of General Staff.

This book does not intend to quote evidence, questions, and examinations from both sides. On February 11, 1948, Prosecutor Keenan read *Part B of the Prosecution's Summation*[6], which is the conspiracy to dominate Asia and the Pacific and Indian Oceans. The outline of this part is as follows:

*I. The conspiracy to dominate Manchuria*

*A. The situation before the Mukden Incident, September 18, 1931*. [Read by UK prosecutor Mr. Comyns Carr.—Author's note]

*1. Obligations that Japan had assumed towards China and others*

*2. The rights which Japan had acquired in Manchuria*

*3. The situation in China*

*4. The situation in Japan before Manchurian Incident*

*B. The Mukden Incident and its aftermath* [Read by Chinese prosecutor Hsiang Che-chun –Author's note]

*1. Events Leading up to the Incident*

*2. The Mukden Incident, September 18, 1931.*

*3. The Military Developments after September 18, 1931.* [Read by Judge Kwei—Author's note]

*4. Economic Domination* [Read by Mr. Crowe—Author's note]

*5. Opium and Narcotics*

The following is a brief introduction to the part read by HSIANG Che-chun.

## *The Prosecution's Summation*

The first part of the prosecution's summation elaborated on many people involved in the Mukden Incident, including some accused. The incident was part of the collusion charged and intended to implement conspiracy. The activity was carried out by the Japanese Army, the Kwantung Army, and civilians. Then it pointed out that in the General Staff, General TATEKAWA was the chief culprit. [He was then head of the First Bureau of the General Staff—The author's note] TATEKAWA strongly advocated that Japan would not become one of the world powers unless it seized Manchuria. Then it revealed a series of conspiracies, including the establishment of Sakuraka, the drafting of a concrete plan by HASHIMOTO, and military action supported by MINAMI, the War Minister, which clearly pointed out that ITAGAKI, ISHIHARA, HANATANI, the staff officers of the Kwantung Army, were undoubtedly the leaders of this clique. And it also pointed out that in the late summer of 1931, the Army's resort to violence in Manchuria was expectant. The summation also analyzed the activities of OKAWA Shumei, pointing out that this incessant plotting, planning, agitation, and publicity had a most serious influence throughout Japan. Although the Japanese government did not approve of their activities then, these radicals used the killing of NAKAMURA Shintaro in Manchuria as an excuse to stir up public opinion.

According to a large amount of evidence in the second part of the summation, it revealed in detail that the Japanese army launched a sneak attack on the North

Barracks where the Chinese army was stationed on the grounds that a section of railway was blown up.

> *As a climax to the mounting tension, there occurred at about 10:00 p.m. on September 18, 1931, an alleged light explosion on the South Manchurian Railroad, as a result of which the Kwantung Army went into immediate action and did not stop until it was completely in control of Manchuria. According to the Lytton Commission, the Japanese version of the incident was that a patrol, on hearing the explosion, discovered that a portion of one rail was blown up, leaving a gap. When they arrived, they were fired on from the east side of the railroad line, but when the fire was returned, the other side stopped and retreated. The Japanese pursued and were attacked by 300 to 400 men, and reinforcements were then sent from Captain KAWASHIMA and Colonel SHIMAMOTO. In the meantime, the southbound train from Changchun passed over the damaged site without stopping and arrived at its destination on time. SHIMAMOTO ordered an attack on the Chinese barracks, which the Chinese contested, but the barracks were captured. In the meantime, Colonel HIRATA decided to attack the walled city, and by 6 a.m., the eastern wall was occupied, and by 7:30 a.m., the arsenal and airdrome were captured. This same version has been repeated before the Tribunal by defense witnesses HIRATA and SHIMAMOTO, and the fact that ITAGAKI approved their plans. The Chinese version, as reported by the commission, was that the attack on the barracks was unprovoked and a surprise. All the soldiers were in the barracks, and since September 6, orders had been received to take special care to avoid any clash with the Japanese, the sentries had only dummy rifles. The Japanese had been carrying on maneuvers around the barracks since the 14th, and on the 18th, they were maneuvering at a village where a train with three or four coaches had stopped at 9 p.m. At 10 p.m., a light explosion and rifle were heard. The Japanese began to attack these barracks and thereafter started to attack with artillery. There was no resistance except for one regiment, which was cut off and had to fight its way through. The Commission, after hearing both sides, concluded that the Japanese had a carefully prepared plan to meet the possibilities of hostilities. The plan was put into operation swiftly and precisely. The Chinese had no plan to attack the Japanese, made no concerted or authorized attack on them, and were surprised by the Japanese attack. There was an explosion, but the damage was insufficient to justify military action. The Japanese military operations could not be regarded as measures of self-*

*defense, although the Commission did not exclude the hypothesis that the officers might have thought they were acting.*

There are more details, such as ITAGAKI secretly installing two artilleries in advance, TATEKAWA Yoshitsugu, who was ordered to stop the Incident, deliberately pretending to be ignorant of it and reaching a tacit understanding with ITAGAKI, etc., all of which clearly show that the Japanese army deliberately did the Mukden Incident.

On February 24, 1948, HSIANG Che-chun read *the Prosecution's Summation against the Defense ITAGAKI, Seishiro*,[7] which is divided into eight sections:

1. *Before the Mukden Incident*
2. *The Mukden Incident*
3. *The Creation of a Puppet State*
4. *Control of "Manchukuo"*
5. *Inner Mongolia, North China, and All China*
6. *War Minister, 1938–1939*
7. *Waging War in China and the Pacific*
8. *Conclusion*

The first four parts revealed ITAGAKI's actions before and after the Mukden Incident, which can be regarded to be a supplement to the summation on February 11.

The Summation pointed out that, in fact, an armed conflict was not inevitable because the Chinese authorities and the Japanese consul were trying to reach an agreement. Still, peace efforts were thwarted by military factions. On the eve of the Mukden Incident, DOIHARA, a close confidant of ITAGAKI, was recalled to Tokyo and preached through newspapers that all urgent problems related to Manchuria should be solved as soon as possible and force should be used if necessary. When public incitement was going on, plans for covert warfare were in place. ISHIHARA, who prepared the battle plan, testified that ITAGAKI knew about the plan. ITAGAKI knew that two artilleries had been secretly planted in Mukden. It was indisputable that these artilleries were actually used to raid the Chinese. Another thing that proves that the Mukden Incident was a prepared action: *That the incident was a pre-arranged one is even more apparent since OKAWA in Tokyo had already learned of it a month beforehand. When drunk, he told Shimizu that ITAGAKI and others would bring about an incident in Manchuria in the near future."*

The Summation gives a more specific description of the process of the Mukden Incident:

> *TATEKAWA, leaving for Mukden, telegraphed ahead that he would like to meet either ITAGAKI or ISHIHARA. In response, ITAGAKI was sent to Mukden with an assignment to meet TATEKAWA and contact the Special Service Organ and Consulate Genera. ITAGAKI admitted that it was customary for an emissary like TATEKAWA to deliver a message without delay. However, he spent two hours with TATEKAWA without any serious desire to learn about the contents of the message that TATEKAWA was to deliver, nor was TATEKAWA in earnest to discuss with him seriously. In fact, ITAGAKI just put him off until the next day. Of course, there was never the next day for the supposedly intended purpose, as the Incident broke out the same evening.*
>
> *As soon as he disposed of TATEKAWA, ITAGAKI went to the Special Service Organ. As he put it, we chatted there for at least one hour and a half. It must be pointed out that this organ is the only link between the outposts and the headquarters of the Kwantung Army headquarters at Port Arthur since only this organ possessed the code to dispatch a telegram to the Commander in Chief.*
>
> *The alleged Incident broke out, and Colonel HIRATA went to the Special Service Organ. Thereupon ITAGAKI assumed the duty of directing the operation, HIRATA, in his testimony, attempted to show that ITAGAKI had no authority to give him orders. However, he admitted that he did ask for ITAGAKI's approval for attacking the Chinese and received such an assurance from ITAGAKI. ISHIHARA also admitted that ITAGAKI did give the field commander either instructions or orders. ITAGAKI himself admitted he gave them a certain pledge.*
>
> *ISHIHARA testified that ITAGAKI had no time to investigate, and ITAGAKI stated that communications were bad and he was unable to ascertain the true nature of the situation. Thus, it is apparent that he arbitrarily approved the field commander's plan to attack the Chinese army without even finding out what was really going on. He was informed that the Chinese made it known that there would be no resistance in the interest of peace. ISHIHARA so testified, KATAKURA, who later investigated it, so confirmed, And ITAGAKI himself so admitted. Yet when*

> *Consul General HAYASHI pleaded with ITAGAKI to stop the military action in view of the non-resistance from the Chinese, ITAGAKI refused. Even though he had not ascertained the actual situation, he bluntly alleged that the regular Chinese challenged the Japanese army without foundation. Even though he had no time to investigate, he told HAYASHI that it was necessary to deal with the Chinese Army thoroughly.*
>
> *Once the approval was given and the operation plan carried out in earnest, the Japanese army began the occupation of Manchuria. Therefore, it is inevitable to conclude that ITAGAKI, one of the central Pictures in the Kwantung Army, had planned and carried out the occupation of Manchuria.*

These statements strongly reveal that the Mukden Incident was by no means accidental but a well-planned conspiracy of Japanese military radicals. The core figure who planned and commanded the battle was ITAGAKI Seishiro, and the conspiracy was supported by MINAMI War Minister, that is, the Kwantung Army.

HSIANG Che-chun cited a lot of evidence in his summation in the Tribunal. In *"the causes and aftermaths of the Mukden Incident,"* read on February 11, 1948, 95 pieces of evidence were cited. On February 24, 1948, 197 pieces of evidence were cited in *Prosecution's Summation against Defendant ITAGAKI Seishiro*. It clarifies the truth of historical events and illustrates the meticulous and difficult work of Chinese prosecutors.

## *References*

[1] *The Judgment of the International Military Tribunal for the Far East*. Translated by Zhang Xiaolin. Retranslated by Xiang Longwan and Xu Xiaobing. 2015. Shanghai Jiao Tong University Press, 255 (49007 of the English court records).

[2] Cheng, Zhaoqi, and Xiang Longwan. 2017. *Transcripts of the Proceedings of the International Military Tribunal for the Far East (Chinese version)*. Vol. 2. Shanghai Jiao Tong University Press, 214 (1817–1818 of the English court records).

[3] Ibid., 268–272 (1948–1959 of the English court records).

[4] Ibid., 2217–218 (1817–1820 of the English court records).

[5] Xiang, Longwan. 2010. *The Tokyo Trial, Chinese Prosecutor Hsiang Che-chun*. Shanghai Jiao Tong University Press, 56 (39083–39084 of the English court records).

[6] Tokyo Trial Literature Committee. 2013. *Transcripts of the Proceedings of the International Military Tribunal for the Far East, Volume 63 (English version)*. National Library of China Publishing House; Shanghai Jiao Tong University Press, 241–416 (38948–39300 of the English court records).

[7] Xiang, Longwan. 2010. *The Tokyo Trial, Chinese Prosecutor Hsiang Che-chun*. Shanghai Jiao Tong University Press, 111–124 (40984–41023 of the English court records).

CHAPTER 6

# PU Yi in Court

## *A Puppet "Emperor"*

In the Tokyo Trial of Japanese aggression against Manchuria, PU Yi, the puppet emperor of Manchukuo, was one of the most important witnesses and attracted worldwide attention.

While planning and carrying out its military operations, Japan had never stopped its effort to find a Chinese proxy. After Chang Tso-lin was murdered by bombs, the Japanese once tried to woo the Young Marshal Chang Hseuh-liang. Prime Minister TANAKA Giichi sent a special envoy, HAYASHI Gonsuke, to talk with Chang Hseuh-liang, demanding Manchuria's independence from China and accepting Japan's support. Chang Hseuh-liang refused the Japanese demands and proclaimed his allegiance to the Chinese Nationalist Party government. On December 29, 1928, Chang Hseuh-liang announced the submission of a power of the four provinces in Northeast China, the Nanking Nationalist Government. The Nanking government then appointed Chang Hseuh-liang as the supreme military and political leader of the northeastern region and announced the completion of the country's unification.

With these failures of both Chang Tso-lin and his son Chang Hseuh-liang, Japan moved to its next target, PU Yi – the last emperor of the Ching Dynasty.

The fourth chapter of this book describes the plot by ITAGAKI Seishiro of dispatching DOIHARA Kenji, his Chief Special Agent, to coerce and threaten

PU Yi in Tientsin. On November 13, 1931, PU Yi arrived in Yingkow under the escort of Japanese soldiers and plain-clothes policemen. On November 20, the army transferred PU Yi to Port Arthur, and ITAGAKI paid him a visit right upon his arrival and made it clear that he intended PU Yi to become the head of the new government, provided that, once established, the new Manchurian regime must employ Japanese as officials and advisors.

On March 9, 1932, the inauguration ceremony of Manchukuo was held in Hsinking (Changchun). PU Yi became the nominal head of Manchukuo, but he was just a puppet of Japan. To PU Yi's own statement, under the influence of the Japanese in Tientsin Concession for the seven years there and officials for more than ten years in the former Ching Dynasty, he was so dependent on the Japanese that he could not survive and or make decisions without them: "*I had to cling to the Kwantung Army for the sake of false self-deceiving dignity, for the sake of my own life, for the illusion of regaining the throne.*"[1] In early May 1932, the League of Nation's investigation team, headed by Sir Victor Bulwer Lytton from Great Britain, went to Changchun to investigate the Sino-Japanese dispute after the Mukden Incident. Defying his own will to follow the order from the Japanese, PU Yi replied gingerly that he was elected by the Manchurian people; Manchukuo was established voluntarily by the Manchurian people.[2]

To have a complete rule over Northeast China, the Japanese decided to meet PU Yi's demand to become the Emperor of Manchukuo so he could be Japan's stooge wholeheartedly. On March 1, 1934, a farce of enthronement ceremony was staged in the suburb of Changchun. Manchukuo was renamed the Empire of Great Manchuria, and PU Yi was crowned the emperor.

The power of the Emperor of Great Manchuria was, of course, in the hands of the Kwantung Army and the War Ministry of Japan. PU Yi had intended to wear the Dragon Robe of the former Ching Dynasty at the enthronement ceremony but was rejected flatly by the Kwantung Army. PU Yi was also reprimanded and told that Japan recognized him as a Manchukuo Emperor, not a Ching Emperor.

From 1932 to 1945, as a puppet, PU Yi always complied with Japan's decree and was an "accomplice" in effect in Japan's invasion of China. PU Yi stated in his book *From Emperor to Citizen*:

> *In the whole fourteen years, in the face of people's resistance and curses, amid resentment and groans, at first, I desired to reign over the whole of China, and then*

*I just wanted to maintain the emperor's signboard. Finally, for my personal safety, I tried my best to please robbers and murderers, serving them obediently, giving them whitewash, and legalizing all the plunder and slaughters.*[3]

PU Yi also admitted that:

*My first give-and-take condition with the Japanese pirates was the Japan–Manchukuo Protocol which was signed by HONJO Shigeru and me. In this transaction, The Japanese allowed me to be the head of Manchukuo; I could implement the 5 five provisions upon taking office.*

1. *Entrusting the national defense and public security of Manchukuo to Japan.*
2. *When the Japanese army considers it necessary for national defense, it can take over rights of the railways, harbors, waterways, and air traffic in Manchukuo.*
3. *In addition, Manchukuo should provide the Japanese army with all necessary facilities.*
4. *Recommending famous Japanese intellectuals to be the counselors of Manchukuo.*
5. *These articles shall be the basis of a formal treaty between Manchukuo and Japan in the future.*[4]

It is obvious that Manchukuo was only a nominal "country" without sovereignty.

On August 9, 1945, the Red Army of the Soviet Union entered Northeast China, and PU Yi fled Changchun. He had intended to escape to Japan, but the Japanese could not even care for themselves. Not only having PU Yi lose his value to the Japanese, but he was also becoming a burden to them. It was not until August 17 that PU Yi fled to Mukden Airport with YOSHIOKA Yasunao. It just so happened that the Soviet soldiers advanced to the airport and led to the capture of PU Yi and his party, who were immediately escorted to Siberia, Soviet Union.

## *A Guilty Conscience*

The Chinese prosecutor thought that, though as a puppet, many of Japan's measures during its invasion of Northeast China were carried out via PU Yi's administration. PU Yi's testimony in court thus would greatly help reveal Japan's war crimes in Northeast China. With the approval of the IPS and the consent of the Soviet Union, PU Yi was extradited to Tokyo from Siberia by the Allied headquarter. Long before the extradition by the Allied, the China War Crime Commission, established in March 1944, already made a resolution on PU Yi's extradition on April 2, 1946: "*First, PU Yi should be tried for the crime of treason. Second, he would be transferred to Nanking for interrogation.*"[5] PU Yi was terrified of being tried as a war criminal. But under persuasion by the Chinese prosecution team, PU Yi testified in court for consecutive eight days from August 16 to 27, 1946, and attracted worldwide attention. There were four hundred and fifty three pages in *The Transcript of International Military Tribunal for the Far East* about PU Yi's testimony in the Tokyo Trial, among them, the interrogations by both the prosecution and defense teams accounted for 764 times recorded on three hundred thirty three pages.

Henry CHIU was Hsiang Che-chun's first secretary, who was responsible for persuading PU Yi to get rid of the troubled mind and to testify in court. When CHIU was interviewed by the media in his old age, he recalled the scene of a meeting with PU Yi[6]:

> *When PU Yi heard that I was a Chinese official and came to Tokyo to participate in the trial, he was very nervous and looked a little restless. There are four Soviets in the court and two Americans. When he spoke, he was very restrained in the serious atmosphere. After being given a brief introduction of the situation, I told PU Yi that Tokyo Trial was to try Japanese war criminals, and he was here to testify and need not be scared.*

To calm down PU Yi, Henry CHIU visited PU Yi frequently at his residence; he became more relaxed gradually the two grew to become friends half a month later.

PU Yi had a habit of giving small gifts as a memorial to all his visitors. He wanted to give a gift to Henry CHIU, but he was sent to Tokyo only for testimony, so he could not find a suitable gift among his belongings. That left PU Yi a little embarrassed. Henry CHIU told PU Yi that, if he insisted, he could give him some calligraphy work on the desk that PU Yi had already written for himself. PU Yi was very excited to hear the suggestion. PU Yi's face blushed and he said to Henry CHIU that he was still learning calligraphy and those were not his best work; however if Mr. Chiu liked it, he could choose whichever he liked. Henry

CHIU took two pieces from the desk: One was "天下为公" meaning that the world belongs to all, and the other was a Chinese character of 斗, commonly to be posted on the door to ward off evil spirits in ancient times. PU Yi used his brush pen and added a footnote of the year 1946 and the place of Tokyo to the two pieces of work, following the Chinese tradition of doing so when giving calligraphy as a gift.

PU Yi was the witness who gave the most and lengthiest testimonies in court during the Tokyo Trial. As he was also the last emperor of China, the news that he testified in the trial became headlines in newspapers and radios all over the world. What did PU Yi testify in the court? What crimes did he reveal against the defense? The following provides an overview of PU Yi's testimony during the Tokyo Trial:

On the morning of August 16, 19, and 20, PU Yi, as a witness for the prosecution, was mainly questioned by Keenan, Chief of Counsel for the prosecution for two and a half days. On the afternoon of August 20, 21, 22, 23, 26, and 27, PU Yi was cross-examined by five American counsels for the defense, namely Ben Bruce Blakeney, Michael Levin, William Logan, Samuel J. Kleiman, Floyd J. Mattice, and three Japanese counsels for the defense.

## *Five Grounds for the Accusations*

PU Yi's testimony comprised five parts – all accusations against the Japanese aggression in China:

The first part of PU Yi's testimony covered how he was coerced and escorted from Tientsin to Dairen by the Japanese with carrots and sticks.

PU Yi was driven out of the Forbidden City in Peking by General FENG Yu-hsiang in 1924. Until 1931, he had lived a relatively quiet and peaceful life in Zhangyuan and Jingyuan, located within the Japanese Concession in Tientsin. After the Mukden Incident in 1931, PU Yi started to encounter a series of incidents, including stray bullets falling into his courtyard and a fruit basket with hidden bombs. In that fruit basket laid a business card of "CHAO Hsin-po (ZHAO Xinbo) from Mukden." PU Yi learned later that there were conflicts between Chinese and Japanese soldiers near Tientsin around that time, DOIHARA was in Tientsin and very active, the basket incident must have been planned under him.[7]

On September 30, KASHII Kohei, the commander of the Japanese garrison in Tientsin, visited PU Yi and warned that it was too dangerous for him to stay in Tientsin. He urged PU Yi to go to Northeast China as soon as possible. On November 10, the Japanese successfully coerced PU Yi and his entourage including CHENG Hsiao-hsu to go to Dairen, along with five Japanese including his translator YOSHIDA Chutaro, and KUDO Tetsusaburo, a Ronin under DOIHARA. PU Yi fled his residence by hiding himself in the trunk of a ragtop. He was later disguised as a Japanese officer in a Japanese army coat and hat and driven straight to Takukow, Tientsin, and then rushed onto the waiting Japanese ship AWACHI Maru. On the morning of November 13, PU Yi and his entourage arrived at the Mantie wharf in Yingkow City, Liaoning Province, and then transited to Port Arthur on November 15. Along the whole journey, the Japanese isolated PU Yi from any other people for the sake of protecting their plan.

PU Yi's second part of his testimony revealed Japan's motivation for forcing him to be their puppet head of Manchukuo.

Upon his arrival in Port Arthur, the Kwantung Army immediately dispatched Colonel ITAGAKI Seishiro to visit and inform PU Yi of their intention to make him the head of Manchukuo. At the beginning of their conversation, ITAGAKI pretended Japan wanted to respect the sovereignty of Manchukuo and that it had no territorial claims; But after PU Yi did not give a quick response, ITAGAKI immediately showed his true and ferocious face. Here is an exchange of questions and answers between Keenan and PU Yi as recorded in the court transcript:

*Q (Keenan): And then what happened after the half year expired?*

*A (PU Yi): After the lapse of half year, the commander of Kwantung Army, HONJO,*

*send his aide, then Colonel ITAGAKI, to see me.*

*Q (Keenan): Was that ITAGAKI Seishiro, one of the accused in this courtroom?*

*A (PU Yi): Yes.*

*Q (Keenan): And what did Colonel ITAGAKI say to you on that occasion?*

*A (PU Yi): He told me that the most eastern political regime, under the General CNANG Hseuh-liang, is the antagonist to the Japanese people as well as Chinese people. He said, as a result of this antagonism on the part of General CHANG Hseuh-liang, the Manchurian people were suffering and that the series of events that happened in that area had impeded the vested rights of the Japanese people.*

*In order to get rid of the Chinese militarists and to secure the social welfare of the -to secure social welfare for the people in the northeastern provinces, he said he was willingly prepared to put up a new political regime in Manchuria.*

*Q (Keenan): you may state whether he told you he was acting for himself or under orders from his superiors in the Japanese Army.*

*A (PU Yi): He said he came to me on the order of the Commander-in-Chief, General HONJO.*

*Q (Keenan): And did he make any specific proposition to you as to any office that he wanted you to take?*

*A (PU Yi): He said he hoped that since I was a Manchurian I should lead this political—this new political regime. He said that the Japanese government has no- has absolutely no territorial design on Manchuria, and that the Japanese government is determined to respect the sovereignty of any Manchurian Regime that would be set up.*

*Q (Keenan): When Colonel ITAGAKI asked you to accept the position as head of a new Manchurian State, did you say, "I will," or "I will not," in substance?*

*A (PU Yi): I refused.*

*Q (Keenan): How long did that conversation between Colonel ITAGAKI and yourself take, approximately?*

*A (PU Yi): In about—over two hours.*

*Q (Keenan): Can you describe the attitude of ITAGAKI after you refused to accept his offer of becoming head of the Manchurian State?*

*A (PU Yi): After I refused, ITAGAKI was very unsatisfied and went back to his hotel. Itagaki asked my advisers, Mr. Cheng Hsiao-hsu and Mr. Wang to his hotel to have a conversation with them. And that time ITAGAKI told my two advisers that this is a determined decision of the Kwantung Army and that in case I refused, they would adopt drastic actions against me.*

Under a threat as such, as well as suggestions from several of his advisers, PU Yi had to submit: *"Firstly, ITAGAKI said that—if I refused, I would be subject to the risk of life. Secondly, my advisers advised me to accept it on the same line of reasoning. They said that if I refused it, my life might be threatened. Thirdly, I was then residing in Port Arthur, where I was in the palm of the Japanese hands. and if I refused them and came out of Port Arthur, the Japanese may think I would spill the secret."*[8]

The third part of PU Yi's testimony is his admission that the head of Manchukuo was a complete puppet of Japan.

Though it might appear that PU Yi was the head of the state, and his ministers from the former Ching Dynasty government held the principal positions of Manchukuo, it was the Japanese who held the real power in the new government: all appointments of officials must be pre-approved by the Kwantung Army, so were all their important policies and measures. CHENG Hsiao-hsu (ZHENG Xiaoxu), who once served as Minister of Home Office in PU Yi's government in the Ching Dynasty, was appointed the Prime Minister of Manchukuo, but all his deputies were Japanese. CHENG Hsiao-hsu convened his State Council once a week, but it was actually hosted by a Japanese, KOMAI Tokuzo, though he was merely the Director of the General Affairs Bureau and one of the subordinators reporting to CHENG Hsiao-hsu. PU Yi's testimony made it very clear: "*In order to deceive the people of the world, Manchukuo is an independent country on paper, but in fact, Manchukuo is manipulated by the Kwantung Army.*"

> *There was always a meeting, called the Tuesday Meeting, composed of the Japanese Director of the General Affairs Bureau, the various Vice Ministers of the ministries, and the Chief of the Fourth Section of the Kwantung Army. In the meeting, they would pass all the rescripts or any other ordinances or enactments that were to be promoted—promulgated by the various ministries. The Japanese Director of the General Affairs Bureau was the Chairman, and the Director of the Fourth Section of the Kwantung Headquarters—Japanese Kwantung Army Headquarters was supposed to be the Vice-Chairman. Any ordinances or enactments to be promulgated would be preferred by the Vice-ministers of the respective ministries, who is a Japanese, and then they will have to be approved by the Kwantung Army. Once it is approved by the Kwantung Army, it is practically passed. Once it is settled and passed by the Kwantung Army Headquarters, they will send these proposed laws or enactments to the National Affairs Bureau of the Manchukuo State, and any rescripts or formal government ordinances are passed in this way. The meeting of the National Affairs Bureau of the Manchukuo State was but a name, for any ordinances to be issued by the National Affairs Bureau or rescripts to be issued by the Emperor will have to be passed by the various vice-ministers—the Japanese vice-ministers, and the Kwantung Army. For some minor matters, the Japanese vice ministers can just pass the law without even informing us. The Chinese absolutely had no right to oppose any of these laws or enactments. They always thought that, since these laws were passed by the Japanese Director of the General Affairs Bureau,*

*the Chinese were not in a position to oppose them. If we persistently oppose their laws, then there might be some danger to our lives.*[9]

PU Yi also mentioned these State Council meetings in his book *From Emperor to Citizen*: "*Every time the National Affairs Bureau of Manchukuo State held meetings, it was him* [KOMAI Tokuzo—Author's note] *who prepared the agenda for Cheng to read it.*" At its first meeting, KOMAI proposed a quota of Japanese officials in various ministries and provincial institutions. HSI Chia (XI Qia), the Minister of Finance, expressed a different opinion. But before His Chia could finish his argument, KOMAI went furious with him immediately with fists pounding the table and cursed: "*You shut up when I tell you not to talk! It is decided by the Kwantung Army, so you have no choice but to agree. You know Manchukuo was established by the Japanese with blood. You are offered everything, yet you still want to make trouble. You should think twice.*" From then on, HIS Chia and other officials simply quit differing.

Even when PU Yi himself had a different opinion at the State Council meetings, he was also reprimanded by KOMAI: "*This is the decision by the Kwantung Army! It can't be changed.*"[10]

Here is another question-and-answer session between Keenan and PU Yi on August 19:

*Q (Keenan): You became the regent or chief executive of the Manchurian State on March 1, 1932, according to the history books. Can you tell us who was in control of Manchuria at that time?*

*A (PU Yi): General HONJO, Commander-in-Chief of the Japanese Kwantung Army in Manchuria, together with his subordinates, and at the same time, on the side of the Chief of Staff, General—Colonel ITAGAKI was a powerful man.*

*Q (Keenan): Do you recall promulgating a series of ordinances covering the Manchurian people on or about—the first day of April 1932?*

*A (PU Yi): None of the ordinances were ever issued by me.*

*Q (Keenan): When you accepted the position as regent of Manchuria on March 1, 1932, what was told to you by ITAGAKI and the other Japanese officers representing the Kwantung Army as to the power that you would have, generally, as such regent?*

*A (PU Yi): At the time when the Manchukuo State was first founded, ITAGAKI and his people assured me that it would be an independent state, and that I would*

> *have the right to administer the State at my own will. But as a matter of fact, I could do nothing whatsoever.*[11]

During PU Yi's 12 years as Emperor of Manchuria State, all his moves were monitored by the Japanese. The Japanese sent a Staff Officer YOSHIOKA Yasunao to arrange all the activities for PU Yi. PU Yi once said that the Kwantung Army was like a powerful high-voltage power supply, he was an accurate and sensitive motor, and YOSHIOKA Yasunao was a wire with good conductivity. As "Emperor," PU Yi didn't even have the freedom to meet his Chinese officials, which he made very clear in answering Keenan's question regarding his freedom after becoming the Emperor of Manchukuo on August 19:

> *I couldn't see them. Once every year—twice every year I was permitted to give an audience to the various ministers. Then the Japanese Director of the General Affairs Bureau was there to supervise us. All the reports the ministers were supposed to make to me were already pre-drafted by the Japanese. They just brought it up to me and read to me, which was nothing, only like drama. To me, the word "freedom" has lost its meaning in the last ten years. I don't have any freedom as I should have as an emperor of the Manchurian State, nor have I any personal freedom. This man, General Yasunoka YOSHIOKA, as I said just now, was ordered by the Kwantung Army to supervise my activities. For any interviews I gave to foreigners, the fellow was there always. Later on, even in interviews, I gave to Japanese people, YOSHIOKA was always there. He even refused to allow me to see the Chinese officials in the Manchukuo State at my own will. I could see the Prime Minister, CHANG King-hui* (ZHANG Jinghui), *and the Chief of the Consular Bureau, TSANG Shih-i* (ZANG Shiyi), *once every week. The rest, say, for instance, the ministers of various miniseries, I couldn't see them.... Twice a year I had the occasion to interview the commanding officer of the military area in Manchuria, who is Chinese, but in this interview, I was also supervised by the Japanese. The reports brought up by the commanding officer were also the same. It was proffered by the Japanese advisers and then read to me by the commanding officer. Also, General YOSHIOKA refused to allow me to talk to these people of my own free will. Even if I am allowed to talk with them, I would have to speak in accordance with penciled notes given to me by YOSHIOKA.... Even my Chinese friends who came to congratulate me on my birthday occasion—were not allowed to see me.*[12]

YOSHIOKA was around PU Yi all the time and watched every move of his, including tour inspections, receiving visitors, ritual ceremonies, going to dinner, and delivering speeches. At first, PU Yi was still allowed to read his letters after being examined by YOSHIOKA but was deprived of such permission after assuming the throne. YOSHIOKA became increasingly unreasonable and rude over time. One time he even said to PU Yi words like: "*The Kwantung Army is your father, I am the representative of the Kwantung Army, I treat you as my nephew.*"[13]

The fourth part of PU Yi's testimony exposed that the Japanese forced the Chinese people in Northeast China to follow Shintoism.

During the trial, the counsels for the defense questioned PU Yi if he was truly a puppet by citing the Japan-Manchukuo Protocol signed by PU Yi himself. Keenan asked PU Yi What, if anything, did he have with that treaty? PU Yi simply replied, "*I didn't even know the existence of such a treaty the day previous to it being signed. On the next day, the Japanese Ambassador to Manchukuo, one named MUTO, came to me and told me, 'Here it is. This is the agreement you have to sign.'… As a matter of formality it was signed by me by that time under the threat of Japanese military force, we lost our freedom completely.*"[14]

PU Yi mentioned several times in his testimony that he had tried to reveal the facts to Lytton, the head of Lytton Commission entrusted by the League of Nations during their investigation in 1931, but Kwantung Army officials were with him, and he could not do anything. In his testimony on August 19, he said:

> *When I met Lord Lytton, we were all under the supervision of Japanese military officers. And wherever Lord Lytton went, he was under the supervision of Japanese gendarmes too. Of course, I admired the spirit of Lord Lytton, and as far as his mission was concerned with Manchuria affairs, I would like very much to have talked thoroughly with him. At that time, I was thinking of meeting Lord Lytton alone or having some party with him, but there was only my wish. It was never realized. When I interviewed Lord Lytton, many of the Kwantung Army officers were beside me supervising. Since Lord Lytton's mission was to inquire into the situation of the oppressed people, if I had told him the truth, I would have been murdered right after the mission left Manchuria. This was just the same as if a robber came into your house and your neighbor tried to come to rescue. What could you do under the pointed gun of the robber? That was not the only case with me, but it is also the case with the Manchurian officials and people who were prohibited by the Japanese, to tell the truth to the Lytton Commission.*[15]

To strengthen their control over people's minds, the Japanese attempted to impose Japanese Shintoism on the Chinese people in Manchuria. Their first target was PU Yi.

On August 19, PU Yi testified:

> *This I was relating to you what was preached to me by General UMEZU Yoshijiro and his people. For that time, they frequently referred to the phrase "Eight corners of the world under one roof." That is the basis of their aggressive idea, the idea of aggression. It was the basis of Shintoism, General UMEZU, pursuant to the Japanese Government's desire to encroach upon the Manchurian State religiously. Their idea was to enslave the people of the whole world, and they started it with their experience in Manchuria. Under their aggression, when we have lost every kind of freedom under their might, as I have said, I have lost all my personal freedom. Deep in my heart, I absolutely opposed the invasion of Japanese Shintoism.*

PU Yi once told the Japanese that China had its own religion and does not need to be introduced to a new one from abroad, but he was reprimanded. During PU Yi's second visit to Japan, the Japanese army failed in the battle with Soviet Russia in Nomonhan. Fearing that PU Yi would vacillate, the Japanese emphasized that Manchuria should have the same religion as Japan, and decided to set up "Founding-State Shrines" all over Manchuria. People must worship the Japanese Emperor or Amaterasu. PU Yi also said in court:

> *The Chinese army people and civilians, civil officials, in schools, in the army, everywhere, were required to set up a temple to respect Shintoism. I, myself, was also included. And it was also provided in law that whoever shows disrespect to Shintoism, will be subject to confinement for more than a year.... Yes. We have no freedom, no freedom of religion here. In the rescript drawn up by the Japanese, it was stated that it was required, that all my descendants were to worship the Shintoism.... General UMEZU ordered me to go to Japan to fetch Amaterasu-Omikami myself. And he told me to make a gesture to the public that I am going to Japan of my own free will. I was feeling very bad, and I always considered that was the worst humiliation that I had ever experienced.*

When talking about a mirror given to him by the Japanese Emperor, PU Yi said:

*It was said that the Amaterasu-Omikami gave the mirror to his issues, to his sons and grandsons, and told them that when you see this mirror, it is the same as when you see me. In the Japanese plan they want to first enslave Manchuria and then China, and then East Asia, and then the whole world.*

On August 22, PU Yi added in the cross-examination by the counsel for the defense Blackney:

*Lieutenant General YOSHIOKA came to me directly and said that now it is decided policy of the Japanese government that Manchuria shall worship the Amaterasu Omikami. He said further that he had come to see me on the order of General UMEZU, and General UMEZU ordered me to go to Japan to fetch the Amaterasu-Omikami myself. And he also told me to make a gesture to the public that I am going to Japan of my own free will. I was then feeling very bad, and I always considered that is the worst humiliation that I had ever experienced.*

On August 26, Counsel for the defense KIYOSE asked PU Yi in the cross-examination: "*You stated, Mr. Witness, that after you had this shrine established [Shintoism shrine established in Manchukuo, author's note] a law had been passed to have the subjects of your country worship it. What sort of law was passed?*" PU Yi answered:

*The law was then like this: it provided that whoever is found to have not worshiped this Shintoism or this temple, showing disrespect, will be punished for not less than a year. There were a few—many religions in Manchuria. Of course, the Japanese couldn't get rid of all these other religions immediately, but I was told by General YOSHIOKA that they would in time come to extinguish the other religions and only leave the religion of Shintoism to prevail. All the students and army soldiers were compelled to worship Shintoism, and shrines were set up in schools and army headquarters—army quarter. And this of course would be construed as a sort of religious invasion.... Once, General YOSHIOKA got a Japanese to lecture me about the Japanese religion, and this Japanese drew a tree and indicated to me that the trunk of the tree is the Japanese Shintoism and the branches are the different kinds of religion, such as Buddhism, Christianity, and others. YOSHIOKA also explained that human beings all the world over were derived from this trunk.*[16]

In the eastern suburbs of Mukden laid the tombs of NURHACHI, the founder of the Ching Dynasty, and his wife YEHENARA Hala, which were built as early as 1651. The tombs were expanded to a grand scale through constructions and reinforcements during the period from Emperor SHUN-CHIH to Emperor CHIEN-LUNG. PU Yi visited Mukden twice and wanted to worship NURHACHI's mausoleum, but was stopped by YOSHIOKA, who told PU Yi that he was the emperor of Manchukuo, not the Ching Dynasty, so he should not pay tribute to the former Ching emperors. YOSHIKA also said that this was the order from UMEZU Yoshijiro. On August 19 and 22, PU Yi testified twice about the incidents:

> *That was the time when I was inspecting—I was on an inspecting tour in Mukden. As my ancestral tomb was then nearby in Mukden, so I proposed to visit that place, YOSHIOKA told me that according to the order of General UMEZU I was not allowed to see the tomb, the reason that the Manchurian Emperor should not go to visit his own ancestral tomb.*[17]

In the fifth part of his testimony, PU Yi accused the Japanese of persecuting him and his family.

He talked about two particular cases.

The first one was the tragedy of LING Sheng and his family—PU Yi's relatives through marriage. LING Sheng was governor of Hsing-An province. His son engaged PU Yi's younger sister. PU Yi said:

> *Once, when there was called a meeting of governors of the various provinces. LING Sheng showed some dissatisfaction attitude with the Japanese. After the meeting, the governors returned to their respective provinces. And after a short while, we heard that Mr. LING Sheng was arrested by the Kwantung Army. After a so-called trial, Mr. LING was sentenced on the ground of revolting against the Manchukuo and anti-Japanese. He was shot immediately. His nephews and some members of his family were also executed."* After this instance, the Chinese in Manchukuo were more frightened, and during all the current and future meetings, none of the Chinese were even willing to speak up. The engagement between LING Sheng's son and PU Yi's sister had to be terminated. PU Yi complained: "*YOSHIOKA told me that since Mr. LING Sheng was already committed, my*

*sister should not be allowed to marry LING Sheng's son. This is but one of the instances I can give you now. There are still many other instances."*[18]

The second case made PU Yi feel the most painful; that was about his beloved concubine TAN Yu-ling who was poisoned by the Japanese.

PU Yi had three wives. When he was 17 years old, he was still living in the Forbidden City; his former ministers of the Ching Dynasty arranged one queen and one concubine for him—the queen is WAN Rung and the concubine WEN Hsiu. But PU Yi did not get along well with them, and the relationship became even worse after PU Yi was driven out of the Forbidden City to reside in Tientsin. In 1931, WEN Hsiu was influenced by the modernization trend in the Chinese society and filed for divorce from PU Yi, and she succeeded. WAN Rung's life was not as fortunate According to PU Yi's statement in *From Emperor to Citizen*, "*Since she forced WEN Hsiu to leave, I took an aversion to her, and seldom talked with her. I don't even pay much attention to her affairs. She was haunted by her internal contradictions. On the one hand, she wanted to live like a normal person; on the other hand, she refused or could not abandon the title of the queen and righteously live a normal life, so she had adultery and was addicted to drugs (opium).*"[19] WAN Rung died of illness in Kirin in 1935.

PU Yi's third wife was TAN Yu-ling, who was also a descendant of Manchu aristocrats. TAN Yu-ling became PU Yi's new concubine in 1937 when she was only 17 years old. PU Yi's life as a puppet emperor was like on the edge of a cliff, empty and uneasy, longing for companionship. TAN Yu-ling brought great comfort to PU Yi's life. On August 19, PU Yi said in court:

*My wife—my late wife—was deeply in love with me. She was twenty—three years of age when she contracted a kind of disease. She was a very patriotic Chinese. She always comforted me by saying that I had to be patient for a time, and then we could revenge—retaliate in the future.*

Of course, the Japanese would not tolerate TAN Yu-ling's lack of loyalty. They wanted to get rid of TAN Yu-ling as soon as possible. TAN Yu-ling contracted the disease when she was 23 years old. PU Yi testified in the court:

*But she was even poisoned by the Japanese and got killed. Who was the man who poisoned her? It was General YOSHIOKA.... At first, she was taken care of by a*

> *Chinese doctor, but later on, General YOSHIOKA recommended a Japanese doctor. At the time the Japanese doctor attended YOSHIOKA had closeted himself with the Japanese doctor for three hours. The sickness from which she was suffering was not a serious one. The next day, after she was attended to by the Japanese doctor, she died. She was supposed to be given an injection of glucose every one hour, but ever since the Japanese doctor arrived, she was given only two injections throughout the night. General YOSHIOKA was staying in our place that night, and throughout the night, the Japanese gendarmes and the nurses were very busy—very busily going about passing information to him.*[20]

Though as the nominal emperor, PU Yi had no freedom. Needless to say, about the ordinary people of Northeast China. This was such an irony to the Japanese, who had been advocating the establishment of an empire of peace and tranquility based on the Royal Way!

PU Yi also exposed Japan's plot to immigrate extensively to Northeast China in an attempt to turn Manchuria into new Japanese territory at no cost. On August 20, PU Yi stated in the testimony:

> *In the time twenty years, there were about six million Japanese immigrants into Manchuria, as a result of which the native Manchurians were squeezed out of their own land. On the surface, they would buy over the land with a certain sum of money, and the farmers who have been on the land for a long time, till the land, would be sent to some unexplored land, and the Japanese would then take over the tilled land. This is proof of the Japanese aggression plan.*

PU Yi also pointed out that there were lots of limitations to the Chinese people, such as being not allowed to travel freely, and being supplied only with low-grade rice—the Chinese would be punished and fined if found to consume fine rice. In the eyes of the Japanese, people were divided by classes. PU Yi said:

> *There was no equality to be talked of. The Japanese were always the first, and then the second came the Koreans, and the third came the Chinese. All the ration system was distributed according to these discriminations. The salaries drawn by the Japanese vice ministers of the various ministries were much higher in amount than even the Chinese ministers.*[21]

PU Yi specifically exposed Japan's crimes of planting poppies and selling opium in Northeast China. On August 20, PU Yi testified, "*there were many kinds of commodities that were under monopolistic control. Opium was one of the main items that were being monopolized under the five-year plan.*" When answering the direct examination by Mr. Keenan, Chief of Counsel for the prosecution, he explained:

> *There were many commodities being monopolized, such as cotton, cloth, and foodstuff. All the matters were in the control of the Japanese Kwantung Army and carried out by the Director of General Affairs Bureau, Manchukuo State. The purpose of distributing the opium on the part of the Japanese—the purpose for Japanese distribution of opium was to break down the Chinese morale and destroy the stamina of Chinese health so that they won't have any chance to resist the Japanese. On the one hand, the Japanese were saying that they suppressed the Opium in Manchuria. And yet, on the other hand, they were encouraging the growth of poppies. The growth of poppies was formerly confined to the provinces of Jehol and the Hsinan West Province. Later on, the area of growth of poppies was extended to Mukden, Chilin, and part of Supin Province. The income they had derived from this sale of opium was increasing year by year, and the latest figure was two billion credited under the name of Special Account in the bank. These two billion represented the net profit for the sale of opium. Two million dollars. The permit for smoking opium was also officially sold in Asia. With those facts, I come to the conclusion that the Japanese were distributing opium in Manchuria so that it could break down the Chinese morale and also make money out of Chinese people.*

Although there were laws restricting drug trafficking and abuse at that time, they were never enforced effectively. PU Yi said:

> *The smoking of opium is not considered an offense by the laws or regulations. This system shows a contradiction in itself. On the one hand, they are trying to oppress the growth of opium. Yet, on the other hand, they don't consider opium smoking an offense. This has been the Japanese policy ever since they came into Manchuria.*[22]

This despicable act of the Japanese had been carried out throughout the period of Japan's invasion of China. Chapter 11 of this book will further expose these crimes.

Many other parts of PU Yi's testimony, would reveal the crimes of Japan's economic plunder in Manchuria, which is the topic of Chapter 9 of this book.

## *A Case of Perjury*

We should also point out here that PU Yi did not reveal all the truth during the Tokyo Trial. When answering the questions from the President, the prosecution, and the defense, he repeatedly prevaricated with excuses such as "*I was too young at that time to have enough experience.*" PU Yi admitted in From Emperor to Citizen: "*Because I was afraid that I would be punished by the motherland in the future, I had many concerns in my heart. Although I did reveal some of the criminal facts of the Japanese aggressors, in order to get away with punishment. I covered up some historical truths with regard to my own crimes.*"

PU Yi even made a false statement. He was still in Tientsin when the Mukden Incident broke out. On October 11, 1931, drafted by CHENG Hsiao-hsu, PU Yi wrote a letter to MINAMI, Jiro, the War Minister of Japan who had just taken office, to express his position on the September 18 Incident. "*The Government of the Chinese Republic, by adopting wrong measures in regard to the recent incident in the Eastern Provinces has opened hostilities against a friendly country, victimizing many people, on whom we take great pity. Hence, we dispatch TOYAMA, Takeo, tutor of the Royal Household, to Japan to give our regards and convey our message of comfort to the war minister, General MINAMI.... "In order to establish stability in East Asia, it is imperative for China and Japan to collaborate and assume in common this responsibility. If we should be half-hearted in our attempts to remove the obstacles confronting us, no end of alarming events would arise to deprive us of the enjoyment of peace.*" PU Yi ended the letter with his stamp of "Emperor Hsuan Tung." CHENG Hsiao-hsu also added a footnote of "Emperor's signature" to the letter with his own signature. PU Yi was so afraid of misjudging the situation, he used a little trick by deliberately adopting different handwriting from his usual one.[23]

During the court hearing on the afternoon of August 21, Major Blakeney, an American counsel, presented this letter as evidence of PU Yi taking initiatives to collude with the Japanese. As DOIHARA had not arrived in Tientsin by the time, PU Yi refused to admit he ever wrote that letter to MINAMI Jiro. Both Webb, President of the International Military Tribunal for the Far East, and Keenan,

Chief of Counsel for the prosecution and Attorney General, participated in that session. The following is an excerpt of the court transcript:

> *Q (Blakeney): I ask you to look at the document which has been placed before you and state whether that is a letter written by you or under your direction, bearing your seal as the Emperor Hsuan Tung.*
>
> *A (PU Yi): Your Honor, this was a fake one. Not only that—*
>
> *The president: Just answer this question: did you write that letter?*
>
> *A (PU Yi): It was not written by me. They should be guilty of counterfeiting this document.*
>
> *Q (Blakeney): Mr. Witness, you read the letter before answering my question?*
>
> *A (PU Yi): Surely, I have read them through, and I am sure it was a fake one.*
>
> *Q (Blakeney): Do you recognize the Imperial Seal of Emperor Hsuan Tung.*
>
> *A (PU Yi): No, it wasn't my one.*
>
> *Q (Blakeney): Do I understand you to say that the seal on this document is not the seal of the Emperor?*
>
> *A (PU Yi): That isn't the one I used. This was not written by me. I don't know.*
>
> *Q (Keenan): May we have this document marked for identification, so we will know what it is?*
>
> *The president: We think that is a wise precaution. It should be tendered for identification.*[24]

At the request of the court, the Chinese prosecution team called for a special expert witness, Professor CHANG Feng-chu who is a handwriting expert of the Chinese military delegation in Japan, to check the authenticity of the signature PU Yi's handwriting was indeed intricate, which Chang Feng-chu was deceived by and concluded not Fu Yi's in his expert opinion to the court. The Chinese prosecution team was also misled that HSIANG Che-chun, the head of the Chinese prosecution team, even adopted CHANG Feng-chu's conclusion in his statement to the court on January 17, 1947. By that time, it was already half a year into the trial, and the procuratorial stage was coming to an end. A great deal of evidence of Japan's invasion of China was made public. Compared with other evidence, this piece was not crucial to the prosecution team did not insist on debating it and dropped the topic. However, PU Yi had felt uneasy about his perjury since the trial. He confessed in 1953 while still in prison at Fushun War

Criminals Management Centre: "*With regard to MINAMI's letter, I had told no one the truth except to my fifth brother-in-law before 1953, whether Chinese or foreigners.*"

Using PU Yi's own words, "*After that, my inner world, which was tightly sealed up in the Tokyo Court, gradually revealed itself. It was a painful process, but it was also the only way to get a new life.*"[25]

## *References*


[1] PU, Yi. 2007. *From Emperor to Citizen.* Qunzhong Press, 253.

[2] Ibid., p254.

[3] Ibid., p243.

[4] Ibid., p244.

[5] File 172-1-0895 (1) on the Tokyo Trial Relationship. Taipei National History Museum. 124.

[6] Ma, Lingguo, and Zhu Huarong. 1996. "Henry CHIU Inside and Outside of the Tokyo Trial." *The Shanghai Bund*, no.116: 31.

[7] Ibid.

[8] Cheng, Zhaoqi, and Xiang Longwan. 2017. *Transcripts of the Proceedings of the International Military Tribunal for the Far East (Chinese version).* Vol. 4. Shanghai Jiao Tong University Press, 83–88 (3957–3970 of the English court records).

[9] Ibid., 102–103 (3993–3994 of the English court records).

[10] PU, Yi. 2007. *From Emperor to Citizen.* Qunzhong Press, 249.

[11] Cheng, Zhaoqi, and Xiang Longwan. 2017. *Transcripts of the Proceedings of the International Military Tribunal for the Far East (Chinese version).* Vol. 4. Shanghai Jiao Tong University Press, 95 (3977 of the English court records).

[12] Ibid., 103–104, 188 (3996–3999, 4190 of the English court records).

[13] PU, Yi. 2007. *From Emperor to Citizen.* Qunzhong Press, 266.

[14] Cheng, Zhaoqi, and Xiang Longwan. 2017. *Transcripts of the Proceedings of the International Military Tribunal for the Far East (Chinese version).* Vol. 4. Shanghai Jiao Tong University Press, 95–96 (3978 of the English court records).

[15] Ibid., 97–98 (3982–3983 of the English court records).

[16] Ibid., 106, 180–182, 226–227 (4004, 4170–4174, 4275 of the English court records).

[17] Ibid., 104, 172 (4000, 4147 of the English court records).

[18] Ibid., 104–110(4000–4014 of the English court records).

[19] PU, Yi. 2007. *From Emperor to Citizen.* Qunzhong Press, 284.

[20] Cheng, Zhaoqi, and Xiang Longwan. 2017. *Transcripts of the Proceedings of the International Military Tribunal for the Far East (Chinese version)*, Vol. 4. Shanghai Jiao Tong University Press, 104–104 (4001–4002 of the English court records).

[21] Ibid., 120–123 (4033–4039 of the English court records).

[22] Ibid., 118–124 (4028–4043 of the English court records).
[23] PU, Yi. 2007. *From Emperor to Citizen.* Qunzhong Press, 203.
[24] Cheng, Zhaoqi, and Xiang Longwan. 2017. *Transcripts of the Proceedings of the International Military Tribunal for the Far East (Chinese version)*, Vol. 4. Shanghai Jiao Tong University Press, 156 (4116 of the English court records).
[25] PU, Yi. 2007. *From Emperor to Citizen.* Qunzhong Press, 310.

CHAPTER 7

# The Lugouqiao Incident

## *The Fierce Battle in Shanghai*

After the Mukden Incident, within six months, almost all of Northeast China fell under the iron hoof of the Japanese army, but military occupation does not mean territorial sovereignty. After the Chinese government appealed to the League of Nations, most members were sympathetic toward her. In order to divert international attention, Japanese militarists decided to cause trouble in Shanghai.

On October 1, 1931, less than half a month after the Mukden Incident, ITAGAKI Seishiro asked TANAKA Ryukichi, then head of Special Service Organ in Shanghai, to come to Mukden and demanded him to cause strife in Shanghai. ITAGAKI indicated that Japan's next step was to occupy Harbin and make Manchuria independent. He had sent Colonel DOIHARA for Tientsin to meet Pu Yi. To prevent the opposition from the League of Nations, ITAGAKI ordered TANAKA to cause strife in Shanghai. Disguised as strife, Japan seized the opportunity to occupy the whole of Northeast China. ITAGAKI was the only representative of the Japanese Army, and the implementation of this conspiracy had to be approved by the highest officials and Navy in Japan. In October of the same year, KONOYE, an advocate of invasion of China who was then the vice president of the House of Peers in 1931, also announced in a group of the Emperor's close confidants that the Kwantung Army was going to start an operation in Shanghai to divert the attention of others, leaving the League of Nations with the illusion that Japan had a desire to make peace and not bring too much humiliation to the League of Nations. With the increasingly serious situation in Northeast China, Japan's strategy became gradually radical, and the idea of causing unrest in Shanghai gradually evolved into provoking war in Shanghai which aroused greater attention.

On January 5, 1932, ITAGAKI Seishiro flew back to Tokyo from Northeast China and was received by Emperor HIROHITO. He reported on the occupation of Northeast China to the Emperor and Army General Staff. Soon after that, ITAGAKI participated in the formulation of the plan to launch a war in Shanghai, and once again ordered TANAKA, Ryukichi to accelerate his plan of action in Shanghai using telegram and allocated 20,000 yen as the activity funds.

Upon receiving the instructions, TANAKA immediately ordered KAWASHIMA Yoshiko, a female spy, to cause strife in Shanghai. From January 18, KAWASHIMA ordered Japanese ronins to cause strife by smashing, looting, and burning Chinese enterprises. In the meantime, the Japanese army sent more troops to Shanghai. Within ten days, the Japanese army assembled 24 warships, over 20 planes, over 1,830 marines, and three or four thousand armed Japanese nationals in Shanghai. On January 21, MURAI Kuramatsu, the Japanese Consul General in Shanghai, made unreasonable demands to the Shanghai Municipal Council, which stated that Chinese authorities should apologize to Japan, punish the offenders, compensate for their loss, and suppress the anti-Japanese movement. On January 27, MURAI issued an ultimatum to the Shanghai Municipal Government, demanding her reply before 6 p.m. on January 28. Although Shanghai Mayor WU Tie-cheng replied at 3:00 p.m. on the 28th, saying that he accepted the conditions put forward by the Japanese, this was not what they really wanted. SHIOZAWA Koichi, commander of the 1st China Expeditionary Fleet in Shanghai, issued a new ultimatum, demanding that the 19 Route Army immediately withdraw from the Chapei area of Shanghai.

In fact, Japan's ultimatum was just a disguise as they were deploying armies. On the night of January 27, Japanese infantry advanced under the cover of ronins, which was stopped and examined by Chinese police. Whilst the ronins were explaining their course of action, the infantry behind suddenly fired, and four Chinese policemen quickly entered the bunker to fight back. On January 28, on the pretext of protecting overseas Japanese, Japan provoked a battle against Shanghai. Before SHIOZAWA Koichi's ultimatum was submitted to the Shanghai Municipal Council, more than 2,000 Japanese Marines had launched an attack on Chapei as planned. The January 28 Incident broke out.[1]

Japanese aircraft carried out the indiscriminate bombing of residential areas and civil institutions for the first time in Chapei as well as other areas in Shanghai.

Japanese warships mercilessly shelled and slaughtered unarmed Chinese civilians, owing to heavy blood debts. The provocation of the Japanese army was resolutely resisted by the 19 Route Army led by general TSAI Ting-kai (CAI Tingkai), the Regimental Commander, and general CHIANG Kuang-nai (JIANG Guangnai), Commander in Chief of the 19 Route Army resulting in the eruption of the Battle of Shanghai.

The next day China made another appeal to the League of Nations. Under the mediation of the United States and Britain, the League of Nations suggested holding a round table conference to arrange a truce in Shanghai. On March 11, 1932, the General Assembly of the League of Nations passed a resolution calling for compliance with international treaties, respect for the territorial integrity and political independence of member states, and peaceful settlement of all disputes in accordance with procedures. At that time, the Nanking government did not want to escalate the situation and decided to relocate the 19th Route Army. On May 5, 1932, the two countries signed the *Shanghai Truce Agreement*. In this battle, the Chinese side dispatched 600,000 troops and suffered about 150,000 casualties. The Japanese side dispatched 300,000 troops and suffered about 70,000 casualties. On May 28, a memorial ceremony was held for the soldiers who sacrificed their lives in battle at Soochow.

TSAI Ting-kai, HO Hsiang-ning (HE Xiangning), CHANG Chih-chung (ZHANG Zhizhong), and other celebrities from all walks of life all offered sacrifices. General CHANG Chih-chung's elegiac address was most touching, which reads:

*What fools, the Japanese.*
*Wolfish, their ambitions*
*Occupying the Northeast*
*Peeping the gates to the East China Sea.*
*Depend on our soldiers*
*To take revenge for national humiliation.*
*Smash the stubborn enemy again and again.*
*Defend the famous city time and time again.*
*The more the enemy, the stronger the iron will.*
*Facing the foemen, we pit one against ten.*

*Roaring, thundering fills the valley*
*Roaring, trembling with the rivers.*
*You can shake the mountain*
*You cannot shake our army.*
*Dark night enveloped Miao Zhen town*
*Whistling wind passing Jiang Wan gulf.*
*Shining are our swords and stars*
*That terrifies the enemy's hearts.*
*Step by step, back, and advance.*
*Running and escaping like falling leaves in the wind.*
*The bombs are falling.*
*The warplanes are diving.*
*Like one man, they stood fire and stood their ground.*
*Brave and devoted, like hunter and hound, they are.*
*Life and death.*
*Sacrifice or success.*
*Fresh blood turning blue*
*Breath becomes a rainbow.*
*We have but one life to lose.*
*But flesh and blood will fertilize the withed grass on the earth.*
*The noble character and indomitable will*
*live on as long as high mountains and vast sea.*[2]

After reading the eulogy, CHANG Chih-chung burst into tears. All the officers and soldiers stood in the wind and rain, paying tribute to the deceased, living in a somber atmosphere.

## *North China Under Iron Hoof*

Although Japan did not win in the Battle of Shanghai, its militarist ambition to expand was incited. On August 19, 1932, the Kwantung Army occupied Nanling in Jehol Province and declared that Jehol was the territory of Manchukuo. On January 1, 1933, Japan attacked Shan-hai Kuan with a pretext. On February 25, the Japanese army attacked Jehol. On March 2, all of Northeast China was occupied by Japan.

On March 27, 1933, Japan withdrew from the League of Nations and relieved itself of the constraints of the League of Nations and many international treaties that it had signed. After that, the Japanese militarists became more unscrupulous, and their next target was vast and rich in resources—North China.

In order to subdue the Chinese government in accepting Japan's occupation of Manchuria and Jehol, China and Japan signed Tangku Truce on May 30, 1933. The chief representative of China was HSIUN Pin (XIONG Bin), Chief of the General Staff, and the chief representative of Japan was OKAMURA Yasuji, Deputy Chief-of-Staff of the Shanghai Expeditionary Army under the aegis of the Kwantung Army. Article 1 of the treaty stipulated that All Chinese troops would quickly retreat to the west and south of the lines formed by Yenching, Changping, Kaoliying, Shunyi, Tungchow, Hsianghe, Paoti, Lintingkow, Ninghe, and Lutai. These lines could not be crossed. Articles 2 and 4 even required that the Japanese army, in order to confirm the implementation of Article 1, would monitor the border at any time, either by aircraft or by any other means, and the Chinese side should be protective of and render support. The police organs of the Chinese side would be responsible for maintaining public peace and order in the areas to the south of the Great Wall Line and areas to the north and east of the line, as stipulated in Article 1. The above-mentioned police organs should not employ the same armed forces that were unfriendly to the Japanese army. The Japanese side's commitment was only to the third Article, which stipulates that if the Japanese army had confirmation that the Chinese army had complied with Article 1, then it would no longer cross the lines mentioned above and would go back to the Great Wall lines.[3]

The Tangku Truce gave the Japanese an opportunity of penetrating Northern China. On June 9, 1935, UMEZU Yoshijiro, Commander of Japanese troops in Northern China submitted a memorandum to HO Yin-chin (HE Yingqin), Chairman of the Peking Military Committee, the supreme organ in charge of the military forces of Northern China through Chief of Staff SAKAI Takashi, demanding a response within three days. The content included the dismissal of YU Hsueh-chung (YU Xuezhong), CHANG Ting-ao (ZHANG Ting'e), CHIANG Hsiao-sien (JIANG Xiaoxian), and other anti-Japanese generals as well as withdrawing the Northeast Army, the Central Army and a gendarmerie regiment stationed in Hopei and prohibiting all anti-Japanese activities.

In the same month, the correspondences between HO Yin-chin and UMEZU Yoshijiro, Commander of the Japanese garrison army, were exposed, known as the

HO-UMEZU Agreement, requiring that all Northeast Army, the Central Army, and the Third Regiment of the Gendarmerie be evacuated out of Hopei province, and a replacement of the chairman of the Kuomintang Hopei Province and the mayors of Peiping and Tien-Tsin, banning anti-Japanese groups and anti-Japanese activities in Hopei Province. This agreement actually gave up the sovereignty of Northern China, which created a greater hidden risk for Japan to launch a full scale war of aggression against China two years later. DOIHARA Kenji, head of the Special Service Organ of the Japanese Kwantung Army, and CHIN Teh-chun (Qin Dechun), chairman of Chahar Province of China, initialed the DOIHARA-CHIN Teh-chun Pact, which included withdrawing SUNG Cheh-yuan (SONG Zheyan) troops, banning anti-Japanese organizations, canceling Kuomintang organizations in Chahar Province, and so on. These two agreements were not officially recognized by the Chinese and Japanese governments resulting in China losing much sovereignty over Hopei and Chahar. After the disclosure of these two secret agreements, public indignation was aroused throughout the whole of China.

While the Japanese army carried out its military plan in Northern China, the Japanese government was also planning to conquer China by diplomatic means. On January 21, 1936, HIROTA Koki, then Foreign Minister, put forward the notorious *HIROTA Sangensoku* (the Three Principles by HIROTA) in his speech:

(1) *Discontinuation of anti-Japanese activities, stop relying on Europe and the United States, and cooperation with Japan on specific issues;*
(2) *Recognition of Manchukuo;*
(3) *Joint action against Communism in the neighboring areas of Outer Mongolia.*

At that time, Japanese Prime Minister OKADA Kaisuke was also a Navy Minister. The Navy did not approve of the Army's policy of military expansion in Asia, which caused resentment among the army extremists. On February 26, 1936, 22 officers and about 1,400 soldiers launched a mutiny, occupying the Prime Minister's residence and the Diet, Home Ministry, War Ministry, Metropolitan Police, and General Staff Headquarters. Thereafter they assassinated TAKAHASHI Korekiyo, Minister of Finance, SAITO Makoto, Lord Keeper of the Privy Seal, WATANABE Jotaro Inspector General of Military Education, and attempted to kill SUZUKI Kantaro, Grand Chamberlain, and OKADA Keisuke, Prime Minister. This incident was called the February Incident or the February

26 Incident. To the astonishment of the world, the Army's ambition was not even suppressed, on the contrary, OKADA's Cabinet resigned, and HIROTA Koki, who supported the Army's tough policy, took over as prime minister. Except for HIROTA himself, all other ministers in OKADA's cabinet were replaced.

However, the measures of HIROTA's Cabinet could not meet the radical demands of the Army's insatiable greed, which were criticized by Seiyu who advocated for the strengthening of the role of the Diet. On February 1, 1937, HIROTA's Cabinet resigned less than one year later, and HAYASHI Senjuro, the General of the Army, formed the cabinet.

HAYASHI Senjuro tried his best to form a military cabinet, with only one of the cabinet members having no military background. Less than three weeks after HAYASHI cabinet came to power, it approved the basic policy towards Northern China, serving as a base for the Japanese military supplies industry and a buffer for anti-Soviet Union. However, these policies conflicted with the bills passed by the previous cabinet and were opposed by Diet. HAYASHI Senjuro immediately announced the dissolution of the Diet for the general election, in an attempt to elbow out political parties and establish a cabinet in which the government and the military colluded with each other. Contrary to his expectations, the party criticizing HAYASHI's cabinet won a big victory in the election, and HAYASHI's cabinet was forced to resign only four months later, KONOYE, an aristocrat in favor of the Army established a new cabinet.

In June 1936, the Emperor of Japan approved the new Imperial Defense Policy and Imperial Army Operation Plan for the War, openly declaring that Japan would dominate East Asia and Western Pacific and finally dominate the world. On August 7, the Five Ministers' Conference composed of the Japanese Prime Minister, War Minister, Navy Minister, Foreign Minister, and Finance Minister adopted the bill of a national policy, which specified the strategic plan of invading China, attacking the Soviet Union, and taking the opportunity to advance to the South. In the meantime, in accordance with the plan of invading China in 1936, the plan of invading China in 1937 was formulated.

There were many unequal clauses in the Boxer Protocol of 1901 signed by the Ching government and the Eight-Power Allied Forces 1901. The 9th Article was to concede the right to the Powers to station troops in the following places: Huangtsun, Langfang, Yangtsun, Tientsin, Chunliangcheng, Tangku, Lutai, Tangshan, Luanchow, Changli, Chinhuangtao, Shanhaikan. The number of troops would be negotiated between the countries and the Chinese government.[4]

In May of 1936, the number of troops stationed in Tientsin from various countries was 1,000 from Britain, 1,300 from the United States, 1,750 from France, 390 from Italy, and 2,100 from Japan. The number of Japanese troops stationed in Tientsin was the largest, but they were still not satisfied with that number. Without China's consent, Japan dramatically increased its troops stationed in Tientsin to 6,000, which greatly exceeded the articles of the Boxer Protocol of 1901.

After that, the Japanese army continually caused problems and frequently conducted military maneuvers, which made the situation in Northern China become increasingly tense. On September 15, 1936, the Japanese General Staff Headquarters issued the Measures against the current situation in China, which clearly pointed out: In case of an incident concerning the prestige of the imperial army in Northern China, the troops stationed in China should receive punishment immediately. To this end, it was decided to add a division, and part of the Kwantung Army was sent from China to Chinchow for standby. The Japanese army should attack and act quickly, give China a strike like lightning in the shortest time, and solve the problem in the local area.[5] It was almost certain that Japan was going to launch a full-scale invasion of China. The peaceful settlement of the Hsi-an Incident, on the one hand, gave a huge blow to Japan's aggressive ambition. On the other hand, it prompted Japan to speed up its determination to appeal to military means.

The Japanese military decided to copy the Mukden Incident, causing strife again, and provoking conflicts to expand wars. The first goal is Fengtai, a strategic fort in Peiping-Tientsin. Fengtai, located on the southern outskirt of Peiping, was called a strategic transportation hub by HASHIMOTO Gun, Chief of the General Staff. Since May 1936, the Japanese army had built military barracks in Fengtai and frequently caused unreasonable provocations. The 29th Chinese Army stationed in Peiping was forbearing and conciliatory and retreated from Fengtai in September of the same year.

When the Japanese army seized Fengtai, their next goal was to another strategic place—Lugouqiao in Wanping County. On the night of July 7, 1937, the Japanese army violated the terms of the Boxer Protocol of 1901 and conducted maneuvers near Lugouqiao in Wanping County, southwest of Peiping. Suddenly, on the pretext that a soldier named SHIMORA Kikuji was missing the Japanese army intended to enter Wanping County to search for him which was sternly rejected by the 29th Route Army. In fact, SHIMORA Kikuji had already returned to the Japanese army but in pretending not to know, the Japanese army fired at the Chinese army and shelled Wanping City.

The 29th Army rose up to fight against the Japanese troops. This was the July 7 Incident, also known as Lugouqiao Incident, which shocked the world. It is often called Marco Polo Bridge Incident in the west.

## *The Beginning of the National Anti-Japanese War*

The Japanese army's rampant attacks aroused the hatred of all Chinese people. On July 8, the Communist Party of China issued three telegrams in succession.

The first telegram was a Letter sent to Compatriots all over China, which was issued to the whole country in the name of the Central Committee of CPC. It pointed out that the attack on Lugouqiao was the first shot of the all-out war of aggression against China, appealing to the Chinese people to be alert that Peiping and Tientsin were in danger; Northern China was in danger, and by extension, the entire Chinese nation was in danger. It pointed out that the only solution for China was to carry out the whole nation's war of resistance, and called on the people, army, and government of the whole country to unite and build a strong Great Wall to resist Japanese aggression. The telegram also issued six slogans: Defend Peiping and Tientsin by armed forces and defend Northern China. Stop imperialists from occupying an inch of China's land and shed the last drop of blood to defend the country, Compatriots, Government, and the army all over the country should unite together to build a solid Great Wall of the national (United Front) and resist the aggression of Japanese pirates. The Kuomintang and the Communist Party cooperated closely to resist the new attacks by the Japanese aggressors to expel the Japanese aggressors out of China.

The second telegram was from the General of the Red Army to Generalissimo CHIANG Kai-shek for the Japanese Invaders' Attack on Northern China, which was sent to CHIANG Kai-shek in the name of seven red army generals: MAO Tse-tung, CHU Teh (ZHU De), PENG Teh-wai (PENG Dehuai), HO Lung (HE Long), LIN Piao (LIN Biao), LIU Po-cheng (LIU Bocheng) and HSU Hsiang-chien(XU Xiamhqian). The main content of the telegraph was that the Japanese invaders attacked the Lugouqiao trying to control Northern China. The officers and soldiers of the Red Army were willing to serve their country and fight against the enemy under the command of CHIANG Kai-shek, so as to protect Chinese territory.

The third telegram was also in the name of the seven Red Army generals which was sent to the four generals of the 29th army SUNG Cheh-yuan, CHANG Tze-chung (ZHANG Zizhong), LIU Ju-ming (LIU Ruming) and FENG Chih an (FENG Zhian) who fought bravely in the front line, which stated that all the Red Army were ready to fight against the Japanese aggressors to the last drop of their blood.[6]

On July 9, CHIANG Kai-shek received another telegram from PENG Teh-wai, LIN Piao, LIU Po-cheng, and HO Lung on behalf of the Red Army which said that the Red Army would like to change its name to the National Revolutionary Army to fight with Japanese invaders. In the meantime, the Communist Party of China sent CHOU En-lai (Zhou Enlai) to Lushan Mountain to talk with CHIANG Kai-shek.

On the morning of July 17, CHIANG Kai-shek issued the Anti-Japanese War Declaration and solemnly declared:

> *We are about to face the extremely tragic situation in which we are the prey of Japanese predators. We have to fight! As for the war, we have nothing to offer but sacrifice and fight to the end. If we are irresolute and delusional, our country will be occupied by the Japanese. If we give up sovereignty, we will be guilty of the Chinese nation through the ages! ... When the war broke out, the whole nation should bear the responsibility of defending our country with the determination to win the victory regardless of the age, occupation, and birthplace.*[7]

The July 7 Incident marks the beginning of the Japanese imperialist war of aggression against China and the beginning of the Chinese nation's comprehensive war of resistance.

## *Mayor and County Magistrate in Court*

As pointed out in the fifth chapter of this book, *the Indictment* divides Japanese aggression against China into two phases. The second phase "began on July 7, 1937, when the Japanese army attacked Wanping near Peiping after the Lugouqiao

Incident, including the continual attacks that followed." After the court completed the part of Japanese aggression against Manchuria, it handled Japanese aggression against the whole of China. Therefore, it was an important task for IPS, especially the Chinese prosecution team, to uncover the Japanese plot to create the July 7 Incident and find proper witnesses from China to testify in court.

When David Nelson Sutton, an American prosecutor, and his party went to China for the investigation, they intended to invite Ching The-chun, undersecretary of the Ministry of National Defense, and Weng Wen-hao, vice president of the Executive Yuan, to testify in court. The *DOIHARA-CHIN Teh-chun Pact* was signed by CHIN Teh-chun and DOIHARA. During the July 7 Incident, he served as the mayor of Peiping and concurrently served as the acting commander of the 29th Route Army, which made him the best candidate. However, during the Tokyo Trial, CHIN Teh-chun was promoted from the Deputy Minister of Military Orders Department to the Deputy Minister of National Defense, and also served as head of the War Crimes Investigation Committee. As a senior official, was he willing to testify in court? Was he mentally and psychologically prepared? Did he collect sufficient evidence? HSIANG Che-chun was in Tokyo at that time. In order to prepare CHIN Teh-chun and other senior officials who might testify in court, he sent an urgent telegram to the Ministry of Foreign Affairs and CHU Shi-ming on June 10, 1946:

*Dear KungLiang,*

*Your telegram has been received so please rest assured.*
*1. The U.S. side authorized Sutton to come to China to consult with the officials concerned, without reaching a specific decision. 2. The U.S. prosecution team had met and invited General CHIN Teh-chun to testify in the court, yet they did not talk about inviting Weng to the court. 3. We have many witnesses, which is helpful to the trial. It is common in a country under the rule of law for senior officials to testify in court. In the same way, the international court could summon the witness. However, the Chinese officials are very busy with their business. The problem is that they have to travel abroad to answer questions frequently. The officials invited will decide if they will go to Japan for themselves. 4. Once they decide to testify in court, it is advisable that they have to bring along with them many documents related to the case and fully prepare for the interrogation. Our witnesses will testify from the end of this month.*

*Sincerely Yours,*
*HSIANG Che-chun*[8]

Finally, the prosecution team invited three witnesses to testify in court for the Lugouqiao Incident.

The first is CHIN Teh-chun. According to the content of the telegraph from HSIANG Che-chun, making full preparations before leaving for Japan, CHIN Teh-chun testified in court for four days in succession from July 22, 1946, to July 25, 1946. Two hundred forty-seven pages in the *Transcript of the International Military Tribunal for the Far East* are about the four days of trial, among which 130 pages are about CHIN.[9] On July 31, the Chinese delegation in Japan translated CHING's testimony in court and the English outlines of the four-day trial and sent it to the Ministry of Foreign Affairs, including the following contents:

*July 22, Court statements*

*I. Facts of Japanese Aggression In North China*

*1. Northern Chahar Incident*

*2. Inducement and Threat Both Prior to and After the Establishment of The Hopei-Chahar Political Council*

*II. A Factual Account of the July 7 Incident*

*1. Prologue*

*2. Factual Account of The Incident*

*III. Witness CHIN Teh-chun cross-examined by OTA Kinjiro, counsel for the defendant, DOIHARA*

*July 23.*

*I. Witness CHIN Teh-chun continued to be cross-examined by OTA Kinjiro, counsel for the defendant, DOIHARA*

*II. Questions and answers between counsel ITO, Kiyoshi, counsel for the defendant, and witness Cheng Teh-chun*

*III. Questions and answers between Franklin E. Warren's counsel for DOIHARA Kenji and HIRANUMA and witness CHIN Teh-chun*

*July 24.*

*I. Witness CHIN Teh-chun continued to be cross-examined by Franklin E. Warren*

*II. Questions and answers between Bruce Blakeney, counsel for the defense UMEZU Yoshijiro and SHIGENORI Togo, and CHING*

*July 25.*

*I. Questions and answers between Okamoto Toshio, counsel for the defense MINAMI Jiro, and CHIN Teh-chun*

*II. Questions and answers between Brooks, counsel for the dense MINAMI Jiro and OKAWA Shumei, and the President of the court*

*III. Questions and answers between Brooks counsel for the defense and CHIN Teh-chun*

*IV. Questions and answers between President and Brooks counsel for the defense*

*V. Direct-examination of CHIN Teh-chun by President*[10]

In the process of testifying in court, besides reading the court statement, he was not only interrogated by the President but also interrogated by six Japanese-American counsels for the defense. CHIN Teh-chun's testimony Documentary of the July 7 Incident[11], which was written neatly with a brush, uncovered the Japanese invasion before and after the Lugouqiao Incident. Its outlines are as follows:

*I. Prologue*

*A. The military and political situations of Hopei-Chahar before the Anti-Japanese War*

*1. Politics*

*2. The place where the July 7 Incident took place*

*B. Stages of Japanese Aggression*

*1. Alienation*

*2. Economic monopolization*

*3. Military Threat*

*II. A Factual Account of the Incident*

In the factual account of the incident CHIN Teh-chun elaborated on the whole process at that time.

*At 12:10 on the night of July 7, 1937, I received the report from the Hopei-Chahar Foreign Affairs Commission, which stated that the said commission had received a telephone call from MATSUI, the Chief of the Japanese Special Service Board, saying: "One company of Japanese troops, in night maneuver in the vicinity of Lukouchiao Bridge just a while ago, seemed to have heard a few gunshots fired by soldiers of the 37th Division of the 29th Army stationed in the city of Wan-Ping. The gunshots brought some confusion to the troops in maneuver. As a result of the roll call, one Japanese soldier was found to be missing. Japanese troops demanded to enter and search the city of Wan-Ping this very evening." The said commission asked for instructions by telephone as to how to deal with the situation. I immediately replied that Japanese troops, maneuvering in Chinese territory at their own will, were in violation of international law. Neither had they notified us in advance nor had they obtained our permission. The Chinese Government has no responsibility whatsoever for the alleged missing soldier. Even if it is true that a soldier was really missing, we shall order the Chinese troops stationed at Lukouchiao Bridge to conduct a search for the Japanese soldier on our own behalf in cooperation with local police forces. My instructions were transmitted to the Japanese by the Hopei-Chahar Foreign Affairs Commission. Soon thereafter, the said commission again telephoned me and reported that after transmission of the reply, both the Japanese Special Service Board and the Japanese troops were not satisfied. The Japanese insisted on conducting a search in the city by force. If refused, they decided to encircle the walled city. I again immediately replied that in case of such unreasonableness on the part of the Japanese, so violent and barbarous, we, for the sake of self-defense, could only take the course of resolute resistance. ...As the Vice-Commander of the 29th Army, I immediately ordered Regiment Commander CHI Hsing-ven (JI Xingwen) to well guard the city of Wan-Ping, that not a single Japanese soldier was to be allowed to come in, that not a single inch of territory was to be allowed to lose, that in virtue of our responsibility as soldiers, to guard our territory, the Wan-Ping city would be, in case of necessity, the most precious and glorious graveyard of our ranks and files, that we should share the same fate with the city. If they did not open fire first, we should not first open fire upon them. If they should first open fire, we were sure to deal them fatal blows... The Japanese, realizing by that time that there was no hope for them to take the city of Wan-Ping without fighting, finally encircled it on three sides. Our forces put up defense works on the walls. Around 06:00, enemy machine gun fire began to attack the city, and enemy forces came towards it. This was the very beginning of the Sino-Japanese War, but the responsibility of the Incident was also definitely fixed (upon Japan).*

At the end of his written testimony, CHIN Teh-chun clearly pointed out: "*Leading Japanese officers who instigated this Incident were: KATSUKI, Seiji, Commander in Chief of the Japanese Garrison Forces in Tientsin, KAWABE, Seiso, Brigadier Commander, MUTAGUCHI, Renyam, Regiment Commander, SAKAI, Takashi, Ex-Chief of Staff of the Japanese Garrison Forces and HASHIMOTO, Kingoro, Chief of Staff at present. But the instigator at the very beginning of Japanese aggression in north China was DOIHARA. All those men should be held responsible for the war of aggression.*"

On July 27, HSIANG Che-chun telegraphed the Ministry of Foreign Affairs and spoke highly of CHING's performance: CHING testified in court for four days and made his testimony terrific.[12]

The second witness to testify in court about the Lugouqiao Incident was WANG Len-chai (WANG Lengzhai), who was the magistrate of Wanping County in that year.

Before the Lugouqiao Incident, when there was a sign that the Japanese were ready to take some measures to occupy Chinese territory, Wang was taking corresponding proactive measures. In his negotiations with the Japanese army, when it came to sovereignty, as a patriot he never gave up his stance and never made any compromise. For example, in order to facilitate future aggression, the Japanese army attempted to build an airport in Taching Village, Wanping County. The Japanese went to Wanping many times with topographic maps drawn in advance, demanding to cede land in accordance with the maps, which was resolutely rejected by WANG Len-chai. The Japanese then colluded with local traitors, ruffians, and hooligans to lure residents to rent and sell their land. When WANG discovered the conspiracy, he made an investigation into the Taching village, arrested the traitors, and publicized patriotism to the residents, so the Japanese army's intrigue was in vain.

WANG Len-chai was a participant in all the negotiations and military defense before and after the Lugouqiao Incident and was also a very suitable witness. At the invitation of the Chinese prosecution team, he testified in court on August 6, 1946.

WANG Len-chai presented the Lugouqiao Incident written by him to the court. He first affirmed CHIN Teh-chun's testimony:

> *Relative to the inception of the Japanese invasion of North China and to the history of the 'Lukouchiao' case, ex-Mayor of Peiping, Mr. CHIN Teh-chun, has already*

*made out a factual report. Mr. CHIN was then one of the high-ranking officials in North China. At the inception of the war Chairman SUNG Cheh-yuen of the Political Council for the Provinces of Hopei and Chahar was on leave at his native place. Mr. CHIN was made to act on his behalf on all matters, diplomatic as well as military. He personally directed and conducted all negotiations and military defense. Therefore, what he has recorded is factual and truthful.*

Then WANG Len-chai told the court his title saying:

*I was then the Executive Supervisor for the 3rd District of Hopei Province and concurrently the Magistrate of Wan-ping Hsien. Lukouchiao, where the Japanese started the initial attack, is within the district of my jurisdiction, and I had personally participated in all of the negotiations and conducted military defense ...*

And then WANG uncovered Japan's ambitions:

*The Japanese by repeating what they had successfully tried out in the North-eastern Three Provinces, hoped to achieve the occupation of North China without sacrificing one single soldier and one single bullet. With this end in view, they started with 'peaceful invasion.' After they had occupied Fengtai and stationed troops there, they tried to take Lukouchiao as well. Had this been successful, Peiping would be under their control with a single pincer movement, and the 29th Army would also be kept under watch... The war of Lukouchiao was started as a consequence of the Japanese military maneuvers, which they performed upon Chinese soil freely without any treaty rights and without notifying the local Chinese authorities beforehand. From the time of my assumption of office up to the outbreak of the Lukouchiao Incident, the Japanese staged maneuvers no less than six times... These showed that the plan of their invasion must have been meticulously studied and that the tempo was being gradually intensified till a certain time when it was ripe for them to wage war.*

WANG Len-chai described the situation of Lugouqiao Incident and the process in detail. A portion of his testimony states:

*The Japanese army had performed several military maneuvers without informing the Chinese authorities before the outbreak of the Lugouqiao Incident. At around 11 o'clock on the night of July 7, 1937, a few shots were heard to have been fired from the outskirts of Wan-ping city. Investigation reports showed that the Japanese troops were then staging maneuvers. I directed close attention to this matter. Soon Mayor CHIN telephoned me that a protest had been lodged by MATSUI, commander of the Japanese Special Service Corps, alleging that one of the Japanese soldiers was found missing after the Chinese garrison forces at Wan-ping had opened fire at the Japanese maneuvering troops, and demanding that the Japanese troops should be allowed entry into the city to conduct searches. I was instructed to investigate the matter at once and submit a report. A number of my men were detailed and sent out to investigate inside as well as outside of the city. But no missing soldier was ever found. I immediately proceeded to Peiping, where I reported to Mayor CHIN. Pressed for a settlement by Commander MATSUI, I was ordered to take up negotiations, in the company of Mr. WEI Tsung-han* (WEI Zonghan), *Chairman of the Foreign Affairs Committee, Mr. LIN Ken-yu* (LIN Gengyu), *member of the Committee, and Mr. CHOW Yun-yieh* (ZHOU Yongye), *Director of the Department of Communications, under the Pacification Headquarters, with the Japanese representatives. Commander MATSUI insisted that it was true that they had one soldier missing and kept on demanding the entry of the Japanese troops into the city to conduct searches by themselves. I refused it out rightly and recalled that the Japanese Consul-General at Nanking, Hr. KURAMOTO, who was claimed to have been missing, was found to have hidden for the purpose of putting the blame on the shoulders of the Chinese government. I hinted that this particular Japanese soldier might have tried to imitate what the Japanese Consul-General had done. Commander MATSUI denied the fact. As a result of the negotiation, it was decided that both Japanese and Chinese authorities should jointly send members out to Wanping to conduct an investigation on the spot and that a satisfactory settlement should be reached. After entering the city, we held a discussion in my office; I had just ordered the Director of the Police Bureau to make his report on the search when a number of gunshots were heard, and bullets were zooming past our heads. Undoubtedly, the Japanese troops had already opened fire. A few minutes later, our guards on the city walls began to return firing. The duel lasted for about another hour. The Japanese started shooting again, and we also returned fire. The skirmishes lasted until 4 p.m., with considerable losses on both sides. By five o'clock in the afternoon, they again attacked us with trench mortars and hit and blasted my office, which was entirely destroyed. Fortunately enough, I had removed all my staff to a safer place a few minutes before this happened. After 6 p.m., the firing quieted down. The Japanese commander, one named KAWABE, Shozo, also sent a note to me and asked me to go out of the city for negotiation, failing which I should see that all the inhabitants be evacuated because they would bombard the city with heavy artillery. I declined the demand. At that moment, our reinforcements from Changhsintien arrived, and that very night, our Big Sword Company fought hand to hand against the Japanese troops at the Dragon King Temple. As this Company of ours was well trained and extremely brave, many Japanese soldiers were killed. The iron bridge which was hitherto occupied by the Japanese was recaptured. Being routed, the Japanese became quiet… Ever since then, fighting was intermittently going on until July 22… On the 26th, they suddenly sent over an ultimatum demanding the withdrawal of our 37th army from Peiping within 24 hours. We were so cornered and pressed.*

WANG Len-chai also briefly mentioned how the Chinese army bravely resisted the enemy:

*A very fierce counterattack was launched by our forces at Lugouqiao and Papaoshan, and an onslaught was made toward Fengtai. On the 27th, the railway station at Fengtai was recovered. But on the 28th, the Japanese concentrated all their forces and attacked us near Nan-yuan, with the help of many planes and artillery. The fight lasted until 2:00 p.m. General CHAO Teng-yu* (ZHAO Dengyu), *Commander of the Division, and General TUNG Lin-kou* (TONG Linge), *Deputy-Commander of the 29th army were killed in action. Chairman SOONG Cheh-yuan, following instructions from the Supreme Commander, left for Paoting to assume his command, while General CHANG Tze-chung, Division Commander, was instructed to stay on in Peiping, to help the various troops coordinate their defense. I was, however, instructed to proceed to Paoting also.*

The conclusion of WANG Len-chai testimony is as follows:

*Judging from the above accounts, one would readily realize that the Japanese invasion was a studied and systematic scheme that was not meted out overnight. They should be made to shoulder the full responsibilities of the war.*[13]

In addition to the two Chinese officials testifying in court, an American witness testified on August 7, 1946. He is Colonel David D. Barrett, the American ambassador to China. When the Lugouqiao Incident broke out, he was an

Assistant Military Attaché to the American Legation in Peking. His executive officer in Peking and acting Military Attaché, was Joseph Stilwell, then a full colonel.

On July 9, 1937, shortly after the Lugouqiao Incident, Stilwell instructed him to go to Wanping County for a field investigation and make a report. Barrett made at least five trips to Wanping from July 9 to 25. His recollections were as follows:

> *On the morning of July 9, 1937, Colonel Stillwell directed me to proceed to Wanping County. Colonel Stillwell directed me to investigate and report on the situation at Wanping, as he had been informed that a clash had taken place there the day before between forces of the Chinese 29th Army and Japanese troops who had been conducting maneuvers in the vicinity for several days. I arrived at Wanping at about 8 a.m. and found the east gate shut and barricaded.... I then walked around the northeast corner of the city wall to the Peking-Hankow railway at a point approximately due north of the city. There I found a battalion of Japanese infantry assembled along the north side of the railway. A few sentries were posted along the top of the railway embankment observing the city of Wanping to the south.... From the Japanese position behind the railway embankment, I then proceeded past the northwest corner of the city wall and into Wanping through the west gate, which was shut, but not barricaded.... Inside the city, I visited the office of the Magistrate where police officials showed me damage apparently caused by mortar fire from outside the walls. The police officials informed me that the county Magistrate was in Peiping consulting with the mayor. The officials gave me an account of what had happened from the night of July 7 to 8. This account was substantially the same as that contained in the affidavit presented by General CHIN Teh-chun and Mr. WANG Len-chai, which I have read. I then returned to Peiping.*

According to what he saw and heard, at first, he and Stilwell both thought:

> *On my return to Peiping, I reported to Colonel Stilwell what I had observed substantially as noted above and stated that as far as I could determine, the clash had been on a very small scale and was not nearly so serious as many other clashes which had occurred since September 18, 1931. I further stated that I believed the incident could easily be settled if the Japanese really so desired, as I had observed absolutely no signs of any aggressive attitude on the part of the Chinese.*

However, the Japanese army reneged on its word and pressed hard step by step. David D. Barrett said in his testimony that their actions in many instances constituted an insult to and direct violation of the sovereign rights of the Chinese nation. Barrett analyzed Japan's actions in Northeast China in those years, and came to the following conclusion:

> *During the first few days of January 1932, Japanese forces attacked and occupied the city of Shanhaikuan. The Japanese alleged they had attacked because of aggressive actions on the part of Chinese forces stationed in Shanhaikuan at the time. I visited Shanhaikuan two or three days after the Japanese occupied the city and made a careful investigation of the situation. I was unable to find any definite proof that Chinese forces had provoked the incident. Here again, the measures taken by the Japanese appeared to be out of all proportion to the importance of the incident itself, regardless of the causes thereof. In my opinion, the action of the Japanese in conducting night maneuvers near Wanping during the first week of July 1937 was deliberately provocative. The Japanese could not but have been aware of the strained relations then existing between Japan and China, and of the chances for misunderstanding and friction which might arise during such maneuvers. The fact that movements of large Japanese forces from Manchuria to areas south of the Great Wall began within a period of twenty-four hours after the Japanese attacked at Wanping inevitably suggests that the Wanping Incident was the carefully prepared excuse for the second stage of Japan's undeclared war on China, the first stage having been begun at Mukden on the night of September 17 to 18, 1931.*[14]

The testimonies of these three Chinese and foreign witnesses are in full accord, which fully shows that the July 7 Incident and the subsequent Japanese aggression were all planned conspiracies.

### *Summary Report*

From February 12 to 13, 1948, HSIANG Che-chun, Nyi, Judson T.Y., D.N. Sutton, and W.G. Brown read out the second part of the Japanese aggressive conspiracy on behalf of the prosecution, entitled *The Expansion of Control and Domination from Manchuria to The Rest of China*[15], and its outline is as follows:

*A. Obtaining Control of North China Prior to July 7, 1937*
*1. The Establishment of the Autonomous Governments in North China*
*2. The February 26, 1936 Incident*
*3. Aggressive Policy toward China March 1936 to July 1937*
*B. The War of Aggression against China 1937–1945*
*1. The Period from July 1937 to January 1938.*
*2. The Period from January 16, 1938, to September 2, 1945*
*C. The Domination of China*
*1. Political*
*2. Economic*
*3. Narcotics*

This book is not intended to elaborate on the summation by the prosecution, so I refer the interested readers to the relevant bibliographies. Essentially, the Lugouqiao Incident is a symbol of the Chinese comprehensive anti-Japanese war, which is the main theatre of the world anti-fascist war in East Asia. Chinese people have made great contributions to saving the nation from peril and striving for world peace. On the other hand, history fully shows that the Japanese militarists are greedy and arrogant, and the fable of "a snake tries to swallow an elephant" is a portrayal of their vain attempt to dominate the world.

History is the best textbook and the best sobering medicament. Throughout the history of the world, the expansion and aggression of other countries by force are bound to fail. This is a historical law. It is the common aspiration of mankind that all countries, big or small, strong or weak, adhere to the path of peaceful development and let the sunshine of peace shine on the planet where mankind lives forever.

## *References*

[1] Hu, Dekun. 2005. *History of Sino-Japanese War (1931–1945) (Revised Edition)*. Wuhan University Press, 26–27.
[2] Chu, Yun. 2011. *Full Disclosure of the Inside Story of Sino-Japanese War*. Current Affairs Press, 80–81.
[3] Chu, Dexin, and Liang De. 1991. *The Treaties between China and Foreign Countries 1689–1949*. Heilongjiang People's Publishing House, 592–593.

[4] History Department of Fudan University. 1977. *Selections on Modern Chinese Foreign Relations*. Vol. 1, bok. 2. Shanghai People's Publishing House, 151.

[5] Hu, Dekun. 2005. *History of Sino-Japanese War (1931–1945) (Revised Edition)*. Wuhan University Press, 103.

[6] Chu, Yun. 2011. *Full Disclosure of the Inside Story of Sino-Japanese War*. Current Affairs Press, 144–145.

[7] Wei, Hongyun. 1981. *Selections of Modern Chinese History*. Vol. 4. Heilongjiang People's Publishing House, 586–587.

[8] Xiang, Longwan. 2014. *HSIANG Che-chun's Letters, Telegrams and Statements at the Tokyo Trial.* Shanghai Jiao tong University Press, 13–14.

[9] Cheng, Zhaoqi, and Xiang Longwan. 2017. *Transcripts of the Proceedings of the International Military Tribunal for the Far East (Chinese version)*. Vol. 2. Shanghai Jiao Tong University Press, 413–510 (2950–2541 of the English court records).

[10] Official Letter No.172 of the Chinese Mission to Japan.

[11] Official Letter No.314 of the Ministry of Foreign Affairs of the National Government.

[12] Xiang, Longwan. 2014 *HSIANG Che-chun's Letters, Telegrams, and Statements at the Tokyo Trial.* Shanghai Jiao Tong University Press, 19.

[13] Cheng, Zhaoqi, and Xiang Longwan. 2017. *Transcripts of the Proceedings of the International Military Tribunal for the Far East (Chinese version)*. Vol. 3. Shanghai Jiao Tong University Press, 318–323 (3317–3332 of the English court records).

[14] Ibid., 336–339 (3355–3364 of the English court records).

[15] Xiang, Longwan. 2010. *The Tokyo Trial, Chinese Prosecutor Hsiang Che-chun*. Shanghai Jiao Tong University Press, 85–94 (39391–39326 of the English court records).

CHAPTER 8

# Crossfire in Court

## *A New Force to the Chinese Prosecution Team*

The first chapter of this book mentioned that four legal counselors joined the prosecutor team of the Chinese Delegation, among whom the associate prosecutors NYI, Judson T.Y., and KWEI Yu appeared and argued cases in court and made important contributions. It was everything but easy for the Chinese team to find these top legal minds in post-war China, where there was a serious scarcity of all kinds of talents.

The court started the witness and evidence stage by the defense on February 24, 1947. In contrast to the stage by the prosecutor, the court is now presented by the defense, and the prosecutor would not be able to rebut effectively if not familiar with the law and the evidence of the case.

By the time, at the beginning of 1947, most of the translation work was completed. Five of the translators were transferred back to the Chinese military delegation in Japan, so the Chinese prosecution team was left with only Prosecutor HSIANG Che-chun, and three secretaries Henry CHIU, LIU T.C., and CHU Ching-ju. To make the situation even worse, the approximately 20 American prosecutors, who had been assisting Chinese prosecutors in the investigation, evidence collection, and court interrogation from the beginning of the trial to the end in 1946, and provided tremendous help, now started to ed the prosecutors tremendously return to the United States one after another. Henry CHIU also resigned later and returned to China due to illness. So, the Chinese prosecution team was seriously short of hands, and the leader, HSIANG Che-chun, was struggling to keep the team's operation.

With the approval of the Ministry of Foreign Affairs, KAW Vurn-ping, one of its interpreters, was added to the team as the secretary. On April 3, 1947, HSIANG Che-chun sent a telegram to China's Ministry of Foreign Affairs.

> *Due to illness, Henry CHIU, secretary of our team resigned. I have telegraphed to get the permission to let KAW Vurn-ping, a law expert from Soochow University, take his place. Since I did not receive your reply for a long time, I am afraid that the telegram was lost. TOJO had begun to make active preparation. Our team needs more hands to deal with a heavy workload. It would be of great help if Mr. KAW could join us. I would appreciate it very much if you could approve of it.*[1]

A more important move was to return home to hire consultants. As early as September 12, 1946, HSIANG Che-chun even stepped up by returning to China himself to hire more counselors. Below is the second telegraph to the Ministry of Foreign Affairs and the Ministry of Justice and Administration HSIANG Che-chun sent for help on September 12, 1946:

> *The case of the Japanese Invasion of China lasted from July 1 to September 10. Various evidence, including Japan's military, political and economic aggression as well as their atrocities in Northeast China and the other parts of China was presented to the International Military Tribunal for the Far East. Furthermore, the witnesses from China, the United States of America, Britain, and Japan were summoned to the court. While the defendants are now collecting related materials, and once the prosecution charges them with aggression against the Soviet Union, Haiphong, Singapore, Pearl Harbor, and the South Seas, they will defend themselves with the assistance of the over 60 Japanese and American counsels and the Japanese government. We do not have sufficient staff to tackle prosecution in Japan, so we are in urgent need of adepts in the language of English, laws, and the economic and political system of Japan and China. What's more, over 20 American assistant prosecutors who handled cases of aggression against China have returned to the United States, so it is necessary for our prosecution team to employ more hands.*[2]

On October 3, He sent another telegram to the Ministry of Foreign Affairs and the Ministry of Justice and Administration:

> *We have presented evidence of Japanese aggression against China to the Tribunal. Twenty seven defenses including TOJO were fully prepared for the cross-examination with the assistance of over 60 Japanese and American counsels. Over 20 American legal experts who handled cases of aggression against China have returned to the United States. China should send more experts who are proficient in legal English and Sino-Japanese situations so as to be well-prepared for the trial.*[3]

HSIANG Che-chun made the trip during the gap to his team when the court heard the case of Japan's invasion of the Soviet Union. His close friend, NYI, Judson T.Y., just happened to return from a European tour. The two met, and NYI, Judson T.Y. agreed immediately to work as the chief adviser to the Chinese prosecution team.

The other three jurists, who had been briefly introduced in the first chapter, AO Daniel S. and KWEI Yu all graduated from the Law School of Soochow University, and WU Hsueh-i was an alumnus of Chaoyang Law School and Kyoto University, and proficient in Japanese. They were all willing to serve as advisers to the Chinese prosecutor.

NYI, Judson T.Y. was a dedicated fan of Chinese operas since his childhood. In Kun Opera or Peking Opera, there are many plays about the trials which fascinated him as justice would be served at the end. NYI, Judson T.Y. recalled them vividly in his memoir *Me and the law*:

> *Fifteen Strings of Cash, one of the famous pieces in Kun Opera tells the story of a court trial in ancient China. The magistrate of Wuhsi County gave the verdict based on his personal preferences which almost caused unjust execution. Fortunately, after private visits and on-site investigation, Kuang Chong, the Mayor of Soochow, finally found the real murderer and served the justice. Similar stories can also be found in Peking Opera, such as The Joint Trial, Judge a Head, Famen Temple, HSIEH Yaohuan, River-viewing Pavilion, and Snowfall in Midsummer, Strange Luck. Influenced by novels and dramas, I think highly of honest and upright officials. This has a great influence on my choice to study law later.*[4]

NYI, Judson T.Y. was particularly good at Kun Opera, and he was close acquaintance with several opera masters like YU Ping-po (Yu Pingbo), YU Chen-fei (Yu Zhenfei), Hou Yung-kuei (HOU Yongkui), Hou Shao-kuei (HOU Shaokui). He kept many handwritten Kunqu music scores that his Kun Opera teachers gave him over 70 years ago. In his late years, he even took to the stage to perform LIN Chong's *Night Fight*, which was adapted from Heroes of the Marshes. Before he proceeded to Tokyo, he had invited HSIANG Che-chun and his wife to enjoy the performance of masters of Kun Opera. One play was about the *Romance of the Three Kingdoms*. KUAN Yu, one of the heroes of that time, went to white vengeance alone with a broad sword. He was a Chinese military general serving under the warlord LIU Bei during the late Eastern Han dynasty of China. The lines of the opera were full of heroic spirit. The two close friends were deeply touched by the play and motivated toward their mission.

NYI, Judson T.Y., and AO Daniel S. made investigations in China. At first, they proceeded to Peiping and visited several traitors in prison. They arrived in Peiping first and interviewed several former officials in prison who worked for the puppet government during Japan's invasion of China.

To their surprise, they were very cunning. LIANG Hung-chih (LIANG Hongzhi), the former President of the Executive Yuan of the Reformed Government of the Republic of China, and WANG I-tang (WANG Yitang), the former member of the Northern China Political Council, malingered to avoid cooperation. Chao Hsin-po (ZHAO Xinbo), the former President of the Legislative Yuan (the legislative branch) of the Manchurian State and legal counsel of the North China Political Council, broker his promise and burnt the documents he prepared for the court. NYI, Judson T.Y., and AO Daniel S. also visited General WU Pei-fu's wife, who revealed that a Japanese spy disguised as a dentist killed her husband by injecting a toxic agent into his treatment which was later accepted by the court as part of the war criminal evidence against DOIHARA Kenji and ITAGAKI Seishiro.

They had an advisory team that had planned to travel to Northeast China but had to cancel the trip because the negotiation between Kuomintang and Communist Party broke down, and a war started in Northeast China.

HSIANG Che-chun needed the advisory team right away. He telegraphed the Ministry of Foreign Affairs and urged the team to get to Tokyo as soon as possible.

*To Ministry of Foreign Affairs:*
*In a few days, the International Military Tribunal for the Far East will be adjourned for two weeks, so that the defense and prosecution would be well prepared for the examinations. Up until now, the prosecution has presented about 2300*

*documents and the pages of the record are over 16,000. Because of the voluminous documents and evidence as well as the complicated procedure, it is necessary for NYI, Judson T.Y., and the other three to come to Japan. Please arrive in Japan before February 1 by ATC.*
*Sincerely Yours,*

The four advisers went to work right away upon arrival in Tokyo.

The court started the defendants' witness and evidence stage on September 10, 1947, which presented their most fierce embattle against the prosecution. The biggest challenge faced by the Chinese prosecution team was how to effectively rebut the defense's arguments for the three defendants, DOIHARA Kenji, ITAGAKI Seishiro, and MATSUI Iwane. As most of their crimes were committed in China, it was natural the Chinese prosecution team would shoulder the assignment to rebut. Here in this chapter, we will focus on the cross-examinations by the Chinese prosecution team on DOIHARA Kenji and ITAGAKI Seishiro by the Chinese prosecution team, and we will provide those details on MATSUI Iwane in Chapter 10.

The Chinese prosecution team was facing two difficult tasks for immediate solutions. The first was how to put forward convincing new evidence when they cross-examined the two defendants. The second was how to have the upper hand during the cross-examination. As the Chinese prosecution team was short of hands seriously, the cross-examination on DOIHARA and ITAGAKI was assigned to Philippine prosecutor Pedro Lopez at one point.

Mr. NYI and his partners worked day and night in reading the court records, evidence, and other relevant materials, and preparing themselves to get familiar with the court process. During their preparations, Mr.NYI was asked to return to China by Minister HSIEH Kuan-sheng to finish his work in Ministry of Justice. HSIANG Che-chun had to telegraph the Minister of Foreign Affairs on May 7 for help:

*The work in the Court is so heavy and we are understaffed. The job in the Court can only be shared by NYI, the chief consultant, and me. It is improper for Mr. NYI to return to China before the task is finished. The Ministry of Justice has sent two telegrams urging him to come back. I would appreciate it very much if you could postpone his return to Peking. Look forward to your reply.*[6]

HSIANG Che-chun's request was approved by HSIEH Kuan-sheng.

HSIANG Che-chun reported to Keenan that the Chinese prosecution team had arranged the resource needed to undertake the cross-examination of DOIHARA Kenji and ITAGAKI Seishiro since both had served as the Japanese commanders in Southeast Asia during the Pacific War following Japan's invasion of China.

Lopez, the Philippine prosecutor, had already prepared for cross-examination. Mr. Keenan hoped that China and the Philippines could cooperate. HSIANG Che-chun and NYI, Judson T.Y. thus suggested cross-examination of the two defendants over their crimes committed in Southeast Asia, and the Chinese team would cover the cross-examination over their overall crimes. Lopez readily agreed. As the cross-examination by the Philippines team was scheduled first, it bought extra time for the Chinese prosecution team to prepare.

The Chinese prosecution team spared no effort in cross-examining DOIHARA and ITAGAKI during their individual defense stage. HSIANG Che-chun kicked off the cross-examination, NYI, Judson T.Y. followed with extensive rebuttal with effective support by LIU T.C. and WU Hsueh-yi who had an excellent command of Japanese and found many pieces of evidence and materials from the Japanese archives. Thanks to their tremendous effort, the Chinese prosecution team accomplished an outstanding job in the cross-examinations. NYI, Judson T.Y. recalled their work many years later:

> *The Chinese prosecution team was determined to fight in the phase of the defendant's individual statement, so as to severely punish the major war criminals who invaded China, which caught the attention of the whole court. It must be stressed here that the trial of Japanese war criminals, in the sense of international law, mainly aims at maintaining world order and upholding international justice instead of blood for blood vengeance. But the death toll caused by the Japanese invasion of China reached 30 million with incalculable property losses, if the major war criminals were not severely punished, how could we maintain the world order and serve international justice? How could we face my compatriots when we return home? With a sober mind, we must try our best to expose the defendant's intrigue and brutal crimes and pave the way for lasting world peace. We shall fight against those cunning criminals for the severely traumatized national feelings.*[7]

## *Nothing to do with "Tiger"*

The defense for DOIHARA Kenji started from September 16 to September 18, 1947.

DOIHARA, a China hand, came to China as early as 1913 and started his more than 30 years of spy career in China by working as an assistant to the spy chief BANZAI Rihachiro.

Japan started to set up its secret service station in Tientsin at the beginning of 1931. and appointed DOIHARA as its chief and later as the chief of the station in Mukden, which became the command center of the stations under the command of Kwantung Army Headquarters after the Mukden Incident. DOIHARA was appointed the mayor of Mukden on September 20 of the same year.

After the Japanese military department approved the plan of the Kwantung Army to establish the puppet Manchukuo, DOIHARA followed Kwantung Army's instruction, went to Tientsin, and kidnapped Pu Yi in Northeast China on October 25, 1931.

DOIHARA was transferred to Harbin to head the Secret Service station there on January 26, 1932. His mission was to stabilize the situation in Northern Manchuria by suppressing the anti-Japanese armed forces in Northeast China and preparing for Japan's occupation of Northern Manchuria. In 1933, DOIHARA was re-appointed as the head of the secret service station and assigned to instigating rebellion and creating unrest in the demilitarized zone designated in *Tangku Truce*.

In June of 1935, DOIHARA was sent to North China by the Kwantung Army to assist TADA Hayao, the Commander of the Japanese garrison in China, in their effort to instigate the warlords to carry out an autonomy movement to create a second Manchuria. Upon his arrival, DOIHARA forced Chahar to sign the *CHIN–DOIHARA Agreement* and seized most of Chahar's sovereignty. He then installed in the ceasefire zone a puppet Eastern-Hopei Government chaired by YIN Ju-keng (YIN Rugeng). He tried it again later with SUNG Cheh-yuan to install the Hopei-Chahar Political Council. But all these efforts by DOIHARA to separate North China did not prevail due to fierce opposition from the Chinese people.

After the Lugouqiao Incident in 1937, DOIHARA's involvement in Japan's invasion of China became direct, and he led the military attacking in North China and slaughtering the Chinese people there.

DOIHARA was summoned back to Japan In June 1938 to participate in the Special Committee on China organized by the War Ministry, the Navy Ministry, and the Foreign Ministry, which established a centralized institution to set up and manage the puppet government in the occupied areas of China—including a new and centralized spy agency—DOIHARA Special Agency in Shanghai. After 1940, DOIHARA was transferred back to Japan to take various assignments, including Supreme War Councilor in General Staff Headquarters, President of Military Academy, Inspector General of Army Aviation, and Commander in Chief of the Japanese Seventh Area Army in Singapore.

DOIHARA, nicknamed by the west as Lawrence of Manchuria, was very cunning. This spy chief was well versed in Anglo-American law, so he chose to involve his right to remain silent in the trial. However, his defense team was large and did not spare any effort.

DOIHARA's first witness from Japan, AIZAWA, was his subordinate when he was the head of the secret service in Mukden. AIZAWA's testimony was mainly to show that the station's duty under DOIHARA was only collecting intelligence and had no other secret activities, and DOIHARA was an honest and straightforward person. NYI, Judson T.Y. rebut DOIHARA's conspiracy in 1935 to organize the "*five-province autonomy in Northern China*" and presented newspaper clips published overseas. NYI asked AIZAWA how could he, as the head of the news department of Kwangtung Army know nothing about it? AIZAWA blushed and did not answer. NYI then presented another exhibit, which was a report signed by AIZAWA himself to his superior about the coverage in foreign newspapers of the matter. AIZAWA had no way but to withdraw his statement.

And NYI, Judson T.Y. went on and presented Exhibit No.3177, an article from the internal publication in 1935 of the secret service station in Mukden 1935, which had DOIHARA's seal on the front page described the details of many activities by the agency in multiple Chinese cities.

The report even mentioned that the names of DOIHARA and ITAGAKI were enough to make the people turn pale in Southern China as if "*they were talking about tigers.*" NYI explained it is a popular Chinese idiom that DOIHARA knew Chinese well and used in the report, which was exactly self-evidence of the brutality imposed on the Chinese people by the secret service agency.

Moreover, the appearance of both names DOIHARA and ITAGAKI in the same document is another self-evidence of the cooperation between the two, which gave the Chinese prosecution team an opportunity to kill two birds with one stone.

There was a funny episode during the cross-examination. Watching AIZAWA did not show any disapproval of NYI's explanation, Warren, the American counsel for the defense, rushed to protest to the court:

> *Your Honor, of course, I cannot read Japanese, but my co-counsel tells me that this interpretation, instead of saying Major General DOIHARA and ITAGAKI, speaks about "the tiger." I don't know what it means.*

The comment by the defense, due to ignorance or ulterior motives, was hilarious. NYI, Judson T.Y. calmly explained to the court:

> *In South China to hear the names of Major Generals DOIHARA and ITAGAKI is something like mentioning a tiger and the people turn pale.*

The judges in the court burst into laughter.[8]

The court went on to hear the next three witnesses of DOIHARA. They were SHIBAYAMA Kaneshiro, the adviser DOIHARA arranged for CHANG Hseuh-liang, KUWAJIMA Kazue, the Consul General of Japan in Tientsin, and YAZAKI Kanju, a former subordinate of DOIHARA.

The testimonies by these three witnesses were mostly for excusing DOIHARA, but they were so vulnerable in facing NYI's cross-examination that they were not adopted by the court.

Among them, KUWAJIMA Kazue's was the most cunning. The Japanese Foreign Ministry had concerned about unfavorable diplomatic reactions by foreign governments when it became known of DOIHARA's plan to hijack Pu Yi in Tientsin and make him the puppet head in Northeast China, so it instructed KUWAJIMA Kazue to dissuade him, and KUWAJIMA Kazue had sent several secret telegrams to the Foreign Minister SHIDEHARA Kijuro, which we had introduced the main contents of them in Chapter 4. To defend DOIHARA, KUWAJIMA Kazue, his words were inconsistent, and he even retracted his words.

KUWAJIMA stated in court:

> *"DOIHARA came to the Consulate General and came to my own room only once and on that occasion, all we did was exchange greetings and nothing more."*

NYI sensed the inconsistency and questioned him right away:

> *Was it true that in your telegrams to Baron SHIDEHARA you mentioned that you had several talks with DOIHARA himself?*

KUWAJIMA replied: "*In none of my telegrams have I ever referred to my talking with General DOIHARA.*"

NYI, Judson T.Y. immediately pulled out two pieces of exhibits, one of them was the telegram KUWAJIMA Kazue sent to SHIDEHARA Kijuro on November 17, 1931, and asked him:

> *"Let me refresh your memory. In Exhibit 287, you said that you talked with DOIHARA and conveyed to him your opinion. In Exhibit 300, you specifically stated that "I have deliberately talked with him several times not to commit such atrocities."*

KUWAJIMA was still trying to deny it and replied: "*I do not have the original of the telegram in my hands, so unless I am shown that particular document it is difficult for me to reply. May I have it shown to me?*" The court judge instructed an assistant to hand the Exhibit No. 300 to him immediately, and asked Major Moore, the Language Arbiter, to read out the content to him:

> *I have fully talked with him twice not to commit such rash acts, but it appears he is continuing plans to overthrow CHANG Hsueh-liang, and there is apprehension that he may start another incident in the Peking-Tientsin area in the near future.*

KUWAJIMA went silent. Mr. NYI went on and asked the last question: "*After hearing this correction in my reading, have you anything to answer, Mr. Witness?,*" KUWAJIMA could only reply, "*Nothing more.*" and stepped down.[9]

## *The Prosecution Team Strike Back*

The debate in the cross-examination aforementioned was one-to-many of NYI, Judson T.Y. alone against multiple witnesses. The debate in the ITAGAKI Seishiro's case on October 6, 1947, was a team one between the prosecutors and the defense. To represent the prosecution were prosecutor HSIANG Che-chun, associate prosecutors Judson NYI and KWEI Yu, and the defense were YAMADA Hanzo, BANNO Kunkichi, KATO Takahisa and American counsels for the defense Owen Cunningham, Floyd Mattice, Alfred Brooks. According to the transcript, the three prosecutors made a total of 122 statements and six defenders 123 statements in court, all within the day.[10]

The entire debate appeared to have three rounds.

The first round was from 9:00 a.m. to 10:45 a.m. and started with a long opening statement by Mattice. He denied all 41 counts of crimes the defendant ITAGAKI was charged with by the prosecution. The real battle between HSIANG Che-chun from the prosecution and YAMADA from the defense.

The National Archives of the United States keeps the documentary film of this debate. A rare scene was seen in the film when HSIANG and YAMADA reached to grab the microphone simultaneously.

YAMADA presented a piece of evidence first and said:

*We offer in evidence defense document No. 2528, a table of political problems towards China, certifying various facts of anti-Japanese movement and resistance against Japan before the outbreak of the Manchurian Incident, which was compiled and published in 1931, based on the materials collected by the Osaka Chamber of Commerce and Industry.*

HSIANG Che-chun stepped onto the podium and refuted:

*If it pleases the Tribunal, the prosecution objects to the admission of this document. This document, dealing with the alleged matters of a wide range that are said to have occurred in periods as early as 1908, 1909, etc., should not be introduced at the present stage. He went on to state his reasons: "We advocate that even if this document is to be accepted, it should be in the summary stage, that is, Manchuria stage. To support our contention, we need only refer to the ruling of the Tribunal announced on the 11 of last September, transcript page 28, 274, which reads as follows: If in the course of an individual case, evidence which might have been received on a general phase is tendered it will not be received in the individual case in the absence of convincing reasons.*

President Webb accepted HSIANG Che-chun's objection and said:

> *This particular Chamber of Commerce is not the body to prepare this statement of disputes between Japan and China on its surface value. Another Chamber of Commerce might take a different view and prepare a different list of disputes.*

Then he turned to HSIANG: "*We heard your objections sufficiently, HSIANG.*" YAMADA contended:

> *This document is submitted to show the causes of the Nanking Incident, Manchurian Incident, and the Osaka Chamber of Commerce went to considerable length and engaged in profound research in order to prepare a table that may be regarded as complete and accurate.*

President said, "*You would have to prove the profound research first. That is only alleged. By a majority, the objection is upheld, and the document rejected.*"

YAMADA then presented several exhibits for the defense, including three speeches made by Foreign Minister SHIDEHARA Kijuro and Prime Minister WAKATSUKI Reijiro, to show the Japanese government's foreign policy towards China at that time was primarily focused on Japan's rights and interests in Manchuria and Mongolia.

It is worth noting about one exhibit was brought by one witness, SHIMAMOTO Masaichi. Who was the Unit Commander in Liuchiaokou when the Mukden Incident broke out? SHIMAMOTO's testimony tried hard to whitewash ITAGAKI. After hearing SHIMAMOTO attending a banquet on the evening of September 18, HSIANG Che-chun immediately refuted:

> *Our Honor, the prosecution objects to this affidavit on the following grounds: First, the affidavit covers matters which should belong to the general phase. The defendant ITAGAKI was only casually mentioned on page 4. Second, evidence of many activities transacted by an alleged drunken officer is not the best evidence. Thirdly, many matters testified to in the affidavit were already tendered in evidence in the general phase. This affidavit is therefore repetitious. In our submission, it should be rejected in its entirety.*

YAMADA went out to defend SHIMAMOTO right away, but President Webb supported HSIANG Che-chun's request and said:

*You won't get much information that is reliable from a man who says he was drunk on the night that it happened, and this man says that. We have had a lot of this evidence that was appropriate to the general phase, and we have had it in the general phase.*

The defense also presented many other pieces of evidence, but only had one accepted by the court under HSIANG Che-chun's effective rebuttal.

The second round included the debates from 11:00 a.m. to 12:00 noon and from 1:30 p.m. to 2:45 p.m. between NYI, Judson T.Y., and BANNO Kunkichi.

BANNO Kunkichi appeared in court menacingly with multiple witnesses, which included Lieutenant Colonel KOKUBU Shinshichiro, FURUNO Inosuke, President of Domei, and YAMAWAKI Masataka, Vice War Minister.

After the testimony by KOKUBU Shinshichiro, NYI refuted:

*May it please the Tribunal, the prosecution objects to this affidavit on the ground that it contains opinions and conclusions rather than facts. It also gives character evidence and recites orders and instructions, the originals of which are not produced.*

In his testimony, FURUNO Inosuke quoted a recorded conversation that he had with ITAGAKI in the front line in Ying County of Shantung Province in April 1938 trying to enumerate his merits and achievements.

*I talked with him several times very confidentially. First when I asked his opinion as to the settlement of the incident. He held very earnestly that we must reach a peaceful conclusion, withdrawing the entire forces from China as soon as possible.*

NYI, Judson T.Y. questioned FURUNO right away by citing a report of Dome:

*Do you know that ITAGAKI, in an interview with your news agency, that is, Domei, on June 26, 1938, after becoming the War Minister, he stated that Japan should be prepared to fight for ten more years, and he asked for popular support?*

FURUNO mumbled: "*While I have no recollection of that at the present moment, it is possible that he may have said that. But the only alternative is to look up the records at that time.*"

NYI immediately presented Exhibit No. 2197 and caught FURUNO in a lie.

In his testimony, YAMAWAKI Masataka depicted ITAGAKI as an angel of peace:

*While I was assisting War Minister ITAGAKI as Vice-War Minister, I became quite familiar with his ideals, executive ability, behavior, personality, and ability to understand.... Here are some of the things he said to me: Japan and China ought not to quarrel with each other but should cooperate. We must devote ourselves most ardently to bringing about peace between Japan and China as speedily as possible by putting an end to the present unfortunate state of hostilities.... In establishing peace between China and Japan, War Minister ITAGAKI approached the problem from a broad point of view. His fundamental idea is mutual respect for sovereignty and territorial right and cooperation in the fields of culture and economy.*

Questioning YAMAWAKI Masataka' words, NYI asked repeatedly:

*Mr. Witness, you have stated that ITAGAKI had an ardent desire for peace with China. Are you familiar with the methods he employed to bring about this peace? Do you know that there was a so-called Special Committee on China Affairs under the Five Ministers' Conference to work out the important strategies in connection with China? You do know that DOIHARA—and you do know that Tang Shoo-i and Wu Pei-fu were approached in connection with the peace movement? Was he sent by the War Minister? Was it one of the strategies advocated at that time to work on retired Chinese statesmen and generals like Tang and Wu in order to bring about the self-destruction of the then existing government? And that was being done in parallel with the intensified military actions, is that correct?*

YAMAWAKI Masataka could only reply: "*I have no recollection*" and "*I do not recall.*"

The third round of debates started from 4:00 p.m. to 5:00 p.m., between KWEI Yu and BANNO.

BANNO tried to defend ITAGAKI's innocence by citing *The Destiny of China*, written by CHIANG Kai-shek:

*CHIANG Kai-shek clearly states that China had resolved to make wholesale resistance against Japan after the outbreak of the Lukouchiao affair, and that she drove Japan into an endless war by colluding with the communist army, and by exercising complete restraint upon Japan strategically and politically, thus bringing Japan's efforts for peace to naught.*

KWEI Yu rebuts:

*In the first place, the book in question was originally written in Chinese. It was written in Japanese. If the English text now presented is a translation from the Japanese version, we should like to refer to the ruling appearing on page 2303 of the record, to the effect that the translation should be from Chinese to English direct. If it were a translation from Chinese, we still would have to object, because there are numerous errors almost entirely distorting the true meaning of the book. Yes. In the second place, neither the name of ITAGAKI nor any of his activities have been mentioned.*

*"The document, if it could be, of any probative value at all, ought to be tendered in the general phase, but not in the individual case,"* said KWEI Yu at the end President Webb announced the rejection of the document despite BANNO's effort to argue,

There is a wonderful story in *the Romance of the Three Kingdoms* of eloquent and witty debating by CHUKE Liang (ZHUGE Liang) against a hall of learned lords., The rebuttals by the Chinese prosecution team in the court of the Tokyo trial were just like a reply.

## *ITAGAKI's Last Rebuttal*

The court debate continued for the next four days. On October 7, it was prosecutor KWEI Yu who cross-exam the witness brought by the defense counsels BANNO and SASAKAWA Tomoharu.[11] From October 8 to 10, it was NYI, Judson T.Y. cross-examine ITAGAKI Seishiro.[12]

ITAGAKI Seishiro had been a fanatical follower of the Japanese Imperil militarism since his youth days.

By the time the Mukden Incident broke out in 1931, he was already a senior staff of the Kwangtung Army and one of the masterminds behind the incident along with ISHIHARA. He was also the architect of establishing the puppet state of Manchukuo. In February 1933, when Kwangtung Army invaded Jehol,

ITAGAKI even joined the battle himself. He also rushed himself from Mukden to Tientsin to set up the Special Committee on Chinese Affairs—an intended puppet government in Norther China, similar to that in Manchukuo, but his plan did not prevail. In August 1934, ITAGAKI was transferred to become Military Advisor to the puppet state of Manchukuo and was later promoted to Vice Chief of Staff of Kwangtung Army, and military attaché in Manchukuo. In 1936 he was promoted to its Chief of Staff. Throughout his tenure in Kwangtung Army, ITAGAKI dedicated himself to strengthening Japan's control over Manchukuo, meanwhile cooperating with DOIHARA to instigate independence of Inner Mongolia and autonomy of Northern China.

After the Lugouqiao Incident in 1937, Japan launched a full-scale war against China. ITAGAKI Seishiro led the Japanese army to invade Northern China again. In 1938 and 1939, ITAGAKI was appointed as the War Minister by the KONOYE Cabinet and HIRANUMA Kiichiro Cabinet. In February 1939, ITAGAKI issued an order as War Minister prohibiting Japanese soldiers from talking about the Japanese atrocities in China after returning to Japan. In June, he had two meetings with WANG Ching-wei, plotting to support the establishment of the WANG puppet regime. He was also a strong advocator of the tripartite alliance of Japan, Germany, and Italy.

After September 1939, ITAGAKI was driven out of the highest decision-making clique in Japan and was dispatched to China, Korea, Singapore, and other places to command military operations. In September 1945, ITAGAKI led his army to surrender to the British army in Singapore.

DOIHARA kept silent during the cross-examination like *A dead pig is not afraid of hot water*, as said in a Chinese proverb. In contrast, ITAGAKI was arrogant and took aggressive defense for himself. Not only had he arranged 15 witnesses to the court, including ISHIHARA Kanji, one of the conspiracy planners of the Mukden Incident, but he also made a statement in the court himself and claimed he would never give up to defend himself in court in an overbearing manner. The Chinese prosecution team was well prepared and struck back right on, and believed the more ITAGAKI bragged, the more of his crime would be exposed.

On October 8, 9, and 10, NYI, Judson T.Y. was questioning ITAGAKI in the court continuously, no less fierce than a bayonet fighting on the battlefield.

On the morning of October 8, NYI, Judson T.Y. started his cross-examine with questions on two contradictory remarks by ITAGAKI.

The first question by NYI, Judson T.Y. was whether Kwangtung Army's plot before the outbreak of Mukden Incident was approved by Tokyo authorities.

> *Q (NYI): You admitted that the Kwantung Army had mapped out an operational plan before the outbreak of the Mukden Incident. Did you take part in drafting this plan?*
>
> *A (ITAGAKI): It appears that it would be necessary for me to explain what an operational plan is.*
>
> *Q (NYI): Now, I want to ask you whether you participated in the drafting, yes or no.*
>
> *A (ITAGAKI): The operational plan is drawn up by the officers in charge of operations in accordance with instructions, orders, and directions from the General Headquarters, issued, that is, by his superiors in that department. Now, I had no direct connection with drawing up this operational plan.*
>
> *Q (NYI): You say, the Supreme Command. Is that the Supreme Command in Tokyo?*
>
> *A (ITAGAKI): It is customary, and it is a common practice in all nations for annual operational plans to be drawn up by the General Staff Headquarters where it is determined.*

NYI immediately fought back using ITAGAKI's own words:

> *But you stated in your affidavit that you drafted this plan without getting assistance from the Central Authorities, and now you stated that you had drafted it with the direction of the Central Authorities. Do you see if there is an inconsistency?*

The second contradiction is the relationship between ITAGAKI and Dai Nippon Kokusui-kai, or Great Japan National Essence Society, which was founded in 1919 as a fanatical group that promoted ultranationalism and gradually became gangster forces.

> *Q (NYI): You have reported that you were closely associated with the members therewith before the outbreak of the Mukden Incident. Did not the consular authorities in Mukden ever take steps to disassociate you or even to check your activities in association with members of the Kokusui Society?*

*A (ITAGAKI): Since you are putting a very strange question, I am hard to make a reply because I have never heard of a Kokusui-Kai, and therefore I know nothing about it.*

*Q (NYI): To refresh your mind, I will read to you a portion of Foreign Minister HIDEHARA's telegram to Consul-General HAYASHI: "We have heard that Colonel ITAGAKI and others of the Kwantung Army at your place are exerting themselves in various activities recently with considerably ample funds and are manipulating Japanese adventurers in China and members of the 'Kokusui-Kai." This telegram was dated September 5, 1931. Does that help your memory?*

*A (ITAGAKI): I have no knowledge as to the contents of the telegram just read by you.*

ITAGAKI's response was in total denial: "*I have no knowledge as to the contents of the telegram just read by you.*"

According to the court record, ITAGAKI replied "*I do not remember*" or words to that effect 90 times to the cross-examination by NYI, Judson T.Y. Below is another example.

The Five Ministers Conference had important influences on Japan's policies during wartime and consisted of the five most powerful ministers in the cabinet, namely, the Prime Minister, the Foreign Minister, the Navy Minister, the War Minister, and the Finance Minister. ITAGAKI Seishiro, as War Minister, attended the conference on July 8, 1938, which by then was more than one year after the outbreak of the Lugouqiao Incident. That meeting made an important decision on Japan's next step in its strategy of invading China.

On the afternoon of October 9, NYI, Judson T.Y. cross-examined ITAGAKI about the decision of the Five Minister Conference on July 8, 1938.

*Q (NYI): Mr. ITAGAKI, this morning you told us that the decisions of the Five Ministers' Conference were mostly in conformity with your views. Did not the Five Ministers' Conference on July 8, 1938, decide the measures to be taken by Japan in case the Chinese Government surrendered?*

*A (ITAGAKI): I do not remember.*

*Q (NYI): Was it not decided that in that eventuality Japan would either adhere to the decision of the Imperial Conference of 11 January or treat the Government of China as one of the local regimes which would participate in the setting up of a new pro-Japanese Government?*

*A (ITAGAKI): I do not remember.*

*Q (NYI): Was it not decided on that occasion that Japan would not try to settle the Incident through negotiations?*

*A (ITAGAKI): That is impossible.*

*Q (NYI): What do you mean by "That is impossible"? They did not decide, or they did decide?*

*A (ITAGAKI): I mean that I have no recollection whatsoever and that at that time, none of us had any such idea as suggested. That is why I said such a thing was impossible.*

*Q (NYI): Was it not decided on that occasion that the Chinese surrender would only be accepted on certain conditions and one of them being the retirement of Generalissimo CHIANG Kai-shek?*

*A (ITAGAKI): That also is not in my recollection at all.*

*Q (NYI): Did not the Five Ministers' Conference on the same day, July 8, decide on the measures to be taken by Japan in case the Chinese Government refused to surrender?*

*A (ITAGAKI): No, I don't remember that at all.*

*Q (NYI): Was it not decided that in case the Chinese Government continued to refuse to surrender, the pro-Japanese regimes would be made to combine so as to set up a pro-Japanese central government?*

*A (ITAGAKI): No, I have no recollection.*

*Q (NYI): Are you following my questions very closely?*

*A (ITAGAKI): I am listening to all that you say.*

*Q (NYI): Did not the Five Ministers' Conference on July 8, 1938, decide on the strategy toward China in conformity with the current situation?*

*A (ITAGAKI): I don't remember whether there was a Five Ministers' Conference on the 8 of July and even if there was a Five Ministers' Conference on that day, I don't remember what we decided.*

ITAGAKI replied nine times in succession yet without any substantial content. Finally, he simply denied the existence of the Five Ministers' Conference. The Five Ministers' Conference was archived, so it was completely futile for ITAGAKI to deny or forget it and his disguise was just a disgusting show.

The defense statement made by ITAGAKI himself was 48 pages long. But it had no substance and presented false claims in many parts that could not stand totally against the evidence presented by the Chinese Prosecution Team.

For example, he said that, after the Lugouqiao Incident, he as War Minister, had always advocated for the withdrawal of the Japanese army and making peace with China. Below was what NYI, Judson T.Y.'s rebuttal in the court:

*Q (NYI): Was the Japanese occupation of Canton and Hankow completed after you became War Minister?*
*A (ITAGAKI): Yes.*
*Q (NYI): Is this retreat or advance?*

ITAGAKI Seishiro had nothing to reply.

In the cross-examination, NYI, Judson T.Y. did not miss DOIHARA, ITAGAKI's accomplice. NYI directed his question right at DOIHARA, although he was not on the witness stand:

*Now I am going to ask you, was this DOIHARA who was sent to China the same one who had been mayor of Mukden, the inaugurator of Henry PU-Yi, long-time promoter of North China autonomy, author of the CHIN–DOIHARA Agreement, and negotiator of Inner Mongolian economy, who is now sitting on this side of the dock (indicating)?*

Although these counts were directed at DOIHARA, ITAGAKI could not escape any of them. ITAGAKI was totally defeated as he stepped down from the stand in frustration. NYI hit two birds with one stone.

During the three-day cross-examination on ITAGAKI Seishiro, NYI interrogated him 122, 202, and 168 times, respectively, with a total of more than 490 questions. Under such an intensified offense by the Chinese prosecution team, the defense witnesses became defenseless and went into limbo. On February 24, 1948, HSIANG Che-chun made a closing statement for the prosecution against the defendant ITAGAKI Seishiro with a total of 190 exhibits of evidence cited.

NYI, Judson T.Y. had an emotional recall in his late years:

*This battle, for me, is a life-and-death battle. Since I was assigned to this task at such a critical time, the result means honor or disgrace for me. When I recalled these scenes, they showed up vividly in my mind. It was a comfort to me amid hardship and bitterness. Upon finishing these words, I failed to calm down with my eyes blurred with tears.*[13]

HSIANG Che-chun highly praised NYI, Judson T.Y., for his marvelous performance in the Tokyo Trial. In a telegram to Foreign Minister WANG Shih-chieh sent on July 16, 1948, HSIANG made a remark specifically: "*Mr. NYI has done an outstanding job in court, with rich legal expertise and experience, which was highly respected.*"[14]

NYI, Judson T.Y.'s success in the Tokyo Trial laid a solid foundation for his great contribution to the field of international law in the future. In the 1980s, he represented the People's Republic of China in the formulation of The United Nations Convention on the Law of the Sea, although he was over 80 years old by then. In 1984, he was selected as a justice of the International Court of Justice at Hague and had served in that post for 9 years. He retired at the age of 88 in 1994.

NYI, Judson T.Y. once gave HSIANG Che-chun a photo of himself in a judge uniform of the international court with an inscription on the back: "*It has been an honor to work with you,*" which reflects the lifelong friendship of the two jurists.

## *References*


[1] Xiang, Longwan. 2014. *HSIANG Che-chun's Letters, Telegrams, and Statements at the Tokyo Trial.* Shanghai Jiao tong University Press, 37.

[2] Ibid., 23–24.

[3] Ibid., 25–26.

[4] NYI, Judson T.Y. 1999. *Me and the Law.* Law Press, 14–15.

[5] Xiang, Longwan. 2014. *HSIANG Che-chun's Letters, Telegrams, and Statements at the Tokyo Trial.* Shanghai Jiao tong University Press, 33.

[6] Ibid., 40–41.

[7] NYI, Judson T.Y. 1999. *Me and the Law.* Law Press, 115.

[8] Tokyo Trial Literature Committee. 2013. *Transcripts of the Proceedings of the International Military Tribunal for the Far East (English version).*Vol. 47. National Library of China Publishing House; Shanghai Jiao Tong University Press, 568–569 in bok. 46, 1–17 in bok. 47 (28602–28626 of the English court records).

[9] Ibid., 39–58 in vol. 47 (28647–28666 of the English court records).

[10] Ibid., 337–454 in vol. 49 (30039–30152 of the English court records).

[11] Ibid., 447–449 (30144–30146 of the English court records).

[12] Ibid., 1-266 in vol. 50 (30292–30549 of the English court records).

[13] NYI, Judson T.Y. 1999. *Me and the Law.* Law Press, 126.

[14] Xiang, Longwan. 2014. *HSIANG Che-chun's Letters, Telegrams, and Statements at the Tokyo Trial.* Shanghai Jiao Tong University Press, 69.

CHAPTER 9

# Economic Plunder

## *Full Control of Manchuria*

During its invasion of China, one of Japan's war crimes was economic plunder. It was characterized by a "trinity" of economic plunder, political domination, and military oppression, which made the economic plunder even more vicious and cruel. As stated in the *Judgment of the International Military Tribunal for the Far East* (referred to as "*Judgement*" below), "*On August 8, 1933, the Japanese Cabinet decided to 'develop Manchuria into an independent state, and this independent state is inextricably linked with the Japanese Empire.' The control of Manchukuo 'was to be exercised by Japanese officials under the command of the Kwantung Army commander.' The goal of the Manchurian economy was to 'unite the economies of Japan and Manchuria in order to establish a firm foundation for the expansion of imperial economic power into the world.'*"[1]

Chapter Five of the *Judgment* also mentioned that as early as 1906, the "South Manchurian Railway Company" established by Japan in Northeast China was an entity that attempted to comprehensively plunder and control the economy and politics of Northeast China. In the *Judgment of the International Military Tribunal for the Far East*, this "trinity" company was mentioned multiple times:

> *Japan organized the South Manchurian Railway Company in August 1906 as a corporation with its shareholders limited to the Japanese Government and its nationals ... This company was authorized to and did, administer the railways*

> *and enterprises pertaining thereto, which had been acquired from Russia, together with any new railroads and enterprises established in Manchuria by Japan. In addition, it was vested with certain administrative functions of government in the leased territory and in the railway zone. In short, it was created as an agency of the Japanese Government to administer the interests of that government in Manchuria.*
>
> *Contrary to the provisions of the Treaty of Portsmouth, the charter of this company provided that* [A treaty signed on September 5, 1905, at the end of the Russo-Japanese War. —Author's Note] *the commander of the Japanese Army in the leased territory should have the power to issue orders and directives to the company in connection with military affairs and in case of military necessity to issue orders involving the business affairs of the company.*
>
> *The Kwantung Army was the Japanese unit maintained in Manchuria under the Portsmouth Treaty for the protection of Japanese interests, including the South Manchurian Railway.*
>
> *Yosuke MATSUOKA, who, like OKAWA, was an official of the South Manchurian Railway Company, published a book in support of the familiar theme that Manchuria was, both strategically and economically, the lifeline of Japan.*[2]

The *Judgment* also quoted the remarks on this company from the *Lytton Commission Report*:

> *She governed the leased territory with practically full rights of sovereignty. Through the South Manchurian Railway, she administered the railway areas, including several towns and large sections of such populous cities as Mukden and Changchun; and in these areas, she controlled the police, taxation, education, and public utilities... There is probably nowhere in the world an exact parallel to this situation.*[3]

The Lytton Commission of the League of Nations was established on January 21, 1932. It was composed of representatives from five countries, including Britain, the United States, France, Germany, and Italy, headed by V.A.G.R. Bulwer-Lytton, 2nd Earl of Lytton from British. It should be noted that the Lytton Commission Report was deeply influenced by the appeasement policy of western powers such as Britain and the United States to Japan at that time. And, as mentioned earlier in Chapter Six of this book, the Lytton Commission received extensive monitoring and interference by the Japanese extensively; even Emperor PU Yi was not allowed to reveal the true situation to the commission. Although the report sealed some historical facts, such as pointing out that Manchuria is China's territory, it did not condemn Japan's aggression, and it even adopted a vague position of "putting the blame on the two parties equally" in its analysis of the causes of "Manchurian Incident." Nevertheless, Japan still did not want to accept the report. On February 24, 1933, with 42 votes in favor of the report and 1 against by Japan, the League of Nations General Assembly adopted the *Report of the Commission of Enquiry*, reaffirming the non-recognition of the puppet Manchukuo. On March 28, 1933, in protest of the report, Japan announced withdrawal from the League of Nations, making the report virtually a dead letter. Research indicates that the activities and investigation reports of the League of Nations failed to stop the Japanese imperialists' aggression in northeast China, and Japan's war of aggression against China was expanding rapidly and preparing to further escalate into a full-scale war of aggression against China.

After Japan occupied Northeast China, it accelerated the pace of its economic plunder. At the end of 1934, the Japanese government created the "Manchuria Affairs Bureau," to fully take charge of foreign affairs and control of the economy, culture, public opinion, and propaganda of "Manchukuo." Many of the defendants in the International Military Tribunal for the Far East were involved in it. For example, ITAGAKI Seishiro, HATA Shunroku, and TOJO Hideki once served as the presidents of the "Manchurian Affairs Bureau," respectively, and OKA Takasumi, SATO Nobuyoshi, KAYA Okinori, SHIGEMITSU Mamoru, and UMEZU Yoshijiro as members, etc.

In early 1935, to further plunder resources in Manchuria, Japan and "Manchukuo" established the "Joint Economic Committee." The first act conducted by the committee was "the integration of Japanese and Manchukuo currencies." In November of 1935, the Yen Bloc was established, and the currency of "Manchukuo" was no longer linked to silver but instead to the Japanese yen. In June 1936, the "Joint Economic Commission" promulgated its second economic act, *The Protocol between Japan and Manchukuo*. The treaty openly declared that "*Japanese subjects shall be free within the territory of the 'Manchukuo' to reside and travel and engage in agriculture, commerce, and industry, and to pursue callings and professions and shall enjoy all the rights relating to land.*"[4]

In October 1937, the Japanese Cabinet further established "the Manchurian Heavy Industry Development Corporation" with the sole purpose of making

Manchuria a workhouse for the production of war goods for Japan. With all these series of measures, Northeast China quickly became a Japanese colony.

Henry PU Yi's testimony in court also included complaints against Japan's economic plunder. Here is an exchange when PU Yi was questioned by Chief Prosecutor Joseph Keenan on August 19, 1946:

*Q (Keenan): Referring to the practices under NAOKI HOSHINO with reference to the industry in Manchuria, can you recall any specific events of importance to relate to the Tribunal?*

*A (PU Yi): At that time, HOSHINO was engaged in exploiting Manchurian industries and controlling economic affairs. The losses incurred to the Manchukuo State were tremendous.*

*Q (Keenan): How was this exploitation affected? Explain in what manner.*

*A (PU Yi): They have put under their control all industries: farm industries, commerce, and others, such as fisheries, telecommunication, and so on. They were all put into the palm of Japanese hands, and none of the Chinese were ever allowed to enter into such enterprises. Consequently, none of the Chinese were in business, and many of them went bankrupt. This situation was simply deplorable and pitiful. The so-called exploitation of industries was that they lay their emphasis merely on the mining industry. I think that was done only to expand their armament industry.*

*Q (Keenan): Can you tell us how many large special Japanese companies were formed for this purpose?*

*A (PU Yi): There were about some sixty-four special companies.*

*Q (Keenan): Were these companies of small capital or medium or very large sums of capital?*

*A (PU Yi): The capitalization of these companies was all in huge amounts, sometimes running into billions. In other words, their planning was to make China bankrupt and expand their influences outward.*

*Q (Keenan): During the time that you were Emperor, who had control of the banks of Manchuria?*

*A (PU Yi): They were also in the hands of the Japanese.*

*Q (Keenan): Were the Chinese or Manchurians at liberty to save money in those banks?*

*A (PU Yi): Yes, they were at liberty in saving money, but they were not permitted to borrow money from banks.*

*Q (Keenan): Who did all the borrowing from the banks?*

*A (PU Yi): Japanese.*

*Q (Keenan): Who put most of the money in the banks by way of savings?*

*A (PU Yi): Naturally, it was Chinese. The banks were trying to absorb all the funds from the Chinese, mostly the labor class. They established a Central Bank, but in various districts, they have the branch office of the Central. There is also another bank, called Industrial Development Bank, which mainly handles matters concerning borrowing money.*

*Q (Keenan): What kind of banks were they? Who named them? Who exercised control over them?*

*A (PU Yi): All these banks were under the control of the Japanese.*

*Q (Keenan): Were the Chinese or Manchurians permitted to go into business, or did they have to get special permits from other people to go into any type of business?*

*A (PU Yi): We are not at liberty—we are not allowed to do business freely.*

*Q (Keenan): Who gave the permits to the Chinese and Manchurians to do any kind of business?*

*A (PU Yi): The permits were issued by the Japanese. So, all these were in the hands of the Japanese. Among the Directors of the Central Bank, there was one Chinese, but still, he had no power whatsoever.*[5]

On August 20, PU Yi continued to answer MR. Keenan's direct examination exposes Japan's economic plunder of Manchuria and its oppression of the Chinese people.

*Q (Keenan): Can you tell us the different commodities that were covered by the monopoly laws and in control of the Japanese?*

*A (PU Yi): Opium was one of the main items that were being monopolized, and under the five-year plan of HOSHINO where the economy was under rigid control, there were many commodities being monopolized, such as cotton, cloth, and foodstuff. As a result of the economic control, all commodities that used to belong to the Chinese were being absorbed by the Japanese, and all different kinds of industries and commerce were controlled by the Japanese.*

*Q (Keenan): Was there a Cotton Control Act passed?*

*A (PU Yi): Yes, it was passed, and that was known to everybody and can be found in the Government Gazette.*

*Q (Keenan): Was that Act enforced?*

*A (PU Yi): All these control laws were enforced, and as a result, the Chinese couldn't get any cotton or cloth during winter days, and in wintertime, many Chinese were found starved—frozen to death. I was personally informed that even private sale or purchase of rice among Chinese was prohibited and considered as in contravention of the control laws.*

PU Yi further exposed Japan's monopoly in the financial field and its oppression of the Chinese people.

*Q (Keenan): Was the national currency of Manchuria paper or coin? Where was that printed or coined?*

*A (PU Yi): They were all printed and minted in Japan.*

*Q (Keenan): Who had control over the amount of currency that was printed, as you stated, in Japan, the national currency of Manchuria?*

*A (PU Yi): Actually, also in the hands of the Bureau of General Affairs, Manchukuo State—Japanese.*

*Q (Keenan): Can you tell us whether there was any compulsory—any compulsion about requiring the deposits—savings deposits—in these banks that you have described previously?*

*A (PU Yi): There was the law of savings by which it was required that all people should save money in the bank. People in the schools and people in the streets, no matter where they were, either were employed by the government or banks; they were all required to save money. (CHINESE MONITOR: Also, schools and offices are also required to save money.) The amount of savings was increased year by year. By the time the Japanese surrendered, there was a total aggregate of some six thousand million in the bank. Averagely speaking, one person was required to save one hundred fifty dollars—one person.*[6]

At the end of World War II, Japan was in a serious shortage of war resources. The Japanese military required all Manchurians, including PU Yi, to "donate" metals of all varieties. In his testimony on August 21, PU Yi revealed this blatant robbery:

*After the outbreak of the Pacific War, the Japanese Army compelled the Manchurian people, the military, as well as me to donate all platinum, non-ferrous metals, brass, steel, or whatever other kinds of metals were in our possession to the Japanese. But one thing I can assure you, that is, as far as my people and I were concerned, we were all objecting to this matter. But then we could do nothing as we were under the oppression of the Japanese Kwantung Army. At the same time, if we were found to have still in our possession some platinum and other metals, we would be guilty of a very serious offense.*[7]

Five high-ranking Japanese officials played crucial roles in Japan's economic plunder of Manchuria. In addition to TOJO Hideki, MATSUOKA Yosuke, president of the Manchurian Railway Company, AIKAWA Gisuke, president of the Manchurian Heavy Industry Development Corporation, HOSHINO Naoki, Director of the General Affairs Office of Manchuria, and KISHI Nobusuke, Chief of the General Affairs Bureau of the Ministry of Industry of Manchuria were known as the "Five Tigers," who controlled the affairs in Manchuria. Three of them, TOJO Hideki, MATSUOKA Yosuke, and HOSHINO Naoki, were charged with war crimes in the Tokyo Trial.

The role of the defendant HOSHINO Naoki was highlighted in Section 2, Chapter Five of the Judgment of the International Military Tribunal for the Far East, specifically.

*HOSHINO was the one more responsible than any other for such success; he stated that Japan took everything out of Manchuria which could be obtained. Since Chinese businessmen were not allowed to enter important industries and were not allowed to make loans, most of them went into bankruptcy. The Chinese farmers lost their lands to Japanese immigrants. The savings law reduced the Chinese laborer to working for mere subsistence. The monopolies on rice and cotton deprived the Chinese of adequate food and clothing in order to furnish the best rice and cotton for Japan's Army.*[8]

When MATSUOKA Yosuke served in the Manchurian Railway Company, he completely supported the Kwantung Army and advocated policies that interfered in China's internal affairs but urged the Japanese government to adopt a deceived approach. He suggested that, while openly claiming no interference in China's internal affairs, the Japanese government should establish policies large-scale instead of small-scale in practice. The "Manchurian Railway Company" itself was one of the main carriers for Japan's economic plunder in Manchuria. Its main source of income was the ill-gotten gains from the transportation of Manchurian specialty soybeans and profits earned through the inhumane and brutal labor system of nearly 100,000 Chinese coal miners at the Fushun.

In 1907, when the Manchurian Railway Company was first established, its profit was at a level of only about 2,000,000 yens, but it increased year after year, rising to ten million yens in 1921 and a record 45 million yen in 1929. The huge economic accumulated gains from the Manchurian Railway Company reinforced its role in Manchuria, also financed the intelligence agency run by MATSUOKA Yosuke, and enable it to carry out unlimited intelligence activities in China.

AIKAWA Gisuke, another rising zaibatsu in Japan, shifted his focus to China after the Manchurian Incident. He established the Manchurian Heavy Industries Development Corporation in Northeast China and made himself its CEO, after taking over the heavy industries operated by the Manchurian Railway Company in the northeast. Under him, the heavy industries, including steel, coal, automobiles, machinery, and aircraft manufacturing in Manchuria had developed significantly and become one of those entities critical to Japan's state policies of its invasion of China. After Japan's surrender, he was once classified as a Class A war criminal.

KISHI Nobusuke once served as Chief of the General Affairs Bureau of the Ministry of Industry of Manchuria and as Deputy Chief of the General Affairs Office of Manchuria. In the Cabinet of TOJO Hideki in 1941, he served as Minister of Commerce and Industry and countersigned the edict declaring war on the United States. After the surrender of Japan, he was also classified as a Class A war criminal and was arrested by the Allies and imprisoned in Sugamo Prison.

## *Expansion of Economic Plunder*

After Japan's full-scale invasion of China, its economic plunder was also expanded from Manchuria to the other parts of China. On December 24, 1937, the Japanese Cabinet adopted the "*Outline Regarding the Settlement of the China Affair*," which set out the objective of economic aggression as "*establishing the base of the Empire's economic development in Central China at Shanghai*." In 1938, Japan decided to establish two economic entities to achieve the above objective: the North China Development Company (NCDC) and the Central China Promotion Company (CCPC).

The purpose of the North China Development Company was to consolidate the various enterprises in Northern China, operating in the areas such as transportation, port construction, electricity, mines, production, and sale of salt. This company was under the supervision of the Japanese government therefore, all major decisions, such as raising funds for shares, changing regulations, mergers, dissolutions, distribution of profits, etc., had to be approved by the Japanese government. The defendant UMEZU Yoshijiro was the director of the company planning its establishment, and another defendant KAYA Okinori was the president of the company for a long period of time.

Central China Promotion Company had very similar functions to Northern China Development Company. It was also under the actual control of the Japanese government.

On November 5, 1940, the Intelligence Bureau of the Japanese Cabinet further proposed the "Outline for the Economic Construction of Japan, Manchukuo, and China." However, the initiation and implementation of these plans were entirely by the Japanese unilaterally. KAYA Okinori once openly claimed that the three of Japan's resource mobilization plans in Northern China are (1) to support Japan's war material supplies; (2) to expand Japan's war material reserves; and (3) to meet Japan's economic development needs in peacetime.

At the same time, Japan went to great lengths to control public utilities and finance in the occupied areas. For instance, Japan took over various public utility companies in Shanghai and established the "Federal Reserve Bank of China" to issue currency for circulation in the occupied areas, and so on. This book does not go into detail.

The main task put in front of the Chinese prosecution team was to investigate these economic plunder crimes, as well as to identify witnesses to testify in court. Compared to atrocities such as murder, arson, and rape, these economic crimes are more insidious and thus more difficult to obtain evidence. HSIANG Che-chun thus sent Secretary Henry CHIU back to China during the trial to collect evidence.

Henry CHIU worked day and night back in China, visiting numerous relevant government departments. His hard work paid off. Upon his trip to the Nanjing National Government's Resources Committee, the Secretary-general TUNG Shu-ming (TONG Shoumin) indignantly provided a long list of cases of Japan's plundering of Chinese resources.

## *Devouring Shanghai Pu-Tung Electric Supply Company*

TUNG Shu-ming was a witness to the history of Shanghai's electricity industry from its birth, development, suffering and re-emergence.

In 1919, TUNG Shih-heng, TUNG Shu-ming's fourth uncle, established Pu-Tung Electric Supply Company in Shanghai with HUANG Yen-pei (HUANG Yanpei) and MU Ou-chu and became its general manager. In the same year, TUNG Shu-ming graduated from Kiang-Su Commercial College in Shanghai and joined the company, then became the deputy manager in 1933 and also the general manager of Hua Shang Electric Supply Company.

Under the effective management of the Tung family, the total share capital of Pu-Tung Electric Supply Company reached 1.5 million yuan in 1936, with the electricity generating and purchasing capacity of 4900 kilowatts covering the power supply area of 1,450 square kilometers. Its operations covered multiple areas including, power generation, purchasing, and distribution, making it one of the most important electric power companies in Shanghai and receiving various honorary awards from the government year after year.

But 1937—a savage year in modern Chinese history—changed the trajectory of this national enterprise forever. One day in September 1937, after the outbreak of the Battle of Shanghai, Japanese warplanes dropped bombs on the Huang-Chia-Tu power plant, which was under construction in Pu-Tung. The explosions were deafening and plunged the entire plant into flames, obliterating the rooftops and leaving only the shells of office buildings standing amongst the rubble.

Pu-Tung Electric Supply Company was forced out of business and was soon forcibly taken over by the Japanese controlled Central China Water and Electricity Company. During this period, the plants and facilities of Pu-Tung Electric Supply Company suffered heavy damage, and plunder its new power plant under construction, with a full new set of equipment just imported from the UK, was dismantled and shipped to Japan after the Japanese soldiers occupied Pu-Yung. In his autobiography, TUNG Shu-ming stated: "*The whole plan off the new factory was for naught, and years of hard work had gone down the drain; looking back on that part of the history, I lament that life is nothing but a mere illusion.*"[9]

TUNG Shu-ming's personal experience witnessed the suffering of China and its people. He had a good command of the English Language which made him a hard-to-find, high-profile witness. Mr. Henry CHIU, the attorney from Shanghai and member of the Chinese division of the prosecution staff, immediately invited

TUNG Shu-ming to testify at the International Military Tribunal for the Far East, and he readily agreed.

On the morning of August 28, 1946, TUNG Shu-ming appeared in the court to give testimony. Mr. Henry CHIU began his direct examination on behalf of the prosecution. The following is a fragment of their question-answer session.

> *Q (CHIU): What happened to your company after hostilities broke out between the Chinese and Japanese troops in August 1937?*
>
> *A (TUNG): We tried by all means to maintain the supply of power during the hostilities. But we stopped the generation of power on August 14, and the supply of power to the inhabitants in the Pu-Tung was affected, and we made arrangements with other power companies in Shanghai. The power supply to Pu-Tung was cut out on or about November 10, 1937, after the withdrawal of Chinese troops.*
>
> *Q (CHIU): Was your company at any time taken over by any person or a company after war broke out in Shanghai?*
>
> *A (TUNG): The company was occupied by the Japanese in November 1937, and operations were resumed by the Japanese in March 1938. In June 1938, the Central China Water and Electricity Company took over the Pu-Tung Electric Supply Company and then put it under the Japanese management. The whole of the company's fixed assets was valued by the Japanese at approximately 470,000 yen against the original value of 1.8 million Chinese dollars and was invested in the Central China Water and Electricity Company. The shares thus acquired were held by the Ministry of Industries of the then puppet Reformed Government under the pretext of the so-called "owner's absence."*
>
> *Q (CHIU): Do you know who operated and controlled the Central China Water and Electricity Company to which you just referred?*
>
> *A (TUNG): To the best of my knowledge, the Central China Water and Electricity Company were one of the affiliated companies of the Central Promotion Company. Namely, on the face, it was a Sino-Japanese concern; but it was actually operated and controlled absolutely by the Japanese, the policy was decided by the Japanese, and all the leading—all the high positions were held by the Japanese.*
>
> *Q (CHIU): What was the general condition of your plant at the time when it was taken over by the Japanese in November 1937?*
>
> *A (TUNG): The company's plant was in good operating condition before the Japanese occupation.*

*Q (CHIU): Did the plant suffer any direct damage as a result of fighting between the Chinese and Japanese troops in battles in and around Shanghai during 1937 or thereafter?*

*A (TUNG): I should say there was no damage during the hostilities in Shanghai.*

*Q (CHIU): Did you take over the company from the Japanese after their surrender?*

*A (TUNG): Yes, I did.*

*Q (CHIU): When did you take over, and in what capacity?*

*A (TUNG): I started to take over the company from the Japanese on September 18, 1945, in compliance with the instructions from the Chinese Government, and l completed the taking over on September 30, 1945, when all the Japanese members of the staff were dismissed.*

*Q (CHIU): What did you find about the conditions of your plant at the time when you took over from the Japanese?*

*A (TUNG): The power plant was in very poor condition. We had installed in the plant one turbine alternator manufactured by Brown and Boveri in Switzerland: B-r-o-w-n and B-o-v-e-r-i, 600 kilowatts, 2,300 volts, 3 phase, 60 cycles; and two water tube boilers manufactured by Babcock and Wilcox, England: B-a-b-c-o-c-k and W-i-l-c-o-x, heating surface about 1,400 square feet each, steam pressure 250 lbs. At the time of taking over from the Japanese, the turbine alternator, boilers, and other accessories were found to be completely lost.*[10]

TUNG Shu-ming later learned from AOKI, the Vice-President of Central China Water and Electricity Company, that the equipment aforementioned had been sold by them to Central China Mining Company at a price of about 120,000 yens, mediated by the Central China Liaison Office of Koain. And the Japanese also said that some of the missing equipment had been moved and installed in a coal mine in Ta Yeh-hsien of Hupei Province.

In the afternoon of the same day, TUNG Shu-ming continued to testify.[11]

Besides being the manager of Pu-Tung Electric Supply Company, TUNG Shu-ming served as the manager of Chinese Electric Power Company in Nan-Ton, Shanghai. He also made accusations about Japan's looting of this company in the court:

*The company operated both the supply of power and tramway service before the war, and the company suspended the tramway service on August 14, 1937; finally ceasing the generation of power on August 20, 1937. After August 20, 1937, the supply of electricity to the inhabitants in Nan-Ton was affected, and through arrangements made with the French Power Company, the supply was cut off on or about November 10, 1937, when the Japanese troops occupied Nan-Ton. In June 1938, the Chinese Electric Power Company, then under the Japanese management, was taken over by the Central China Water and Electricity Company. The fixed assets of the company were valued by the Japanese at about 1.7 million yen against the original value of about eight and half million Chinese dollars. These assets were invested by the Japanese in the Central China Water and Electricity Company and the shares acquired were held by the Ministry of Industries of the then puppet reformed government under the pretext of so-called "owner's absence."*

*We had installed in the power plant ten water tube boilers and three steam turbo-alternators, the total capacity of which was sixteen thousand kilowatts; at the time of taking over from the Japanese, these ten boilers and three turbo-alternators were found completely missing.*

TUNG Shu-ming was also involved in overtaking the Chinese Electric Power Company in Nan-Ton after the war. In his testimony, TUNG Shu-ming revealed the looting spree of this company by the Japanese as well.

*The company had twenty-two kilometers of tramway rail and about six hundred and thirty steel poles, and about fifty cement poles carrying the trolley wires, and these tramway rails and poles were found completely lost at the time of taking over. There we have recovered these materials only to the extent of twenty percent. We also had fifty-four train cars, twenty-seven trailers, and three converters, a total capacity of twenty-one hundred kilowatts and three transformers and three switchboards, and this equipment has not been recovered so far. Many of the buildings were badly damaged. The company also had a large tram shed capable of accommodating about 100 tram cars and trailers, which were found to have been completely demolished by the Japanese, remaining only a vacant lot of ground.*

TUNG Shu-ming also had knowledge of the situations of other power companies in Shanghai during the Japanese occupation. He revealed in his testimony that:

> *The Chinese-owned company—the Chapei Water and Electricity Company, was also taken over by the Japanese immediately after the withdrawal of the Chinese troops. The company had a total generating capacity of 36 thousand kilowatts. It was so badly damaged in the condition that it is currently unable to generate electricity. The company also suffered heavy losses in transmission and distribution equipment and other facilities. The American-owned Shanghai Power Company was also taken over by the Japanese after the outbreak of the Pacific War. Its total generating capacity was 183 thousand kilowatts, but now only 136 thousand kilowatts are left, representing a decrease of 47 thousand kilowatts. That is about 45% of its pre-war power generation. One-sixth of the transmission and distribution line was destroyed, and only a small part of the equipment in storage was taken over from the Japanese. The other company—the French Power Company—was not taken over by the Japanese, but it was, of course, operated under the manipulation of the Japanese during the war, with the generating capacity reduced from 28 thousand kilowatts to 16 thousand.*

At the end of his testimony, TUNG Shu-ming provided evidence of a severe shortage of electricity for civilian and industrial uses in Shanghai during the Japanese occupation. He stated:

> *The supply of electricity for domestic use in Shanghai was repeatedly curtailed until finally each family—irrespective of the number of members—was allowed to use only 7 kilowatt-hours of electricity per month. Obviously, this is not enough for a family of any size. Excesses in consumption would entail a very heavy fine, and the supply would be cut off if a breach of the laws was committed twice or thrice. The supply of power to the factories was likewise time and again curtailed until finally all the Chinese factories were not allowed to use electric power, with the exception of the few factories whose products were required by the Japanese military. And the application for a supply of this nature was very difficult to be approved.*

During the testimony on the day, Tung was also cross-examined by American defense lawyers Brooks and Levin. He fully prepared himself and responded excellently in the court. He was able to produce photos of each case and counterargued with evidence of the facts, as suggested by Assistant Prosecutor Henry Chui when facing aggressive questions from the defense attorneys.

As an example, defense lawyer Levin suggested that, based on the exchange rate of 4:1 between the Japanese yen and the Chinese yen, it would be reasonable for Japan to acquire 1.8 million Chinese yens' worth of real estate with 470,000 yens. Tung immediately replied with a concrete figure:

> *I have stated already the original value at the time of taking over by the Japanese in 1937, the assets of the Pu-Tung Electricity Supply Company were about 1,800,000 Chinese dollars, and the value of the assets of the Chinese Electric Power Company at the time of taking over by the Japanese was about eight and a half million Chinese dollars. Before the war, the ratio of Chinese dollars to Japanese yen is one to one dollar—the Chinese dollar is equal to about 95 cents in yen. The Pu-Tung Electricity Supply Company's assets were valued at about 43,000 yen at the time. It represented only about twenty-five percent, I believe.*

TUNG Shu-min was praised both inside and outside of the courtroom for his eloquent exposure of the barbaric acts of the Japanese on Chinese soil. As an entrepreneur, he used concrete and persuasive instances in court to show the world how Shanghai, the heart of China's economy, had been robbed and suffered during the Japanese invasion of China. Those testimonies by Tung Shu-ming had become indelible historical evidence in the Tokyo Trial.

## *Sabotaging North China Iron and Steel Company*

Another Chinese witness in the Tokyo Trial was CHEN Ta-shou (CHEN Dashou), who provided evidence of Japan's economic blundering in China. Mr. CHEN graduated from Peiyang University in Tientsin in 1915 with a bachelor's degree in science and then worked as an engineering intern and assistant engineer in Nan Yang Iron and Steel Works and Yangtze Iron and Steel Works. In 1920 he went to America to pursue his postgraduate studies at the University of California and obtained a master's degree in Science in Metallurgy in 1921. He took further study in coal mining and coal preparation and coking at the University of Illinois. In the autumn of 1922, he returned to China and worked as a mining engineer and a mine manager of Mantoushan Coal Mine in Anhwei Province, and then as a mining engineer of the Construction Commission of Chekiang Province from 1928 to 1930.

From 1931 to 1938 CHEN Ta-shou worked in the National Construction Commission of the National Government of China as a mining engineer, Chief of Mining Section, Director of Hunan Coal Mine, and Director of the Enterprise Department, successively. He was sent to Europe in 1933 to study the coal mines and iron-steel works in France, Belgium, the British Isles, and Germany. In the summer of 1938, he joined the National Resources Commission of the National Government of China and was appointed Director of Pingkwei Mining Administration of Kwangsi Province. In 1940 he was appointed by the National Resources Commission of the National Government Vice-President and Chief Engineer of Yunnan Consolidated Tin Corporation. In February of the same year, he was sent by the National Resources Commission of the National Government to Peiping to investigate the iron and steel works in Northern China. In March of the same year, he was appointed Executive Director of the Preparatory Committee of North China Iron and Steel Corporation to take over the company that was operated by the Japanese during wartime.

On September 9, 1946, the International Military Tribunal for the Far East examined Japan's economic exploitation in China. The prosecutor summoned CHEN Ta-shou to give testimony in the court. Mr. CHEN provided detailed and accurate data to reveal economic plunder in China by Japan, thanks to his expertise in the related professional fields and his fluent English. The following was part of the written records of the Q & A by Henry A. Hauxhurst, an assistant prosecutor from the U.S., and Mr. CHEN. The translator for them was Mr. FANG F.S. mentioned in Chapter 3, a secretary of Chinese justice MEI Ju-ao.

*Q (Hauxhurst): Mr. Chen, for what purposes was the North China Iron and Steel Corporation formed, and what is its business?*

*A (CHEN): The North China Iron and Steel Corporation is a Chinese corporation organized to take over the Japanese-operated iron and steel works and iron mines in North China.*

*Q (Hauxhurst): From your own knowledge, will you state where the subsidiary companies are located and describe them briefly?*

*A (CHEN): This corporation has iron and steel works that smelt pig iron. These companies are North China Iron Manufacturing Company, Tsingtao Iron Manufacturing Company, Tientsin Iron Manufacturing Company, Tientsin Steel Company, Ito Steel Company at Tientsin, Tangshan Steel Company at Tangshan, and also has three coal mining—iron ore mining companies. The iron ore mining companies are the Lungyen Iron Ore Mining Company, the Chinling Cheng Iron Ore Mining Company, and the North China Mining Company. For iron smelting, the North China Iron Manufacturing Company has eleven 20-ton blast furnaces, one 200-ton blast furnace, one 380-ton blast furnace, and one 600-ton blast furnace under construction. The Tsingtao Iron Manufacturing Company has two blast furnaces, each of 250 tons. The Tientsin Steel Company has one 25-ton open-hearth furnace and two rolling mills, small rolling mills. The Tsun Shan Steel Metallurgy Company has two 8-ton electric furnaces and two small rolling mills. The Lungyen iron mine has ten 20-ton blast furnaces at Hwuanwha and two iron mines, one at Yen-tung-Shang and another at Lung-Chia-Pao. The Chingling Cheng Iron Ore Mining Company has iron mines at Chingling Cheng near the Kuang-hsi Railroad. The North China Mining Company has iron mines at Lan-hsien in Hopeh Province, iron mines in Honan Province, and a coal mine in Shantung Province.*

*Q (Hauxhurst): Mr. Chen, from your personal inspection and investigation, will you state what you found as to the conditions of the plants when they were taken over by this corporation after the surrender?*

*A (CHEN): The blast furnaces are of no use for temporary, but big furnaces, one hundred tons in capacity, are either frozen solid without tapping out the molds or materials during the time of surrender or under repairing or under construction. The small furnaces of twenty tons capacity serve only for the war purpose, of no use whatsoever now. Furthermore, the two 250-ton furnaces at Tsingtao use only wooden head frames for the blast furnaces, and they have only four hot blast stoves for two furnaces.*

*Q (Hauxhurst): Did your company come into possession of the books and records of the Japanese operations from the time of the occupation up to the surrender of these various companies that you have named?*

*A (CHEN): I not only examined all the books and records; I personally visited a number of the iron—steel works.*

*Q (Hauxhurst): Will you state what these records disclosed as to the consumption of coal and iron ore in the operations during the period of the Japanese occupation?*

*A (CHEN): Of 4,300,000 tons of ore mined during the time of Japanese operation, only about 700,000 tons were used in smelting—in producing pig iron. They used about two tons of iron ore and 2.2 tons of coke to produce one ton of pig iron.*

*Q (Hauxhurst): As an expert, Mr. Chen, in the manufacture of iron and steel, will you state what your experience as to the practice is of the use of coke and iron ore in the manufacture of iron?*

*A (CHEN): The amount of iron ore used is variable according to the percentage of the iron ore content. While for coke, usually one ton of coke is consumed for every ton of pig iron produced.*

*Q (Hauxhurst): You spoke about using 4,350,000 tons of ore, and spoke of a certain amount that had been used. Did you make a personal inspection of the books and records to determine what became of some of the ore during that operation?*

*A (CHEN): Yes, I do. I examined all the books, and I found out that 1,400,000 tons were exported to Manchuria, 1,000,000—and about 1,030,000 tons of iron ore were exported to Japan.*

*Q (Hauxhurst): What effect did the use of this ore during the period of that occupation have on the ore reserves in that district?*

*A (CHEN): A little over four percent of total reserve in these regions was depleted.*

*Q (Hauxhurst): Did you have any other connections with any other mines in China? If you did, will you give their names and describe their operations?*

*A (CHEN): I have connections with the Man-Toushang Coal Mine and Wai-Nan Coal Mine and Railroad Company. This mine used to produce 400 tons of coal per day. It is situated very near to the Yang-Tzu River. There is a railroad of several kilometers using light railroad tracks with locomotives hauling 400 tons of coal per day. It has a power plant of 540 kilowatts. It is operated with electricity. All the mining machinery, such as pumps, hoisting engines, air compressors, and so forth, are operated by electricity. It is four to twelve feet thick in the coal seam. It gives good semi-anthracite of eleven percent ash and a heavy value of 12,000 B. T. U. I went there in December of 1945 to see the mine. When I went there, I found nothing but a piece of flat land. All the buildings were demolished, and all the machinery, railroads, and equipment, as told by the natives of the region, they were all demolished and taken away. All the heavy pieces were cut into small pieces and taken away. As to Wai-Nan Coal Mine has a railroad of 212 kilometers. It can produce 2,000 tons of coal daily on an average. It has a neighboring mine called the Ta-Tung Coal Mine. It was inaugurated—completed together with the Wai-Nan Coal Mine to form the new Wai-Nan Mining Company. The Ta-Tung Coal Mine used to produce 1500 tons of coal a day. At present, after the consolidation of these two mines, they can produce only 1100 tons of coal per day. The director of the*

> *mining company told me that during the time of occupation by the Japanese forces, they had mined coal without doing any development work, so all the coal above the 180-meter level was either mined out or put in a situation that cannot make access at present because they pay no attention to the maintenance of the archway, and they have mined out a part of the pillars in the archways. So, these mines cannot recover their original output without sinking new shafts.*[12]

The above are just two cases of Japan's economic aggression against China.

In Chapter Five "Japan's Invasion of China" of the "*Judgment of the International Military Tribunal for the Far East*," there are two sections dedicated to the topic of Japan's economic aggression against China.

The second section is titled "*Consolidation and Exploitation of Manchuria*," accounting for as many as 30 pages in the record written in English. It clearly states: "At the very outset of the military occupation, the Japanese seized control of the economy of Manchuria." The subtitles in this section include "*Economy of Manchuria seized*," "*Kwantung Army's economy plan for guiding Manchukuo*," "*Economic construction program for Manchukuo*," "*Japan-Manchukuo joint economic committee*," "*Yen bloc organized*," "*Industrial Bank of Manchukuo*," "*Second period construction plan*," "*Control of industry*," "*Manchurian heavy industry development cooperation*," "*Manchukuo—A workhouse for Japan*," "*Opium and narcotics*," etc., which elaborated Japan's economic plunder of Northeast China.[13]

The seventh section is titled "*Japan's Economic Domination of Manchuria and Other Parts of China*," accounting for 18 pages in the record written in English, it revealed that Japan adopted the same economic plundering policy in Manchuria and North, Central, and South China:

> *The Japanese policy in Manchuria was to consolidate the territory under a government subservient to Japan and then by means of agreements with that government and by other means to obtain much-needed basic materials required to carry out the program adopted in Japan and to obtain control of the communications and a substantial part of industry and commerce, all of which were of great value to later Military Operations. In North China, the same plan was followed for the same purposes and particularly to fill the demand for supplies that at the time were not obtainable in foreign markets and which were badly needed in the campaign against the whole of China and were necessary to facilitate the over-all plan. The same policy was adopted as the war progressed into Central and Southern China.*

> *Furthermore, the subsections, such as "General economic matters," "Particular industries," "Transportation and communications," "Natural resources," "Public utilities,"* "*Banking,*" and "*Narcotics in China,*" all demonstrated more details of the process of Japan's economic plunder of China.[14]

## Planting and Selling Drugs

Japan's despicable growing and selling of opium in Northeast China was mentioned in the sixth chapter of this book. In fact, the drug trade had always been an extremely sinister and vicious way of Japanese militarism during the 14 years of Japan's invasion of China, which was, however, unknown to the world.

On August 15, 1946, HSIANG Che-chun, the Chinese prosecutor, made a specific prosecuted remark in his opening statement about "*the atrocities against civilians and other persons, and the use of opium and other narcotic drugs in China.*" He pointed out:

> *As a part of their plan to subjugate China, the Japanese leaders used opium and narcotics as weapons to prepare for and to further aggression in China. This was in violation of obligations of the three Conventions relating to the suppression of opium and narcotic drugs, which are now in evidence as Exhibits No. 17, 18, and 19, of which Japan was a signatory.*
>
> *Our evidence will prove that in advance of Japanese armed aggression in any area, Japanese agents, military and civilian, engaged in widespread illegal traffic in opium and narcotics, not only in Japanese concessions but in all parts of China. Such agents introduced the production of Heroin, morphine, and other opium derivatives into areas where such use had not been prevalent before. They operated almost with immunity because of the then existence of Japanese extra-territoriality rights in China. The intent and the effect of this illegal activity were to neutralize or completely defeat Chinese attempts to control the drug menace. The physical effect of drug addiction is so well known as to make it clear that the Japanese intended to render millions of Chinese listless and incompetent to resist aggression.*
>
> *The official character of this illegal activity is indicated by the repeated failure of Japanese consular authorities to take positive action to prevent Japanese nationals from engaging in narcotic traffic or punish adequately Japanese nationals apprehended for narcotic violations by Chinese or other police. This failure is in*

*sharp contrast with the drastic action taken by Japanese authorities in cases where Japanese nationals sold narcotics to Japanese.*

*It will be shown that as the Japanese achieved domination of each area in China, that area served as a basis of operations for a narcotics offensive against the next area marked for that form of armed aggression, which the Japanese called" Pacification." In this connection, it will be shown that beginning with the creation of the puppet government of Manchukuo and then successively through North China, Central China, and South China, Japanese controlled puppet governments followed a uniform pattern of abrogating Chinese law in respect of opium and other narcotics and in creating opium monopolies designed to appear as opium suppressing agencies, but which in fact became the sole traffickers in opium and in narcotics in their several territories. There ensued a large increase of opium dens in areas under Japanese control, an increase of areas assigned for the cultivation of the poppy, large importations of opium and narcotics, and a failure to adopt suppressive measures in line with the purported purpose of the opium monopolies.*

*Under the guise of control of opium for the purpose of suppression, Japanese controlled puppet governments received huge revenues from the opium and narcotic traffic. It will be shown that in "Manchukuo" a Japanese loan for the purpose of financing the operations of the puppet government, was secured by a pledge of the profits of the opium trade.*

*In short, the evidence will show that the opium and narcotic traffic was sponsored by Japan for two purposes:*

*(1) To weaken the stamina and undermine the will to resist on the part of the Chinese people;*

*(2) To provide substantial revenues to finance Japanese military and economic aggression.*[14]

In Chapter 5, *"JAPANESE AGGRESSION AGAINST CHINA"* of the *International Military Tribunal for the Far East*, there are two sections that were dedicated to revealing Japan's war crimes in this regard.

In Section 2, *Consolidation and Exploitation of Manchuria*, there is a subsection titled *OPIUM AND NARCOTICS*, which clearly points out Japan's purpose as "*In order to finance her operations in Manchuria and also in order to weaken the power of resistance, of the Chinese, Japan sanctioned and developed the traffic in opium and narcotics.*" It continued to state:

> *Wherever the Japanese Army went in China, Korean and Japanese drug peddlers followed closely upon its heels vending their merchandise without hindrance from the Japanese authorities. In some cases, these traffickers were sent ahead of the invading Army to prepare a way for it by engaging in intrigue, espionage, and sabotage.... Japan's real purpose in engaging in drug traffic was far more sinister than even the debauchery of the Chinese people. Japan, having signed and ratified the Opium Conventions, was bound not to engage in the drug traffic, but she found in the alleged but false independence of Manchukuo a convenient opportunity to carry on worldwide drug traffic and cast the guilt upon that puppet state. A large part of the opium produced in Korea was sent to Manchuria, where opium grown in Manchuria and imported from Korea and elsewhere was manufactured and distributed throughout the world. In 1937, it was pointed out in the League of Nations that ninety percent of all illicit white drugs in the world were of Japanese origin, manufactured in the Japanese concession in Tientsin Dairen and other cities of Manchuria, Jehol, and China, always by Japanese or under Japanese supervision.*[15]

Section 7 subtitled "NARCOTICS IN CHINA" further revealed the crimes by Japan:

> *A policy similar to that adopted in Manchuria was adopted from time to time as military operations succeeded in North, Central, and Southern China. This traffic is related to the military operations and political developments in that by means of it substantial funds were obtained for the various local governments set up by the Japanese, funds which would otherwise have to be furnished by Japan or found by additional local taxes. Incidentally, the effect on the morale of the Chinese population by the tremendous increase of drug addicts can be well imagined. Connected with the opium traffic in China from 1937 were the Japanese Army, the Japanese Foreign Office, and the Asia Development Board.*[16]

The puppet regime in China during Japan's invasion would do a mere show from time to time by setting up anti-narcotics institutions, which only turned out to expose itself while trying to cover up its misdeeds. There was evidence cited in the *Judgment*:

*The explanation may be found in the cryptic evidence of Harada, Kumakichi, and Japanese Military Attaché at Shanghai from 1937 to 1939. He says, "When I was head of the Tokumu Bu, I received instructions through military channels to provide opium for the Chinese people by establishing an opium suppression board."...After the occupation of Tientsin in 1937, there was a notable increase in the use of narcotics. The Japanese concession in Tientsin became known as the center of heroin manufacturing. No less than two hundred heroin factories were established in the Japanese concession, and it was stated before the League of Nations Advisory Committee on Traffic in Opium in 1937 that it was common knowledge that almost 90% of all illicit white drugs in the world were of Japanese origin manufactured in Tientsin, Dairen and the other cities of Manchuria and North China.... In Shanghai, Fukien Province, and Kwantung Province in South China and elsewhere after 1937, upon occupation of each province and large center by the Japanese, the traffic in drugs increased on a scale corresponding to that in other parts of the country which has already been described.*[17]

In short, Japan's scale of drug cultivation, manufacturing, and trafficking during its invasion of China was unmatched by today's drug lords' activities. During that period, "90% of the illegal white drugs" in the world were under the control of the Japanese empire, which might have made a record in human history.

To defend its invasion of China and other countries in the Asia-Pacific area, Japan had successively concocted various "thesis," such as "Hakko Ichiu" ("eight crown cords, one roof," i.e., "all the world under one roof"), "Dai Asia shugi" ("Greater Asianism"), "Manchuria-Mongolia Lifeline," "Sino-Japanese Economic Cooperation," and so on. In July 1940, after the Second KONOYE Cabinet came into power, it launched the "Greater East Asia Co-prosperity Sphere" plan, arrogantly including Japan, China, East Asia, Southeast Asia, South Asia, Oceania, and the Russian Far East. On November 11, 1942, the so-called "Greater East Asia Ministry" was established, and Kazuo Aoki was named the first "Greater East Asia Minister." On September 9, 1946, just before Chen Ta-shou testified, the prosecutor read Kazuo Aoki's "Inauguration Statement" in the court:

*This war of construction is aimed at establishing a new order based upon morality and righteousness by realizing the basis of the fundamental principle which guided the founding of our Empire, the great principle of Hakko Ichiu, throughout Greater*

*East Asia so as to enable all countries and peoples in the Greater East Asia sphere to have each its proper place with Japan serving as the pivot.... From this standpoint, I intend to render still closer and stronger, in conformity with the stipulations of treaties, our nation's cooperation with these countries in the sphere of co-prosperity such as Manchoukuo, the Republic of China, Thailand, and French Indo-China, which have special relations with Japan. At the same time, it is my fervent hope that these countries also, understanding the real meaning of the present war, will extend further their cooperation for the realization of the idea of establishing the new order of Greater East Asia."*[18]

It is obvious that the so-called "Greater East Asia Co-prosperity" was just an excuse for a "Japan-centric" world. Despite the slick rhetoric of "stay united with friendly countries," it was in sharp contrast to Japan's vicious economic plunder in the area. What Japan had done was the most ironic interpretation of the "Greater East Asia Co-prosperity Sphere."

On November 5, 1943, Japanese Prime Minister TOJO Hideki presided over the "Greater East Asia Conference." The representatives of "Manchukuo," WANG Ching-wei's "National Government," Thailand, the Philippines, Myanmar, and the Provisional Government of "Free India" were ordered to participate in the event to further whitewash the "Greater East Asia Co-prosperity Sphere."

Even the Japanese scholars scoffed at the farce. As early as April 1948, KAINO Michitaka from Tokyo Imperial University published a short essay, *The Legal Theory of War Trial* in *Historical Review*, pointing out sharply that:

*What the Greater East Asia Co-prosperity Sphere actually means is something that the residents of the Japanese-occupied territories during the war could not be clearer about. Besides, the officials involved in the local administration just needed to think in conscience for a second and then would figure out whether what they had done was really for the "autonomy and independence," "respect for sovereignty" and "coexistence and co-prosperity" of the local aborigines. It is conceivable that TOJO's hypocritical representations of the Greater East Asia Co-prosperity Sphere certainly aroused great indignation across Asia, headed by China, which had directly suffered from Japanese aggression.*[19]

## *References*


[1] *The Judgment of the International Military Tribunal for the Far East.* Translated by Zhang Xiaolin, retranslated by Xiang Longwan and Xu Xiaobing (2015). Shanghai Jiao Tong University Press, 309 (49136 of the English court records).

[2] Ibid., 25–30, 49, 51 (48462–48463, 48516, 48523 of the English court records).

[3] Ibid., 255–256 (49008–49009 of the English court records).

[4] Ibid., 317 (49153 of the English court records).

[5] Cheng, Zhaoqi, and Xiang Longwan. 2017. *Transcripts of the Proceedings of the International Military Tribunal for the Far East (Chinese version)*, Vol. 4. Shanghai Jiao Tong University Press, 111–112 (4021–4022 of the English court records).

[6] Ibid., 118–120 (4028–4032 of the English court records).

[7] Ibid., 158 (4121–4122 of the English court records).

[8] *The Judgment of the International Military Tribunal for the Far East.* Translated by Zhang Xiaolin, retranslated by Xiang Longwan and Xu Xiaobing (2015). Shanghai Jiao Tong University Press, 319 (49158–49159 of the English court records).

[9] Wu, Yuzhen. 2014. "Discover the lost history of the Tokyo Trial." *Wenhuibao* (9), November 12, 2014.

[10] Cheng, Zhaoqi, and Xiang Longwan. 2017. *Transcripts of the Proceedings of the International Military Tribunal for the Far East (Chinese version)*, Vol. 4. Shanghai Jiao Tong University Press, 291–293 (4425–4429 of the English court records).

[11] Ibid., 294–299 (4432–4448 of the English court records).

[12] Cheng, Zhaoqi, and Xiang Longwan. 2017. *Transcripts of the Proceedings of the International Military Tribunal for the Far East (Chinese version)*, Vol. 5. Shanghai Jiao Tong University Press, 85–86 (5196–5201 of the English court records).

[13] *The Judgment of the International Military Tribunal for the Far East.* Translated by Zhang Xiaolin, retranslated by Xiang Longwan and Xu Xiaobing (2015). Shanghai Jiao Tong University Press, 309–321 (49135–49164 of the English court records).

[14] Xiang, Longwan. 2010. *The Tokyo Trial, Chinese Prosecutor Hsiang Che-chun.* Shanghai Jiao Tong University Press, 15–16 (3889–3892 of the English court records).

[15] *The Judgment of the International Military Tribunal for the Far East.* Translated by Zhang Xiaolin, retranslated by Xiang Longwan and Xu Xiaobing (2015). Shanghai Jiao Tong University Press, 320–321 (49159–49164 of the English court records).

[16] Ibid., 383–390 (49309–49326 of the English court records).

[17] Ibid., 388–390 (49322–49326 of the English court records).

[18] Cheng, Zhaoqi, and Xiang Longwan. 2017. *Transcripts of the Proceedings of the International Military Tribunal for the Far East (Chinese version)*, Vol. 5. Shanghai Jiao Tong University Press, 83–84 (5191–5193 of the English court records).

[19] TOTANI, Yuma. 2016. *The Tokyo Trial, Pursuit of Law and Justice after WWII.* Translated by Zhao Yuhui. Shanghai Jiao Tong University Press, 227–228.

CHAPTER 10

# The Rape of Nanking

## *A Killing Competition*

The Tokyo Trial revealed a large number of crimes from the Japanese aggression. Among the most shocking was the Nanking Massacre, which was extremely cruel in the human world.

From August 13 to November 2, 1937, China and Japan fought a three-month "Battle of Shanghai" in the Shanghai area. Although it ended in the fall of Shanghai, the tenacious resistance of the Chinese army along with civilians made the Japanese army's arrogant plan of quick victory come to naught.

The Japanese army was shamed into a rage. On August 15, the Japanese government, reversing right and wrong, issued a statement brazenly: "*In order to punish the violence of the Chinese army and prompt the awakening of the Nanking government, we have to take drastic measures today.*"[1]

MATSUI Iwane, Commander of the Shanghai Expeditionary Army, put forward plans to march into Nanking repeatedly. He said in the *Field Diary* on August 15 that "*We have urgent needs to lift the hammer to awaken the Shina authorities.*" The next day, he advised the War Minister SUGIYAMA Hajime: "*It is advisable to make every effort to aim at Central Shina, especially Nanking government, and make progress towards the overall situation through all-round oppression by force and economy.... Our army should send the necessary troops (five divisions) to Central Shina for the purpose of attacking Nanking and destroying the Nanking government in one fell swoop.*" On September 17, MATSUI wrote a letter to the Deputy Chief of the Army General Staff, and proposed "*in my personal opinion*" *that the third stage of the war was "raiding Nanking.*" On September 23, he wrote in his diary: "*On this day, Major NAKAYAMA of the War Ministry returned to the capital, and I entrusted him with a letter to Minister SUGIYAMA, the main purpose of which is: ... 3. The target of war in the South of Yangtze River should be Nanking anyway ...*"[2]

On November 14, the Japanese army captured Taitsang, then on the 17th, it broke through Kunshan outside Suchow; on the 19th, Suchow and Changshu fell; and on the 27th, Wu-hsi fell.

On November 28, the General Staff in Tokyo ordered: "*pursue and attack Nanking.*" Then on December 1, another order was issued ordering the Central China Area Army, the Shanghai Expeditionary Army, and other troops to attack from land and water to "*conquer Nanking jointly.*"

After fierce fighting, the Japanese army occupied Chiangyin, Ch'int'an, Tanyang, Liyang, and Lishui on December 2; they occupied Chüjung on December 5 and Chenkiang on December 8. The Chinese and Japanese armies began to fight ferociously around the walls of Nanking.

The Japanese army marched aggressively from Shanghai to Nanking, burning, killing, raping, and plundering along the way, which became more and more savage as they committed a series of atrocities. In the postwar memories of many Japanese soldiers, they revealed many atrocities of the Japanese from their personal experiences. To name a few:

TADOKORO Kozo recalled: "*Before going to Nanking, it could be said that it was like two weeks without food or water. At first, there was rice, but the supply couldn't keep up. Seeing farmers eating red rice, without understanding the language anyway, we hit their heads with guns and then grabbed red rice to eat. Once the head was smashed, the people mostly died ... We burned one village after another along the way.*"

In *Personal Records of Nanking Massacre – War Stories Not Recorded in the History of War*, SONE Kazuo recorded the process of how they gradually lost their humanity as they committed barbaric acts of burning, killing, and raping: "*With the adaptation to the battlefield, the devil's heart grew gradually, and the captured enemy soldiers were beheaded occasionally.*" "*I thought I was human, but when I marched into Chüjung near Nanking, I killed innocent villagers.*" He also described how they raped and killed a woman in Chüjung Village.[3]

Chapter Four mentioned the report of the "Killing Contest" that Mr. KAW Wen-pin discovered. It took place during the Japanese invasion of Nanking.

MUKAI Toshiaki and NODA Tsuyoshi, two junior officers of the 16th Division, started this inhuman competition after the Japanese army's capture of Wuhsi on November 27, with the winner being the first to finish killing 100 Chinese people with a saber. The Japanese newspaper "*Nichi Nichi Shimbun*" actually carried out follow-up reports.

On November 30, the newspaper published the report of special correspondents ASAKAI, MITSUMOTO, and YASUDA for the first time, with the title "*The 100-man Killing Contest! Two Sublieutenants Have Already Killed Over 80 People*": "*It is said that after leaving for Wuhsi, one has already killed 56 men and the other 25.*"

On December 4, the newspaper published the report of ASAKAI and MITSUMOTO for the second time entitled "*Rapid Progress, the Process of 100-man Killing Contest*":

> *Since sending troops to Changchow, we have doubled our efforts and captured Tanyang City at 6:00 p.m. on the 2nd. Before that, Sublieutenant MUKAI had killed 86 people, while NODA 65 and the two launched a fierce competition.*

On December 5, special correspondents ASAKAI, MITSUMOTO, and SUZUKI issued the third report at the foot of Purple Mountain, which was entitled "*The 100-man Killing Contest, How Heroic!*":

> *When capturing Chüjung City, the two 2nd lieutenants rushed to the front and fought bravely. Until the capture, they achieved close results: MUKAI 89 and NODA 78.*

On December 13, these three special correspondents made a fourth report, titled "*Incredible Record in the Contest to Behead 100 People*":

> *The warriors of the Katagiri unit, 2nd lieutenants MUKAI Toshiaki and NODA Tsuyoshi, set a precedent for the 100-man Killing competition in front of Nanking. In the frenzy raid of Purple Mountain on the 10th, they set a record of 106:105. ... The two reached an agreement immediately: "Then let's call it a draw. But what if we continue to reach 150 kills?" On the 11th, the competition to kill 150 people really started.*[4]

These murderous maniacs and gruesome news reports were unprecedented in the history of human civilization. The two bestial soldiers did not escape the punishment of the law. On January 28, 1948, they were executed by shooting after being tried by Nanking War Crimes Tribunal.

Facing the menacing Japanese army, on November 20, the Nationalist Government issued *The Declaration of Relocation to Chungking*, which declared the purpose of moving to Chungking, the "secondary capital," and the determination to persist in the War of Resistance against Japan.

However, Nanking is still the "capital" legally, and Dr. SUN Yat-sen's mausoleum is also on the Purple Mountain. Therefore, whether Nanking should be defended or abandoned has aroused the debate among the decision-makers of the Nationalist Government. Chiang Kai-shek was very conflicted at that time. He wrote in his diary on November 26: "*Nanking can't be defended, but it can't be abandoned either. Otherwise, we can't pacify the upper class and lower class as well as the country and the people.*" At that time, the "Nine-Power Treaty Conference" was being held in Brussels, the capital of Belgium. Chiang Kai-shek hoped that western countries such as Britain and the United States would impose sanctions on Japan at the meeting; Trautmann, the German Ambassador to China, also conveyed Japan's armistice conditions to China secretly. Therefore, Chiang Kai-shek made the policy of "Short-term Defense" and appointed General TANG Sheng-chih (TANG Shengzhi), who advocated defense, as the commander of the Nanking garrison.[5]

Although the battle of Nanking was very fierce and the Japanese army paid the price with heavy casualties, due to a shortage of troops, long defensive line, and poor command, eventually, Nanking fell. On December 11, Chiang Kai-shek issued withdrawal orders twice, and on the 12th, TANG Sheng-chih held a meeting of officers and there announced the retreat. At that time, Nanking was besieged by Japanese troops on three sides, and they had to break through from the Yangtze River. However, there were quite a lot more people than ships along the river, so it was extremely chaotic. As a result, a large number of disorganized troops were stranded along the river or returned to the city, many of whom became prisoners.

## *An Unparalleled Atrocity*

On December 13, the Japanese army conquered Nanking. The next six consecutive weeks witnessed a terrible holocaust; the atrocities of the Japanese army were beyond count, mainly in the following categories.

The first category of violence is organized massacres.

On December 13, a group from the Japanese army arrived in Hsiakuan District when they found out that many of the Chinese soldiers and civilians were trying to cross the Yangtze River to flee the fallen city. Immediately, the Japanese soldiers began to fire at them with their cannons, machine guns, guns in the armored vehicles, and other weapons. Almost all of the Chinese soldiers and civilians were killed on the bank or in the water. In fact, even before the fall of the city, the headquarters of the Japanese army had already issued a "mopping-up order." That is why the Japanese army slaughtered so many Chinese soldiers who had already surrendered, as well as other ordinary civilians in Hsiakuan District. Although the Japanese army prohibited their soldiers from exposing their beastly behaviors, many of them still left authentic records in their diaries or letters. Here are just a few examples.

On December 14, TAKAHASHI Ichirou, a soldier of the 33rd infantry regiment in the 16th Division of the Japanese army, wrote in his diary:

> *The first team had captured more than 200 defeated soldiers. "Drag them somewhere and kill them all, no matter whether there are 200 or 500 of them!" said Adjutant Oshima. So, they were sardined into some empty carriages at the station. His team was ordered to help the heavy machine gun team deal with the captives on the riverside ... A total of 1200 people were pulled out of the warehouse and were driven to stand or sit in the muddy soil which had already buried their knees, and they were made to face the Yangtze River. On the command, several heavy machine guns hiding in the back trenches all fired together. People fell down like dominoes, and their bodies were blown to pieces.*[6]

On December 16 and 17, KAJITANI Kenrou, a Sergeant of the Japanese Army Headquarter at the Second Anchorage in Nanking, described in his diary the scenes that had frightened him:

> *Around 2:00 a.m., I heard the sound of intensive machine guns, and about 2000 defeated soldiers were killed. This was done in Hsiakuan near the Yangtze River.... And one of the victims seemed about only 15 years old. There were countless bodies, and the scene was beyond description. I saw with my own eyes the shooting of 2000 defeated soldiers started around 1:00 a.m. and lasted for about an hour.*[7]

Before the Japanese army captured Nanking, more than 20 westerners who stayed in the city spontaneously established the "International Committee for Nanking Safety Zone," which was designated as a neutral "safe zone" in the western part of Nanking city for innocent citizens and refugees to escape the war. But the Japanese soldiers broke into it all the same to do evil. George A. Fitch, an American missionary, wrote in his diary on December 15:

> *The Japanese army captured and shot all 1300 people in a refugee camp near our headquarters. It was hard for us to imagine that we would witness with our own eyes the unparalleled cruelty and barbarism of our time.*[8]

John H. D. Rabe, chairman of the "International Committee for Nanking Safety Zone," described the Japanese atrocities in his diary. In his diary entry of January 5, 1938, he wrote, "*The Gate of Hanhsimen opened yesterday and was closed today. Kroeger saw about 300 bodies lying in a dry ditch outside the gate, all of them civilians killed or executed by machine guns.*"[9] The diary on January 22 quoted a letter from a German expatriate Edward Sperling to the Secretary of the German Embassy in China, George F. Rosen: "*About 500 civilians were shot dead in a similar way outside the Gate of Hanhsimen. I estimated that 5,000 or 6,000 people had been brutally killed, all of whom are homeless and unarmed.*"[10]

The second category of Japanese atrocities is scattered slaughter.

There were many more cases than could be numbered of this kind. From December 12, 1937, to February 5, 1938, John G. Magee, an American missionary, wrote many letters to his wife, Irving H. Forster, exposing a large number of Japanese atrocities that he witnessed, which have been archived in the Divinity School Library in Yale University. They exposed a large number of Japanese atrocities that he witnessed. In his letter of January 30, he mentioned the horrifying experience of an 8-year-old girl and her family:

*The Japanese soldiers came to a house in the southeast of the city. They killed a total of 13 people in the house, with only an 8-year-old girl and another 3- or 4-year-old surviving. The 8-year-old girl was stabbed three times in the back and side but survived. Among the deaths were the 76-year-old man and the 74-year-old woman, and the mother and her three daughters. The two elder daughters were 16 and 14 years old, respectively, and the little one was only one year old. The two girls were raped three times, then the Japanese soldiers killed them in the cruelest way, and the 1-year-old child was also stabbed to death.*[11]

The 8-year-old girl, named HSIA Shu-chin (XIA Shuqin), survived by a fluke. For the rest of her life, she kept denouncing the blood debt of the Japanese soldiers to her family and never gave up doing so.

AZUMA Shiro was at that time a Private First Class in the 20th infantry regiment of the 16th Division of the Japanese army. In his diary, he recorded the Japanese brutality he witnessed on December 21, 1937.

*At this time, a Chinese man was dragged out of nowhere. Hashimoto put forward a cruel and wicked plan, which is to shove him into a bag, pour gasoline on it, and then have it ignited. In the extreme panic voices of his crying and shouting, the man was shoved into a mailbag, and the bag was then tightly tied. He was desperately yelling and crying in it. Our soldiers kicked the bag around like a football, and then urinated on it, like watering vegetables. Hashimoto got gasoline from a dilapidated car, poured it on the bag, then banded a long belt to the bag and dragged it around to play. People with conscience frowned when watching the cruel scene. Those who have no conscience clapped their hands to echo it with applause. Hashimoto ignited the bag and the gasoline flared up. There was a panic cry in the bag, and the Chinese jumped up with all his strength, and the bag jumped and rolled. Hashimoto, holding the bag, said, "Wow! If you're so hot, I'll let you cool off!" Then he attached three grenades to the belt and threw the bag into the pond. The fire went out, the bag sank, and just as the waves were about to calm down, the grenades exploded. As soon as the water splashed, everything returned to calmness and the game was over.*[12]

HIGA Shiro is known as "a man troubled by his conscience." In December 1987, at the age of 75, he opened up the diaries he kept during his stay in China into "*My Nanking Platoon*" and "*Note of HIGA Shiro,*" which were published in Japan. Better known as the "*The Diary of HIGA Shiro*"[13], the book which brought the brutal acts of the Japanese army to light was his gesture of atonement to the Chinese people. Braving the attack, rebuke, and intimidation of the Japanese right-wing forces, he paid seven visits to China, during which he was found testifying in Nanking, Peking, Shenyang, Shanghai, and other places, reflecting upon and telling the crimes committed by the Japanese army against Chinese civilians and prisoners and testifying on the very spot where the massive massacre of the Chinese took place.

During the Nanking Massacre, about ten to twenty charities in Nanking were carrying out charitable activities such as providing relief, medical care, and handling the burial of the deceased. For example, the Nanking Branch of the World Red Cross, set up a team and started burying corpses on December 22, 1937. In 1945, the organization disclosed the detailed statistics of the bodies they buried from December 1937 to October 1938, which was "a total of 43,071," the original documents of which are now kept in Nanking Archives.[14]

Chongshantang was another private charity that assembled and buried dead bodies in Nanking. CHOW I-yu (ZHOU Yiyu), chairman of Chongshantang, stated in his testimony in the Nanking Trial that "According to my count 112,266 bodies were buried at that time."[15] Based on the statistics of these two organizations alone, in the Nanking Massacre, the number of unnatural deaths had exceeded 150,000.

On August 3, 1954, in a court in Fushun, China, OTA Hisao also mentioned the burial of bodies on the part of the Japanese troops in his statement as the defendant. After enumerating various burials, he had handled or witnessed, he came to the conclusion that "Nanking anchorage depot handled the burial of about 100,000 corpses, and the troops attacking Nanking handled about 50,000, which brought the number of corpses handled during the invasion of Nanking to 150,000 in total."[16]

Sexual violence on a large scale was the third category of atrocities committed by the Japanese army.

During the Japanese occupation of Nanking, they subjected Chinese women to brutal and inhuman sexual violence, regardless of their age, job, or status, and even pregnant and sick women were not spared. Tens of thousands of Chinese women suffered from rape and gang rape, many of them were even tortured to death, and these atrocities were appalling. In the tragic experience of Hsia Shuchin's family mentioned before, among the ten people killed, two women and one young girl had undergone agonizing rape before they were killed.

From the accusations, diaries, correspondence, and media reports of victims as well as from Western witnesses, numerous cases have been made public. For example, Ms. CHEN, who lived in Shuangcha Town was only 12 years old when she was raped at home; Ms. JIN, who lived in Pagoda Mountain was pregnant when she was repeatedly raped by the Japanese soldiers; and hiding in the air-raid shelter did not keep MA a 14-year-old girl of Hui nationality from being gang-raped by Japanese soldiers, her mother was also raped.

The Japanese army even invaded the safety zone on many occasions, taking women into captivity in large numbers for sexual abuse, or sneaking in at night to forage for women to violate. Rabe wrote in his diary on December 17, 1937, that,

> *According to an American, "the safety zone has turned into a brothel for the Japanese." These words are in line with the facts. Last night, about 1,000 girls and women were raped; at the Kinling Women's College of Arts and Sciences alone, the number reached more than 100. All that falls on our ears at the moment are the news of rapes. Once brothers or husbands intervened, they would be shot by the Japanese. What I have heard and witnessed are nothing but the brutal and barbarous crimes of Japanese soldiers.*[17]

In early 1938, in a report to the German Ministry of Foreign Affairs, Rabe estimated that "*Within a month after the fall of Nanking, more than 20,000 women were raped by the Japanese army.*"[18]

In addition to large-scale rapes, the Japanese army also filled their atrocities with perversions and sadism. For instance, many women were raped before they were killed, local Nanking people were forced to rape each other, monks were compelled to conduct rape, and even family members were forced to have sexual intercourse. Countless cases are simply too cruel to read, hence its exclusion from this book.

The inhumanity shown by the Japanese army can be attributed to the instigation of the authorities. Japanese soldiers were once instructed that "*In order to avoid causing too much trouble, they can be handled either by offering money or killing them afterward.*"

The fourth category of atrocities committed by the Japanese army was robbery and plunder.

Before the Japanese conquered Nanking, there was growing evidence of indiscipline among the troops. The order that the food supply on the front line should rely on "requisition on the spot" was in fact the command for the troops to rob local civilians. After the fall of Nanking, the Japanese troops were even more unscrupulous. Large-scale looting involving all officers and soldiers took place across every corner of the city, from the residences of high-ranking officials of the National Government to the residences of the common people. NAKAJIMA Kesago, Commander of the 16th Division of the Japanese Army, once broke into Chiang Kai Shek's private residence and seized antiques and fine artworks as his own. These items, together with stolen goods from other places, were packed into 32 packages and sent to Tokyo.

The busy and affluent commercial streets were the main targets of the Japanese army. On January 15, 1938, Rosen, the Secretary of the German Embassy in Nanking, described the horrible situation he witnessed on Taiping Road and Hsinchiekow Square in a report named "*The Condition of Nanking and the Atrocities of the Japanese*," which says,

> *Weeks of the Japanese rule have witnessed terrifying lootings have turned the city's commercial areas, namely the Taiping Road area and the entire area south of the so-called "Potsdamer Plaza" into rubbles, leaving only broken walls of some buildings. More than a month has passed, and the fire set off by the Japanese army during their occupation is still burning.*[19]

On January 27, 1938, Rabe expressed his worries about the future of Nanking in his diary[20]:

> *This morning, Dr. Rosen and I [G.F. Rosen, secretary of the German Embassy in China—Note from the author] went to the east of the city. Passing Beimen Bridge, Gofu Road, and other places along the way, we saw all the houses had been ransacked, and about one-third of them had burned down. How to bring the stores back to life is still a mystery to us.*

Ignoring diplomatic conventions, the insatiable Japanese soldiers even broke in and plundered the innocent foreign embassies in China. On December 14, 1937, the second day Nanking was captured, the British Embassy was the first target; the Japanese troops broke into it and looted all of the contents inside. Subsequently, other embassies such as America, France, and Spain were all looted and damaged by Japanese troops. As Japan's allies, Germany and Italy couldn't spare their embassy staff from the suffering. For instance, on December 30, 1937, two Japanese soldiers broke into the residence of an Italian embassy official, and stole all his property; On January 8, 1938, Rosen, the secretary of the German Embassy, and Scharfenberg, the administrator, had their residences thoroughly looted.[21]

A number of church buildings built before the war by western churches were also looted and badly damaged. For example, the Episcopal Church on Taiping Road was also looted on the second day of the Japanese occupation of Nanking, and then on December 17, all the houses of the American Presbyterian Church located around Moch'ou Road suffered the same disaster.

Nanking, as a well-known ancient capital of six dynasties, preserved in abundance the precious books and cultural relics. The plunder of books and relics was a top-down decision of Japanese troops. At the very beginning of a full-scale war of aggression against China, Japan set up the "Books and Documents Reception Committee of Central Branch Occupied Regions," serving particularly for the collection of Chinese books. After the capture of Nanking, nine Japanese secret agents rushed to Nanking from Shanghai to make a large-scale investigation of the book collection in Nanking. They searched and pillaged more than 70 institutions, including the Executive Council of National Government, the Civil Affairs Department, the Ministry of Foreign Affairs, the Examinations Authority, the Central Party Office, the Ministry of Communications, the Ministry of Education, the Provincial Library, the Compilation Hall, the Purple Mountain Observatory, and the Academia Sinica. In 1941, Japan published the *Business Profile of Central Branch Construction Data Arrangement Committee,* which revealed the scale of Japanese troops' book plunder in Nanking.

> *A dozen truckloads of books were loaded into the investigation agency every day, and more than 200 book mountains were piled up on the first, second, and third floors of the main building.*

In August 1938, the aforementioned committee classified the books they plundered into "separate edition of foreign books," "periodicals of European countries," "periodicals of China and Japan," "Han documents," "magazines" and so on, amounting to approximately 900 thousand volumes, which was more than the whole book collection of 850 thousand volumes in Tokyo Library, Japan's largest library.

In addition, the Japanese troops plundered the Nanking Scientific Research Unit of more than one hundred thousand scientific specimens, as well as countless private collections of antiques.[22]

The fifth category of Japanese atrocity is arson.

As mentioned above, the plunder of Japanese troops in and around Nanking was accompanied by arson, which was not an individual act but an organized atrocity. The Japanese troops had been setting fires even before the invasion of Nanking. Takashima, a Japanese soldier in the third regiment of the sixteenth Infantry division, recorded in his diary on November 14, 1937, that "*Following the regiment commander's order 'if you find any suspicious village, set it on fire,' the soldiers in our regiment set fire to everything for fun.*" On the day of the Japanese occupation of Nanking, Yanagawa Heisuke, Commander of the 10th army, gave the order: "*Wipe out the enemy army by all means, and if necessary, burn down the whole city to reach the end.*" Accordingly, the Japanese troops burned down numerous business districts after looting, leaving many block buildings and residences reduced to ashes.

On December 21, 1937, Rabe recorded in his diary: "*Undoubtedly, the Japanese are burning the city, probably just to erase the traces of their plundering and looting.*"

On the same day, Robert O. Wilson, an American doctor, gave a similar account in his diary: "*So far, more than half the city has been burnt down and the whole business district has been set on fire.*"

Additionally, Nanking was a city for its religious culture. Yet, a large number of Buddhist temples and Taoist temples were left in ruins under the arson of Japanese troops. For example, the Japanese invasion of Nanking suburbs on December 10, 1937, temples and Caves on Niushou Mountain in the south of the city, such as the Temple of Immortal Cave, the Temple of Solitary Roost, the Cave of Wenshu and the Cave of Kuanyin, together with the old trees all over the mountain, were all burnt down by the Japanese troops. Many Islamic mosques in places such as Hsiakuan Street, West Street, Hsike Street, and Little West Gate, were totally destroyed as well.[23]

Many other ancient buildings and cultural relics also suffered irreversible damage. In summary, the atrocities of the Japanese troops during the Nanking Massacre were too numerous to record. According to Justice MEI Ju-ao: "*The Nanking Massacre was no doubt striking atrocity committed by Japanese troops during World War II, its cruelty being only next to the Holocaust at Auschwitz.*"[24]

There was immediate media coverage of the Nanking Massacre both at home and abroad.

On December 15, 1937, the second day after the Japanese occupation of Nanking, a report by journalist A.T. Steele was published on the front page of *Chicago Daily News* in America. The report was entitled "Nanking Massacre Story," which was written on USS Oahu when he was evacuated from Nanking. It described: "*'Four Days in Hell' are the best words to describe the capture of Nanking. As we left Nanking, our last sight was a group of 300 Chinese was being executed in an orderly fashion in front of the riverside wall, with knee-high bodies lying around. The fall of Nanking was also an unspeakable act of terror and confusion for the Chinese city defenders trapped in the city, and a reign of terror under the ensuing Japanese occupation forces, who caused the massacre of tens of thousands of lives including abundant innocent civilians.*"[25]

On December 18, *The New York Times* in America also covered a special telegram by F. T. Durdin from the warship Oahu, under the headline "*The Fall of Nanking, the Massacre*," followed by several subtitles such as "*The Massacre of All Prisoners*," "*Terror Spreading in Nanking, and the Massacre of Civilians*," "*The Attack of American Embassy*," "*The Disaster of Nanking Fall*," "*Heavy Civilian Casualties*," and so on.[26]

## *Witnesses from Different Countries*

The Japanese army had blocked the news and destroyed all evidence of their criminal acts, which left the world ignorant of the magnitude of the Nanking Massacre; the Prosecution's evidence and media reports alone were not sufficient enough to be convincing. Therefore, providing sufficient human and physical evidence for the court became the key task of China's investigation team. The International Prosecution Section attached great importance to the investigation of the Nanking Massacre.

As early as March 1946, Henry CHIU accompanied HSIANG Che-chun and two U.S. assistant prosecutors, Morrow and Sutton to conduct a field investigation in China. Over the course of five weeks, they interviewed 31 witnesses and jointly wrote a report entitled "*The Report from China: Atrocities against Civilians.*" After the Tokyo Trial opened, they returned to Nanking and other places to collect evidence. From May 31 to June 12, 1946, they collected a large amount of evidence and invited several witnesses to testify in Tokyo. Henry CHIU also conducted a special check on six topical cases.

Henry CHIU recalled that personal experience in his later years.

> *From March to June 1946, in order to make the trial of the Nanking Massacre by the Japanese invading forces proceed smoothly, and to sentence the war criminals to due punishment, we went to Nanking twice to look for witnesses and evidence. As the hearing was only two months away and the task was urgent, I didn't take the opportunity to go back to Shanghai to visit my parents. Instead, I took a direct flight to Nanking, the capital of China at that time, and found YANG Chao-lung, the director of the Criminal Department of the Ministry of Justice, and asked him to cooperate in the collection of evidence, especially on the Nanking Massacre. At that time, various notices were posted at the gate of the Supreme Court of China, calling on survivors, witnesses, victims, and their relatives to file complaints. On hearing that the International Military Tribunal for the Far East had sent personnel to Nanking to collect evidence to punish Japanese war criminals and redress injustice for the victims, the gate of the Supreme Court of China was crowded with angry protestors. We searched and registered tens of thousands of complaint materials all night, selected a dozen particularly egregious examples from among them, and made "affidavits" in accordance with the internationally accepted Anglo-American legal procedures, that is, witnesses, local lawyers, and foreign lawyers signed and sealed the documentary evidence together.*[27]

Both the Chinese officials and civilians attached great importance to the Nanking Massacre. In June 1946, the *Nanking Massacre Investigation Committee* was set up, with a total of 51 members from all over China headed by CHEN Yu-kuang (CHEN Yuguang), the president of the Nanking Provisional Senate, and CHEN Yao-tung (CHEN Yaodong), vice president of the Senate. Among the committee members were 16 senators, including WU Chong-hsueh (WU Chongxue), YANG Chao-lung (YANG Zhaolong), and YANG Yun-chu (YANG Yunzhu), directors of the Ministry of Foreign Affairs, as well as eminent figures in law and journalism. The Committee hired 17 consultants, including WEI Tao-ming, vice president of the Legislature, WU Ting-chang (WU Dingchang), minister of Civil Affairs, CHEN Li-fu, minister of Education, CHEN Cheng, minister of Military Affairs, Wang Shih-chieh, minister of Foreign Affairs,

WANG Chung-hui, secretary-general of the National Defense Council, HSIA Chin (XIA Qin), president of the Supreme Court, and CHENG Chun (ZHENG Jun), chief procurator.

The investigation committee held its first meeting on June 23. On September 12, CHEN Yu-kuang and CHEN Yao-tung issued an official letter to the Ministry of Foreign Affairs, reporting on the preliminary results.

> *So far, more than 1,840 cases have been investigated and deemed sufficient to prove guilt. Two of them, PAI Hung-en* (BAI Hongen) *and YIN You-yu, had a narrow escape and were seriously injured when the Japanese carried out a mass massacre. Another one, LULI Hsiu-ying* (LuLi Xiuying), *fought hard against several Japanese soldiers who attempted to rape her, suffered 33 knife injuries, and sustained near-fatal injuries, but ultimately survived due to the assistance of doctors in the Drum Tower Hospital. The circumstances of these three cases are extremely serious, and the evidence is conclusive. With the resolution of the Standing Committee of the Investigation Committee, we requested Mr. YAO Keng-sheng* (YAO Gengsheng) *of the Shanghai Communications Office of the Chinese Delegation to Japan to submit in evidence the investigation documents of the cases of PAI Hung-en and other three victims, including photographic evidence, to Mr. HSIANG Che-chun, China's Prosecutor in Japan, to the Tokyo War Crimes Tribunal. There are many other cases of this type, and they are now being sorted out and reviewed, to be sent for testimony in due course.*[28]

On August 21, 1946, the Committee forwarded the document "*Statistics of Male and Female Deaths and Injuries*," "*Statistics of Categories of Enemy Crimes*," "*Table of Victims' Names and Addresses Available for Testimony*," and "*Summary of the Nanking Massacre*" to China's prosecutor HSIANG Che-chun in Tokyo.

After four months of investigation, a total of 2,784 pieces of evidence on the Japanese atrocities were listed in the "*Statistics of Enemy Crimes*." Among them, there were 1,159 cases of shooting, 667 bayonet assassinations, 315 cases of mass killings, 285 cases of enslavement, 136 cases of burning, 69 cases of beating to death, 33 cases of torture followed by killing, 20 cases of rape followed by killing, 19 cases of bombing, 16 cases of rape, 14 cases of collective punishment, among many others.

From mid-July to mid-August of 1946, the court heard the case of the Nanking Massacre committed by the Japanese army. There were 11 witnesses for the prosecution in court, eight of whom accompanied Henry CHIU from China to Tokyo.

On July 25, the witness in court was the aforementioned American, Mr. Wilson. He was a surgeon at Kinling University Hospital. After the fall of Nanking in 1937, many of the patients admitted to the hospital were either victims or survivors of Japanese atrocities, including the elderly, women, and children. Many of the injured died in hospitals. He accused the Japanese army of a number of crimes based on his personal experience and recollections.

> *One case that comes to my mind is that of a woman of forty who was brought to the hospital with the back of her neck having a laceration severing all the muscles of the neck and leaving the head very precariously balanced. From direct questioning of the patient, and from those who brought her in, there was no doubt in our minds that the work was that of a Japanese soldier.... A young boy of eight was brought in with a deep penetrating wound of the abdomen, which pierced his stomach. A man came into the hospital with a bullet through his jaw, barely able to talk. About two-thirds of his body was very badly burned. His story, as nearly as we could make it out, was that he had been seized by Japanese soldiers, shot, covered with gasoline, and set afire. He died two days later. Another man was admitted with a very severe burn covering his entire head and shoulders. While still able to talk, he told us that he was the only survivor of a large group who had been bound together, had gasoline sprayed over them, and were set afire. We have pictures of these particular cases that I have mentioned so far. An old man of sixty was admitted with a bayonet wound in his chest. His story was that he had gone from the safety zone back into the other part of the city to look for a relative. He met a Japanese soldier who bayoneted him in the chest and threw him in the gutter for dead. He recovered consciousness six hours later and was able to get to the hospital. Cases like this continued to come in for a matter of some six or seven weeks following the fall of the city on December 13, 1937.*[29]

Before the Japanese occupation, it was a capital offense to sell opium; thus, Wilson had never seen a shop with a sign on the outside showing the sale of opium in Nanking. However, one year after the occupation he found out that there were twenty-one places openly selling opium on one of the main streets. Wilson testified until July 26. On July 26, four Chinese testified in court as witnesses.

The first was Dr. HSU Chuan-ying (XU Chuanyin), the chief of the Housing Commission within the International Committee for the Nanking Safety Zone. He acquired a Ph.D. from the University of Illinois in the United States and had been living in Nanking since 1928. When the Japanese army occupied Nanking, he was in charge of the Housing Commission within the International Committee for the Nanking Safety Zone and the Chairman of the Red Swastika Society.

On the third day of Nanking's fall, he saw the streets strewn with corpses in Nanking City. He attempted to count the number of corpses lying on both sides of the main street, but the number climbed to more than 500 quickly, so it was impossible for him to get the exact number. On another day, HSU Chuan-ying saw the Japanese soldiers break into the safety zone, tie the hands of the refugees together with ropes, and take them away. It was not until he heard machine guns near the headquarters of the International Committee the following morning that he realized the refugees had been executed, and then their corpses were thrown into the pond. HSU Chuan-ying also accused many Japanese soldiers of their atrocities of raping and slaughtering women: "*The Japanese army's behavior towards Chinese women is more atrocious, and we can hardly imagine this is happening in the civilized world.*" "*One day, the Japanese soldiers came with three trucks to one of the camps, attempted to truck all the girls in the camp to a place where they could rape them. I went – tried to stop them, but no effect. Now these girls, these women, ranges from thirteen years old up to forty years old.*"

HSU Chuan-ying also told of the Red Swastika Society's experience of burying corpses.

He said:

> *There is around two hundred regular staff doing this sort of work. We buried over forty-three thousand, but the number is really too small. The reason is we are not allowed to give a true number of the people we buried. At first, we did not dare to give a number, nor did we dare to keep any records, and later, we just kept private records. This number represents only what we have buried. These are all civilians, not soldiers.*[30]

Next, three Nanking residents appeared in court to testify as victims. They were SHANG Teh-i (SHANG Deyi), WU Chang-the (WU Changde), and CHEN Fu-pao (CHEN Fubao).

SHANG Teh-i was a retailer. He was arrested by the Japanese army and kept in a refugee camp, bound with more than 100 male civilians was taken to the bank of the Yangtze River. Before the Japanese soldiers started executing them, he slumped to the ground by a fluke and was covered with piles of corpses, which saved him from death.

WU Chang-teh was a policeman, while CHEN Fu-pao was an ordinary folk of Nanking. Sharing identical experiences with SHANG Teh-yi, they were arrested by the Japanese army, barely escaped from being executed, and bayoneted to death.[31]

On July 29, Miner Searle Bates, an American professor in the History Department of Nanking University, was called to the court as a witness on behalf of the prosecution. He was a founding member of the International Committee for Nanking Safety Zone, whose purpose was to provide a refuge for Chinese civilians. He cited numerous atrocities of Japanese soldiers he had witnessed.

He said:

*Large parties of Chinese soldiers laid down their arms and surrendered. Within the first 72 hours, they were immediately taken to the outside of the walls of the city and cut down by machine gun fire, mostly on the bank of the Yangtze River. Our International Committee hired laborers to carry out the burials of more than 30,000 Chinese soldiers.*

When he was asked by Assistant Prosecutor Sutton, "*What was the conduct of the Japanese soldiers toward the women in the city of Nanking*?" He said:

*That was the roughest and saddest part of the whole picture. In the homes of my three nearest neighbors, women were raped, including the wives of university teachers. On five different occasions, I came upon soldiers in the act of rape, and I managed to pull them away from the women. The case reports of the safety zone, which were previously referred and my records of refugees submitted to the Japanese authorities with exact details, revealed many hundreds of cases of rape. My reports involved 30,000 refugees from various grounds and in different buildings of Nanking University. One month after the occupation of Nanking, the Chairman of the International Committee, Mr. Rabe, reported to the German authorities that he and his colleagues believed that at least 20,000 cases of rape had occurred. A little earlier, based on reports from the safety zone, my conservative estimate of rape*

> *was some 8,000 cases. Every day and night, a large number of different gangs of soldiers, usually in groups of 15 to 20, went about through the city and broke into houses to hunt for women. At Nanking Theological Seminary, right under the nose of a friend of mine, a Chinese woman was gang-raped by 17 Japanese soldiers in a flash. I am not willing to repeat the cruel and perverted behaviors in connection with the raping of occasional cases, but I want to stress that it was only at Nanking University that a 9-year-old little girl and a 76-year-old lady were raped.*[32]

Bates also testified on Japan's crimes of robbing personal property, burning buildings, and selling opium.

On August 7, Captain LIANG Ting-fang, a Chinese military surgeon, appeared in court to testify. Before the fall of Nanking, he and the medical corps were given orders to stay in Nanking and take care of the Chinese wounded. Dressed in civilian clothes, they lived in a refugee camp. He detailed the mass murder after they were taken from the refugee camp to the Yangtze River by the Japanese soldiers:

> *We were in a refugee camp when the Japanese army took the city. On the 16, we took an order from the Japanese army to proceed to Hsia Kwan, on the bank of the Yangtze River in Nanking. I estimated that there were more than 5,000 people who marched in four columns, and each column was 3/4 of a mile long. When we arrived there, we were placed in a line on the bank of the river while Japanese soldiers and their machine guns lined up on both sides of the line and in front of the line, with machine guns pointing at the line. There were also two trucks loaded with ropes, and men were bound five in a group with their wrists tied below their backs by the Japanese soldiers. I saw the first person of each group was shot to death by Japanese soldiers and then thrown into the river.... My friend and I decided to escape after the shooting had been going on for 4 hours, and at about 23:00, my friend and I made a dash for the river and jumped in it. The Japanese soldiers fired at us, but we were not hit. There was a steep bank on the river, and we found the water there was only waist-deep, so we hid under the steep bank. Under cover of the shadow, the Japanese soldiers did not see us. However, they kept spraying bullets into us with machine guns and hit me in the shoulder. It was not until 2:00 a.m. that they stopped shooting prisoners. However, I fainted from excessive blood loss.*[33]

Thus, LIANG Ting-fang also managed to have a narrow escape by luck.

On August 15 and August 16, the prosecutors' last witness, the aforementioned American missionary John G. Magee, who served in the Protestant Episcopal Church in Nanking from 1912 to 1940, appeared in court. He cited a large number of shocking Japanese atrocities that he experienced.

For example:

> *I passed columns of men being taken out to be killed. These people were being killed by rifle fire and machine gun principally. Also, we knew of groups of several hundred being bayoneted to death. One woman told me that her husband's hands were tied in front of her, and he was thrown into a pond, and she stayed there, and they wouldn't let her rescue him. On December 16, they came to a refugee camp that I knew very well because it was one of my Christian congregations and took out fourteen men from that congregation, including the fifteen years old boy of the Chinese pastor. Four days later, one member of that fourteen, a coolie, came back to tell us the fate of the others. They had been gathered together with about a thousand men and marched to the bank of the Yangtze River and there mowed down with cross-fire machine guns from either end.... The rapings continued day by day. Many women were killed and even children. If a woman resisted or refused, she was either killed or stabbed. I took pictures, moving pictures of the wounds of many of these women – women with their necks slit, stabs all over their bodies. If the husband of the woman tried to help her in any way, he was killed.*[34]

What is commendable is that Priest Magee filmed a 105-minute film with a 16-millimeter movie camera at the risk of his own life, documenting the Japanese troops' burning, killing, looting, and raping atrocities, which made an indelible impression on us. Documentary No. 4 offered a detailed account of the atrocities the HSIA Shu-chin family suffered. Not long ago, Magee's son, following his father's will, donated the film and the movie camera to the Memorial Hall of the Victims of the Nanking Massacre by Japanese invaders.

## *Japanese Army—A Criminal Gang*

In addition to the witnesses who testified in court, the prosecutors provided several written documents. The most notable were the files provided by the International Committee for the Nanking Safety Zone.

The International Committee for the Nanking Safety Zone has 15 members, including seven Americans, four Britons, one Dane, and three Germans. The chairman of the committee is John Rabe, a German who has worked in China for 30 years. During the Japanese occupation and slaughter in Nanking, he and some international personages tried every means to prevent the Japanese slaughter during the hard times. The Safety Zone provided temporary shelter for some 250,000 Chinese civilians. From the perspective of the westerners, John Rabe recorded a very rare page of human history in the form of a diary. In 1942, he compiled the diary he kept in Nanking from 1937 to 1938 into a manuscript named "*Bombing Nanking.*" Sixty years after gathering dust, it was published as a book in Germany. In 2009, the Chinese version of *The Diaries of John Rabe* was published in Nanking. The book has been largely referred to in the above-mentioned part of this paper.

Secretary Dr. Lewis S.C. Smythe, an American, was a professor of sociology at Kinling (Nanking) University. During the Japanese occupation of Nanking, he and chairman John Rabe negotiated with the Japanese Embassy in China almost on a daily basis. In the spring of 1938, he conducted a survey in Nanking concerning the damage caused by the war. The Nanking International Relief Committee published the result of the survey in June of 1936 titled "*The Disaster of War in Nanking: From December 1937 to March 1938.*"

From August 29 to 30, 1946, Sutton, an American Assistant Prosecutor, read out in court a *LIST OF INTERNATIONAL COMMITTEES FOR THE SAFETY ZONE*, including ten files dating from December 16 in, 1937 to January 4 in 1938, included letters by Rabe, Smythe and another more than 20 foreign residents to the Japanese Embassy in Nanking, in which they severely condemned the Japanese atrocities in the Nanking Safety Zone.

Sutton also read out other written evidence, including *The Report of the Chief Prosecutor of the Nanking District Court*, *The 1938 Telegram from the U.S. Embassy in China*, *The Letter from John Moore Allison to the U.S. Ambassador, a communication from Trautmann to the German Foreign Office in Berlin marked "Strictly Confidential,"* and *The Transcripts of the Interrogation of the Defendants Iwane MATSUI and Akira MUTO*, and *The Testimony of 18 other prosecutors' Witnesses*. Among these witnesses were three American witnesses and 15 representatives of the Nanking residents who were victims.[35]

Some of the testimonies have been quoted earlier and thereby will not be enumerated one by one. I hereby quote the top-secret telegram sent by Trautmann, the German Ambassador to China in Hankow, Wuhan, on February 16, 1938, to the German Ministry of Foreign Affairs, in which Trautmann, as a diplomat of the Japanese Allies, reported on what happened in Nanking from December 8 in 1937 to January 13 in 1938:

> *The picture of the city has changed completely under Japanese rule. No day goes by without new cases of arson. It is now the turn of the Taiping Lou, the Chung Shan Tung Lou, Go Fu Lou, and KioKian Lou. The entire southern part of the city and Fudse Miave are completely burned and plundered down. Expressed in percentages, one could say that 30 to 40 percent of the city has been burned down. Although no shot was ever fired on the Japanese by the Chinese in the city, the Japanese shot dead at least 5,000 men. Among the people who were shot were harmless workers of the city administration, electrical undertaking, and the waterworks. Another sad chapter is the maltreatment and violation of many girls and women. Unnecessary barbarities and mutilations, even on small children, are not uncommon.*

The top-secret telegram also showed that even the German diplomat did not tolerate the atrocities committed by the Japanese army. He concluded: "*It is not a single soldier who is undisciplined and committing a brutal crime; it is the entire Japanese army that committed the atrocities.*"[36]

## *"Brotherhood"—A Fallacy by MATSUI*

Despite the irrefutable proof of the atrocities committed by the Japanese troops in "the Nanking Massacre," as the Anglo-American legal system requires, the tribunal still granted the defendants and their lawyers the opportunity for self-justification and evidence presentation.

From May 2, 1947, to October 22, 1947, 17 defense witnesses were called to the stand successively. They were: Liaison Officer between the Japanese Navy and Army, AOKI Takeshi, Commander of the Japanese 2nd combined Naval air corps, MITSUNAMI Teizo, Councilor of the Japanese Embassy in China, HIDAKA Shinrokuro, Chief of the Judicial Department of Shanghai Expeditionary Force, TSUKAMOTO Hirotsugu, Staff Officer of the Central China Area Army, NAKAYAMA Yasuto, Battalion Commander of the 13th Field Heavy Artillery Regiment, OBATA Minoru, Director of the Bureau of East-Asiatic Affairs of the Foreign Office, ISHII Itaro, Lord Keeper of the Privy Seal of Japan and also one of the defendants, KIDO Koichi, Leader of the observation section of the artillery regiment of the third division, OSUGI Hiroshi, Chief of Staff of the 16th Division, NAKASAWA Mitsuo, Acting Commander of the 7th Battery of the 9th Mountain Artillery Regiment of the 9th Division in the Shanghai Expeditionary Force, OUCHI Yoshihide, Commander of the 36th Regiment of the 9th Division, WAKISAKA Jiro, Battalion Commander of the 1st Battalion of the 19th Infantry Regiment, NISHIJIMA Takeshi, Chief of Staff of the Shanghai Expeditionary Force, IINUMA Mamoru, Chief of Legal Affairs Section of the 10th Army, OGAWA Sekijiro, Staff Officer of the Expeditionary Force to Shanghai, SAKAKIBARA Kazue, non-regular official attached to MATSUI's headquarters, OKADA Takashi.

All these witnesses were Japanese officers, except Kido and OKADA. Their testimony was nothing more than the claim that they had not seen any violence or was simply attempting to exonerate MATSUI Iwane, which had no effect on dismissing the prosecution's evidence.

Some witnesses even concealed the truth deliberately. For example, IINUMA Mamoru mentioned in his diary many times that MATSUI Iwane was the advocate of the advance of Nanking. When Japan was forming the Shanghai Expeditionary Force after the Shanghai Incident, MATSUI, as the Commander, said: *"We must resolve to order troops into action as needed based on our traditional spirit of 'instant engagement, instant victory' by shifting our main forces from northern China to Nanking," "We should capture Nanking in a short time."* However, IINUMA Mamoru spoke none of that when he appeared before the tribunal.

The two defendants, MUTO Akira and MATSUI Iwane, also defended themselves.

On November 13, 1947, American lawyer Roger F. Cole read MUTO Akira's self-justification statement. In this brief affidavit, he began with the vindication for MATSUI Iwane by stating that he gave orders to strictly maintain military discipline and morale. Meanwhile, he tried to clear his own name by implying that he had no power to make a decision at all, serving as the Assistant Chief of Staff of the Central China Area Army. MUTO's self-justification had played its part to a certain degree. Working together with other exhibits, MUTO was sentenced to hang by the International Military Tribunal for the Far East, yet the responsibility for "the Nanking Massacre" was exempted from his charges.

It was stated in *the Judgement* that: "*MUTO was an officer on the staff of MATSUI from November 1937 to July 1938. It was during this period that shocking atrocities were committed by the Army of MATSUI in and about Nanking...MUTO, in his subordinate position, could take no steps to stop them. MUTO is not responsible for this dreadful affair.*" However, during his tenure as Chief of staff to Yamashita Tomoyuki in the Philippines, the Japanese troops later waged continuous massacre, torture, and murder of the civilian population. It was concluded in the Judgement that: "*MUTO shares responsibility for these gross breaches of the Laws of War.*"[37] He was sentenced to death for these Counts.

Unlike MUTO Akira, MATSUI Iwane had a much longer affidavit, which took the American defense lawyer Floyd Mattice half a day to read on November 24, 1947.

The priority of MATSUI's affidavit is to put the blame on the Chinese:

> *Before their retreat, the Chinese troops adopted the so-called "scorched earth tactics" and either destroyed or burnt main transportation facilities and buildings. Some of them changed their uniforms to plain clothes and turned into guerrillas, sniping at our soldiers and threatening our rear. The local people also cooperated with their troops by cutting telegraph wires or arranging signal fires, jeopardizing our troops to no end. However, it is a well-known fact that, in wartime, the Chinese troops and some outlaws almost always commit acts of violence and looting by taking advantage of the confusion.*

Then he tried to shirk his responsibilities as the Supreme Commander:

> *It is possible that a great number of Chinese soldiers and civilians were killed or wounded by bombs, artillery shells, and rifle bullets during the Nanking campaign, but I do believe that there is not a bit of truth in the prosecution's charge that there were cases of a planned massacre in the fight of Nanking. Nothing can be farther from the truth than the slander that the staff of the Japanese Army ordered or tolerated the above deeds...I was sick in bed at Suchow when Nanking was captured; I stayed only five days in Nanking before leaving the city; as the Commander of the Central China Area Army, I had no direct authority over the officers and men in the field.*

What's more preposterous is that MATSUI constructed the "brotherhood" argument:

> *I was always firm in the belief that the strife between Japan and China was a quarrel between brothers in the so-called "household of Asia" and that it was unavoidable expedience for Japan to rescue by forcing the Japanese residents in China and to protect our endangered rights and interests. It was no different from an elder brother thrashing his young and recalcitrant brother after putting up with him for so long.*[38]

From the afternoon of November 24 to 25, Canadian prosecutor Brigadier Nolan cross-examined MATSUI. MATSUI had a weak case and could not justify himself, so he frequently resorted to answers like *"no," "I had heard rumors," "I don't recall the exact date," and "I know nothing at all about that"* to prevaricate.

## *Lessons for All*

Thanks to the efforts of Chinese prosecutors and American counterparts, the horrific atrocities of The Rape of Nanking by the Japanese Army were revealed to the public and shocked the world. 37 pieces of evidence from the prosecution and 23 pieces of evidence from the defense were accepted by the tribunal. On this basis, the section entitled *The Rape of Nanking* in Chapter 8 *Conventional War Crimes* of the *Judgment,* is nine pages long, describing the atrocities of the Japanese Army in detail. The excerpts are as follows:

> *When Nanking fell on December 13, 1937, all resistance by Chinese forces within the city entirely ceased. After the Japanese soldiers, under the command of General MATSUI, were in complete control of the city an orgy of violence and crime by the soldiers began and continued for more than six weeks. Among the offenses committed by the Japanese troops were (1) murder and massacre, (2) torture, (3) rape, and (4) robbery, looting, and wanton destruction of property.*
>
> *Small bands of two or three or more Japanese soldiers roamed at will the entire city. It was the killing, raping, and looting of these soldiers that perpetrated the worst of the terrors on the city.*
>
> *At least 12,000 civilian men, women, and children were killed by the Japanese soldiers in Nanking during the first few days after its fall on the ground that they had formerly been soldiers.*

> *In the month following the fall of Nanking, not less than 20,000 women and girls had been raped by Japanese soldiers. It was later estimated that more than 200,000 civilians and prisoners were massacred in and around Nanking during the first six weeks of Japanese occupation.*[39]

The Court reached a verdict that MATSUI Iwane, the commander of the Japanese Army in The Rape of Nanking, could hardly absolve himself from the blame. The verdict in the *Judgment* was as follows:

> *Before the fall of Nanking, the Chinese forces withdrew, and the occupation was of a defenseless city. Then followed a long succession of most horrible atrocities committed by the Japanese Army upon the helpless citizens. Although the extent of the atrocities was denied by Japanese witnesses, the contrary evidence of neutral witnesses of different nationalities and undoubted responsibility is overwhelming. In this period of six or seven weeks, thousands of women were raped, upwards of 100,000 people were killed, and the untold property was stolen and burned. At the height of these dreadful happenings, on December 17, MATSUI made a triumphal entry into the city and remained there for five to seven days. The Tribunal is satisfied that MATSUI knew what was happening. He did nothing, or nothing effective, to abate these horrors. He must be held criminally responsible for his failure to discharge this duty.*

The Tribunal holds the accused MATSUI guilty under Count 55 and death by hanging.[40]

Another defendant involved in The Rape of Nanking was HIROTA Koki, the verdict in the Judgment was as follows:

> *As to Count 55, the only evidence relating him to such crimes deals with the atrocities at Nanking in December 1937 and January and February 1938. As Foreign Minister, he received reports of these atrocities immediately after the entry of the Japanese forces into Nanking. After these assurances had been given reports of atrocities continued to come in for at least a month. HIROTA was derelict in his duty in not insisting before the Cabinet that immediate action be taken to put an end to the atrocities, failing any other action open to him to bring about the same result. He was content to rely on assurances that he knew were not being*

*implemented while hundreds of murders, violations of women, and other atrocities were being committed daily. His inaction amounted to criminal negligence.*

The Tribunal finds HIROTA guilty under Count 1, 27, and 55 and death by hanging.[41]

The prosecution and trial by the International Military Tribunal for the Far East of the atrocities committed by the Japanese Army in Nanking was not only a just trial, redressing the grievances of hundreds of thousands of victims, but also a truly international trial, a trial that followed the principles of civilization and legal principles. The victims and witnesses included Chinese residents, foreign residents, and diplomats. Besides the prosecution, the defense and judges who participated in the trial were of different nationalities. These archives in black and white, as well as the trial in international form, enabled the Tokyo Trial to write the atrocities of the Japanese militarists on the scroll of human history based on ironclad facts, which could never be altered and erased.

However, some Japanese scholars shut their eyes to the historical facts; they even believed that The Rape of Nanking was an invention. For example, YOSHIMOTO Ei, the author of *Smash the Fiction of The Rape of Nanking*; FUJI Nobuo, the author of *How the Rape of Nanking Was Made Up: The Deception of the Tokyo Trial*; TANAKA Masaaki, the author of *The Fiction of The Rape of Nanking*; MATSUMURA Toshio, the author of *The Great Questions about The Rape of Nanking*, etc. If these could be tolerated, what cannot?

In fact, the Chinese government and scholars have never stopped their follow-up investigations and academic research on The Rape of Nanking. In the 1980s, many salvage investigations were conducted in Nanking. In 1984, 1,756 survivors were investigated in six urban districts and four suburban counties of Nanking. During the summer holiday of 1991, the Memorial Hall of the Victims in The Rape of Nanking by Japanese Invaders and Nanking Education Bureau organized high school students to visit these survivors, finding out that more than 1,300 of them were still alive. In 1997, 14,000 college students and high school students surveyed 5.2 million people in 15 districts and counties of Nanking, finding that there were still 1,213 survivors and systematically sorting out the exhibits and oral materials of survivors. By December 2017, there were still 100 survivors.

Scholars in Nanking have done a lot of work in excavating, sorting, editing, and publishing the documentary materials of The Rape of Nanking, including

*Collection of Historical Materials on The Rape of Nanking* (72 volumes, Jiangsu People's Publishing House, 2005–2011), *The History of the Rape of Nanking* (Nanking University Press, 2014), *Selected Historical Documents of the Rape of Nanking* (Jiangsu People's Publishing House, 2014), *Selected Documents and Evidence of The Rape of Nanking* (Phoenix Press, 2014) edited by ZHANG Xianwen, *Series of Books on the Studies and Documents of the Rape of Nanking* (31 volumes, Nanking Press, 2007–2014) edited by ZHU Chengshan, *Human Memory: the Solid Evidence of the Rape of Nanking* (2 volumes, People's Publishing House, 2016) co-edited by ZHANG Xianwen and ZHANG Jianjun, etc. Many archival materials in this chapter are quoted from the literature mentioned above.

In the late 20th century, overseas scholars gradually paid attention to The Rape of Nanking. In 1997, Iris CHANG, a young Chinese American scholar, wrote a monograph, *The Rape of Nanking: The Forgotten Holocaust of World War II in English*, which shocked western mainstream media and ordinary people. Soon, it was reprinted ten times and was named the most popular book of the year by The New York Times. In 2014, the translation of the book was published[42].

CHENG Hung, a professor of applied mathematics at Massachusetts Institute of Technology in the U. S. and British writer David Michael Davies wrote *Nanjing Never Cries,*[43] and *The Storm Flower, Nanjing, 1937*[44], respectively: both novels about Nanking Massacre. Professor CHENG wrote a poem at the end of the book to express his strong feeling about the Rape of Nanking. Davis also said, "*It's a good way to manifest this part of the history in the form of novels so that people all over the world will realize that Nanjing Massacre is not only the trauma of the people in Nanking or that of the city. It is not only the historical memory of the Chinese people but also the record of the bloody disgrace of mankind. All human beings are supposed to remember and reflect upon it.*"

On October 9, 2015, UNESCO announced that the 12th Conference of the International Advisory Committee of its Memory of the World Program decided to inscribe *Documents of the Rape of Nanking* on its *Memory of the World Register*. So far, *Documents of the Rape of Nanking,* together with *Witness Archives of the Jerusalem Massacre, Diaries of Anne Frank,* and *Warsaw Ghetto Archives,* have become the universal memory of the people of the world of the Fascist violence committed by Germany and Japan during WWII.

The 80th anniversary of the Rape of Nanking was in 2017. Chinese scholar and professor Cheng Zhaoqi's monograph *Research on the Rape of Nanking—Refuting the Japanese Fabrication School* was published. The book was based on historical materials, including the battle logs and diaries of MATSUI Iwane and other Japanese officers. It refutes the lies of the Japanese right-wing one by one. The arguments of the book have been cited in this chapter. Now we'll quote one more research finding mentioned in the book. OGAWA Sekijiro, who was appointed Chief of Legal Affairs Section of the 10th Army gave testimonies at the Tokyo Court on November 7, 1947, in which he said, "*On 4 January 1938, when I met General MATSUI at the Headquarters in Shanghai, the General said laying much stress, 'Judgment of crimes shall be fair and strict.' I faithfully followed his advice and discharged my duties very strictly.*" Time, place, and people are so accurate that the procuratorate can hardly question its credibility. However, Cheng Zhaoqi found in OGAWA's diary that he wasn't in Shanghai on January 4. Instead, he was in discussion with Lieutenant General Yanagawa Heisuke, Commander of the 10th Japanese Army in Hangchow, and attended a farewell party there. He didn't leave Hangchow for Shanghai until January 7 and met MATSUI Iwane in Shanghai on January 15. Cheng Zhaoqi also pointed out, "*The diary of the January 15 recorded in detail the meeting with Iwane MATSUI. Iwane MATSUI vehemently talked about policies and strategies toward China, how to overthrow the regime of Chiang Kai-shek, how to establish a pro-Japan regime, and how to achieve the century-long plan of immigrating large numbers of Japanese to China, and so on. They didn't mention anything about the discipline of the army,*" which clearly indicates that OGAWA had been making false testimonies in court.[45]

On February 27, 2014, the 7th session of the Standing Committee of the 12th National People's Congress of the People's Republic of China made the following decision: December 13 will be designated as the National Memorial Day for Nanjing Massacre Victims. On December 13 that year, the first National Memorial Day ceremony was held in the Memorial Hall for the Victims of the Nanjing Massacre by Japanese Invaders. President XI Jinping was present at the ceremony and delivered an important speech in which he said:

> *The Japanese invaders occupied Nanking on December 13, 1937. They committed the atrocious Nanking Massacre, in which more than 300,000 Chinese were killed, countless women were raped, and numerous children died a violent death. One-third of the buildings were destroyed, and lots of property was pillaged. The inhuman massacre committed by the Japanese invaders is one of the Three Great Atrocities in the history of WWII. It is an appalling anti-human crime and a dark chapter in human history.*

*Both The International Military Tribunal for the Far East and the Chinese Military Tribunal for war criminals have conducted investigations into the Nanking Massacre, determined its nature, and made their final conclusions about it in a legal aspect. A band of Japanese war criminals whose hands were stained with Chinese people's blood was sentenced and punished severely by law and justice. They are forever nailed on the Post of Disgrace in history.*

*We hold the Memorial Ceremony for the Nanking Massacre Victims to arouse the yearning and persistence of peace in the heart of every kind person instead of continuing hatred. The Japanese and Chinese people should be friendly to each other throughout the generations, take history as a constant mirror and make contributions to world peace together.*[46]

On December 13, 2017, President XI Jinping attended the ceremony of the National Memorial Day for Nanking Massacre Victims. After the ceremony, he met with some of the Nanking Massacre survivors, among whom is the 89-year-old HSIA Shu-chin, and representatives of the relatives of international friends such as the son of Wilson and grandson of Rabe. According to XI Jinping, history must be true for its beauty or disasters. We need to polish the mirror of history, wipe off the dust, take history as a mirror and steadily walk towards the future.

## *References*

[1] Zhang, Xianwen, Zhang Lianhong, and Wang Weixing. 2014. *The History of Nanking Massacre*. Nanjing University Press, 39.

[2] Cheng, Zhaoqi. 2017. *Research on the Rape of Nanking—Refuting the Japanese Fabrication School.* Shanghai Jiao Tong University Press, 89–90.

[3] Zhang, Xianwen, Zhang Lianhong, and Wang Weixing. 2014. *The History of Nanking Massacre*. Nanjing University Press, 319, 387, 402–405.

[4] Zhang, Xianwen, Cui Wei, and Dong Weimin. 2014. *Selected Documents and Evidence of the Rape of Nanking*. Phoenix Press, 99–104.

[5] Zhang, Xianwen, Zhang Lianhong, and Wang Weixing. 2014. *The History of Nanking Massacre*. Nanjing University Press, 45–46.

[6] Ibid., 93–94.

[7] Ibid.

[8] Ibid., 100–101

[9] Rabe, Johan. 2009. *Rabe's Diary*. Translated by Translation Team of this book. Jiangsu People's Publishing House; Jiangsu Education Press, 295.

[10] Ibid., 397.

[11] Zhang, Xianwen, and Lv Jing. *Selected Historical Documents of the Rape of Nanking*. Jiangsu People's Publishing House, 103.

[12] Zhang, Xianwen, Cui Wei, and Dong Weimin. 2014. *Selected Documents and Evidence of the Rape of Nanking*. Phoenix Press, 49.

[13] HIGA, Shiro. 1999. *The Diary of HIGA Shiro*. Translated by Zhang Guoren and Wang Ping. Jiangsu Education Press.

[14] Zhang, Xianwen, and Zhang Jianjun. 2016. *Human Memory One: The Solid Evidence of the Rape of Nanking (China & Japan)*. People's Publishing House, 56–57.

[15] Zhang, Xianwen, Cui Wei, and Dong Weimin. 2014. *Selected Documents and Evidence of the Rape of Nanking*. Phoenix Press, 327.

[16] Sun, Zhaiwei. 2005. *Corpses Processed in Nanking Massacre*. Bok. 5 of *Collection of Historical Materials on the Rape of Nanking*. Jiangsu People's Publishing House; Phoenix Press, 337–348.

[17] Rabe, Johan. 2009. *Rabe's Diary*. Translated by Translation Team of this book. Jiangsu People's Publishing House; Jiangsu Education Press, 156.

[18] Zhang, Xianwen, Zhang Lianhong, and Wang Weixing. 2014. *The History of Nanking Massacre*. Nanjing University Press, 132.

[19] Zhang, Xianwen, and Lv Jing. *Selected Historical Documents of the Rape of Nanking*. Jiangsu People's Publishing House, 566.

[20] Rabe Johan. 2009. *Rabe's Diary*. Translated by Translation Team of this book. Jiangsu People's Publishing House; Jiangsu Education Press, 425.

[21] Zhang, Xianwen, Zhang Lianhong, and Wang Weixing. 2014. *The History of Nanking Massacre*. Nanjing University Press, 191–199.

[22] Ibid., 199–204.

[23] Ibid., 204–207.

[24] Mei, Xiao-ao, and Mei Xiaokan. 2013. *The Tokyo Trial Manuscript of MEI Ju-ao*. Shanghai Jiao Tong University, 405.

[25] "The Nanking Massacre Story." *The Chicago Daily News*, December 15, 1937.

[26] "The Fall of Nanking, the Massacre." *The New York Times*, December 18, 1937.

[27] Zhu, Chengshan. 2004. *Series of Books on the Studies and Documents of the Rape of Nanking*. Nanjing University Press.

[28] File No. 172-1-0899. Ministry of Foreign Affairs of the National Government, 28–32.

[29] Cheng, Zhaoqi, and Xiang Longwan. 2017. *Transcripts of the Proceedings of the International Military Tribunal for the Far East (Chinese version)*. Vol. 2. Shanghai Jiao Tong University Press, 505–510 (2527–2541 of the English court records).

[30] Ibid., Vol. 3, 11–14 (2561–2570 of the English court records).

[31] Ibid., 25–30 (2598–2610 of the English court records).

[32] Ibid., 42–48 (2634–2651) of the English court records).

[33] Ibid., 340–342 (3369–3374 of the English court records).

[34] Ibid., Vol. 4, 55–59 (3893–3905 of the English court records).

[35] Ibid., 307–373 (4458–4604 of the English court records).

[36] Ibid., 370–373 (4597–4604 of the English court records).

[37] *The Judgment of the International Military Tribunal for the Far East.* Translated by Zhang Xiaolin, retranslated by Xiang Longwan and Xu Xiaobing (2015). Shanghai Jiao Tong University Press, 607–608, 623 (49820–49821, 49856 of the English court records).

[38] Tokyo Trial Literature Committee. 2013. *Transcripts of the Proceedings of the International Military Tribunal for the Far East (English version).* National Library of China Publishing House; Shanghai Jiao Tong University Press, 344–377 (33784–33881 of the English court records).

[39] *The Judgment of the International Military Tribunal for the Far East.* Translated by Zhang Xiaolin, retranslated by Xiang Longwan and Xu Xiaobing (2015). Shanghai Jiao Tong University Press, 510–514 (49604–49612 of the English court records).

[40] Ibid., 604–606, 623 (49814–49817, 49856 of the English court records).

[41] Ibid., 595–596, 622 (49791, 49855 of the English court records).

[42] Chang, Iris. 1997. *The Rape of Nanking—The Forgotten Holocaust of World War II.* Translated by Yang Xiaming (2004). Oriental Press.

[43] Cheng, Hong. 2016. *Nanjing Never Cries.* MIT Press.

[44] Davies, David Michael. 2018. *Nanjing 1937.* Jiangsu Phoenix Literature and Art Publishing.

[45] Cheng, Zhaoqi. 2017. *Research on the Rape of Nanking—Refuting the Japanese Fabrication School.* Shanghai Jiao Tong University Press, 239–246.

[46] *People's Daily*, December 14, 2014.

CHAPTER II

# Historical Legacy

## *Court Debate*

During the Tokyo Trial, the Chinese prosecuting team left a large number of written records that serve as historical evidence of their adhering to legal principles. In addition to *the Indictment* written jointly with colleagues of the International Prosecution Section, their most direct work that should be known to the world is the prosecution, direct examination, cross-examination, and debate in the court. From the trial records of the International Military Tribunal for the Far East, the dates, themes, and pages of the Court speech by the Chinese prosecutor team are listed in the following table:

| Year | Month | Date | Present in court | Theme | Volume | Pages in English |
|---|---|---|---|---|---|---|
| 1946 | 5 | 14 | HSIANG Che-chun | The supplemental plea to the jurisdiction; a refutation of the defense lawyer YAMAOKA's viewpoint that before Japan's declaration of War against China, there was peace between the two countries; Japanese leaders misled the Japanese people, fooled them, and destroyed them. | 1 | 272–277/6 |
| | 7 | 22 | HSIANG Che-chun | Views on providing Chinese translation; a refutation of the defense motion that General Cramer is ineligible to sit as a Member of this Tribunal. | 4 | 2350–351/3 |
| | 8 | 15 | HSIANG Che-chun | Opening statement in respect of atrocities against civilians and others and use of opium and other narcotics in China. | | 3885–3892/8 |
| | | 26 | HSIANG Che-chun | Remarks and suggestions of the translations provided by the Court. | | 4299–4302/4 |
| | | 27 | HSIANG Che-chun | Objection to FUJII Goichiro's cross-examination on Henry PU Yi; reading evidence of abduction of the dethroned Emperor Hsuen Tung to Northeast China. | | 4324–4326; 4360–4369/10 |
| | | 28 | Henry CHIU | Direct examination on TUNG Shu-ming about the Japanese economic plunder | 8 | 4423–4442/20 |

*(Continued)*

| Year | Month | Date | Present in court | Theme | Volume | Pages in English |
|---|---|---|---|---|---|---|
| 1947 | 1 | 17 | HSIANG Che-chun | Reading a report by Professor Chang Feng-chu, handwriting expert, on the Study of Pu Yi's handwriting. | 26 | 15543–15554/12 |
| | | 20 | HSIANG Che-chun | Reading an affidavit by Professor Chang Feng-chu, a handwriting expert. | | 15707–15712/6 |
| | 2 | 27 | HSIANG Che-chun | Objection to the admission of the document concerning the so-called treaty of 1915 between China and Japan. | 29 | 17432/1 |
| | 4 | 23 | NYI, Judson T.Y. | Cross-examination on defendant HASHIMOTO Kingoro. | 34 | 20637–20667/31 |
| | | 28 | NYI, Judson T.Y. | Cross-examination on defendant FURUYAMA Katsuo. | | 20945–20959/15 |
| | 5 | 1 | NYI, Judson T.Y. | Cross-examination on defendant OKAMOTO Toshio | 35 | 21200–21241/42 |
| | 5 | 7 | HSIANG Che-chun | No cross-examination on MATSUDA Kanetoshi. | | 21634/1 |
| | | 8 | HSIANG Che-chun | Views on the written evidence of three prosecution witnesses. | 36 | 21804–21807/4 |
| | 6 | 11 | NYI, Judson T.Y. | Cross-examination on defendant KAGESA Sadaaki (read by HSIANG Che-chun). | 39 | 24007–24149/143 |
| | | | HSIANG Che-chun | Reading the confidential telegram of Wang Ching-wei's removal plan by Japan. | | 24151–24162/12 |

*(Continued)*

| Year | Month | Date | Present in court | Theme | Volume | Pages in English |
|---|---|---|---|---|---|---|
| | 9 | 16 | NYI, Judson T.Y. | Cross-examination on AIZAWA Makoto. | 46 | 28607–28608/2 |
| | | 17 | NYI, Judson T.Y. | Ibid. | 47 | 28609–28626/18 |
| | | | HSIANG Che-chun | No cross-examination on HATTORI Takushiro. | | 28709/1 |
| | | 18 | NYI, Judson T.Y. | No cross-examination on KAWABE Torashiro; asking about the reasons why DOIHARA received a decoration from Germany. | | 28747–28749/3 |
| | | | HSIANG Che-chun | Cross-examination on defense witness TATSUMI Eiichi, interrogating DOIHARA's behavior in POW camp. | | 28755/1 |
| | 10 | 6 | HSIANG Che-chun | Refutation of pieces of evidence and witnesses for ITAGAKI Seishiro. | 49 | 30047–30071, 30144/26 |
| | | | NYI, Judson T.Y. | Cross-examination on defendants KOKUBUN Shinshichiro, FURUNO Inosuke, YAMAWAKI Masataka, MADOKORO Shintaro. | | 30078–30142/65 |
| | | | KWEI Yu | Submitting Prosecution evidence. | | 30144–30145/2 |
| | | 7 | KWEI Yu | No cross-examination on defendant Sawada Shigeru. | 50 | 30157/1 |
| | | | NYI, Judson T.Y. | Cross-examination of defendant ITAGAKI Seishiro. | | 30252/1 |

*(Continued)*

| Year | Month | Date | Present in court | Theme | Volume | Pages in English |
|---|---|---|---|---|---|---|
| | | | NYI, Judson T. Y. | Ibid. | 50 | 30338–30383/46 |
| | | | NYI, Judson T. Y. | Ibid. | | 30385–30459/75 |
| | | | NYI, Judson T. Y. | Ibid. | | 30461–30519/59 |
| 1948 | 1 | 13 | HSIANG Che-chun | Refutation of ITAGAKI Seishiro's defense with Japanese telegram. | 60 | 37306–37307/2 |
| | | 14 | HSIANG Che-chun | Reading several pieces of evidence for the Mukden Incident; debate with a defense lawyer about ITAGAKI Seishiro's crimes. | | 37311–37341/31 |
| | | | NYI, Judson T. Y. | Ibid. | | 37341–37401/61 |
| | | 15 | NYI, Judson T. Y. | Refutation of ITAGAKI Seishiro's lies with German diplomatic documents. | 61 | 37403–37412/10 |
| | 2 | 9 | NYI, Judson T. Y. | Cross-examination on defense witness UGAKI Kazushige | 63 | 38801–38833/33 |
| | | 11 | HSIANG Che-chun | Reading the prosecution's summation "*The Mukden Incident and its aftermath.*" | 63 | 39083–39111/29 |
| | | | KWEI Yu | Ibid. | | 39111–39120/10 |
| | | 12 | KWEI Yu | Reading the prosecution's summation "Japanese Domination of Manchuria." | | 39122–39135/14 |

*(Continued)*

| Year | Month | Date | Present in court | Theme | Volume | Pages in English |
|---|---|---|---|---|---|---|
| | | | NYI, Judson T.Y. | Ibid. | | 39135–39165/31 |
| | | | HSIANG Che-chun | Reading the prosecution's summation "Obtaining Control of North China Prior to July 1937" and "The War of Aggression against China 1937-1945." | | 39191–39218/28 |
| | | | NYI, Judson T.Y. | Reading the prosecution's summation "The Domination of China." | | 39278–39300/23 |
| | | 19 | NYI, Judson T.Y. | Reading the prosecution's summation on DOIHARA, Kenji. | 65 | 40617–40662/46 |
| | | 24 | HSIANG Che-chun | Reading the prosecution's summation on ITAGAKI Seishiro. | 66 | 40984–41024/41 |
| | 4 | 16 | HSIANG Che-chun | Reading the prosecution's reply to the defense summation on behalf of the accused DOIHARA. | 78 | 48215–48248/34 |

"Volume" here refers to the volume number in the book *Transcripts of the International Military Tribunal for the Far East* (jointly published in July 2013, by Shanghai Jiao Tong University Press and National Library Press); pages refer to the source pages in the English transcripts.

The table above shows that HSIANG Che-chun made 20 statements during the trial, covering nearly 300 pages; NYI, Judson T.Y, 18 statements, covering nearly 700 pages; KWEI Yu, four statements, covering 27 pages; Henry CHIU, one statement, covering 20 pages.

HSIANG Che-chun made his first statement on May 14, 1946, which was the beginning stage of the prosecution, and his last statement was made on April 16, 1948, the last day of the prosecution phase.

In the second chapter of this book, I quoted his first speech refuting the defense attorneys' fallacy that there was no war between China and Japan before the official declaration of war. In that speech, he made another important statement when the defense attorneys, at the beginning of the court sessions, had seized on the "jurisdiction of the court" to challenge the legitimacy of the trials themselves.

On May 13, 1946, KIYOSE Ichiro, deputy chief defense counsel, made a statement in court. He argued that the trials of "crimes against peace" and "crimes against humanity" had no precedents and thus were matters of the "ex post facto" justice. He also offered many other reasons in an attempt to deny the legitimacy of the Tokyo Trials. In order to rebut KIYOSE Ichiro's argument, the American Prosecutor Keenan and the British Prosecutor Comyns-Carr made lengthy statements one after another.

In his first speech, HSIANG Che-chun also made a solemn statement:

> *Up to now, in this proceeding, our learned counsels on the defense have first tried to question the jurisdiction of this Tribunal and also challenge the Members thereof. My associates on the prosecution have answered them on various points in addition to this. I would ask for the Court's permission to add a few observations of my own. This Tribunal was duly created by a general proclamation of the Supreme Commander for the Allied Powers in accordance with authority delegated to him by the Allied Powers, and the Members thereof, having been designated by their respective governments concerned, were appointed by the Supreme Commander under the Charter under which we are functioning. I submit that we are not making new laws as charged by members of the defense to the contrary. The Charter simply embodies law and the principles already in existence.*

In this same speech, HSIANG made a clear distinction between the Japanese people and their leaders:

> *Then I think the Chinese people had all along with the most friendly feelings toward the Japanese people. But we submit to the Court that their leaders misled them, fooled them, and destroyed them—ruined them. These leaders ought to be held responsible as a matter of justice, not only to the oppressed among the Chinese people, not only in the interest of world peace but also in the interest of the Japanese people. That is my submission.*[1]

It was admirable to have a broad and open mind like this at that time.

The vast majority of the court statements and debates of all members of the Chinese Prosecution Team were based on evidence, and they spoke for the prosecution or made refutations against the defendants in accordance with legal principles. There were very few emotional words. This book has quoted many of their statements on other occasions, which will not be repeated here.

## *Letters and Telegram Records*

The second way the team of Chinese prosecutors left their important records was through official letters and telegrams they sent back home during the Tokyo Trials. At present, 83 official letters and telegrams were sent by HSIANG Che-chun to the Chinese Ministry of Foreign Affairs and the Chinese Ministry of Justice and Administration. Among them, 28 were sent in 1946, 25 in 1947, and 30 in 1948.

The subjects and dates of these letters and telegrams are listed as follows:

**1946**

(1) [English Telegram] Reporting that Secretary Henry CHIU and he arrived in Tokyo and met with Chief Prosecutor Keenan (February 9).

(2) [English Telegram] Providing evidence for the loss caused by the Japanese invasion of China (February 1).

(3) [English Telegram] Request for evidence of atrocities committed by troops led by Matsui Iwane and HATA Shunroku and that of Japan's opium-related facts in our country (February 12).

(4) [English Telegram] The Indictment urgently needs the crimes committed by Japanese troops in China, Hong Kong, Singapore, Thailand, and other East Asian regions (February 21).

(5) [Telegram] Reporting that Chief Prosecutor Keenan would visit China and other parts of the Pacific area to investigate Japanese atrocities and collect evidence (March 8).

(6) [Telegram] Reporting having accompanied Keenan had been accompanied from Shanghai to Peiping (March 21).

(7) [Telegram] Reporting having accompanied Keenan to Chungking (March 23).

(8) [Telegram] Reporting having accompanied Keenan on a visit to Shanghai, Peiping, and Chungking, and paying a visit to Chairman Chiang Kai-shek in a few days (March 24).
(9) [Telegram] The date of establishment of the Inner Mongolia Autonomous Committee is required, and a report that Sutton is to come to Nanking and Shanghai to negotiate for witnesses, and the documents of the murder of YANG Kuang-sheng are required (June 7).
(10) [Telegram] American prosecutors Sutton and Colonel Morrow will meet with Vice Minister CHIN Teh-chun and WENG Wen-hao to negotiate how to testify in court (June 10).
(11) [Official Letter] English documents containing several conversations of Keenan's after he returned to China from Japan, and other prosecutors are quite dissatisfied with his excessive speeches (June 9).
(12) [Express Mail as Telegram] Reporting the gist of the Indictment by Chief Prosecutor Keenan and the statement of the British prosecutor (handwriting in pencil) (June 21).
(13) [Telegram] Notifying he has submitted to the Court the evidence of Japan's invasion of North China (July 4).
(14) [Official Letter] Reporting a total of 15 transcripts of the International Military Tribunal for the Far East from April 29 to June 21, 1946 (July 10).
(15) [Official Letter] Continuing to report the indictment gist stated by Chief Prosecutor Keenan, one in English and one in Japanese (July 10).
(16) [Telegram] Reporting the Vice Minister of CHIN Teh-chun to have testified in court four times with complete success (July 27).
(17) [Official letter] Proving that SHANG Teh-yi testified in court (July 29).
(18) [Telegram] Requesting the related documents of the massacre in Benxihu Coal Mine in July 1942 (August 5).
(19) [Telegram] Asking for the Chinese names of the seven Manila victims including YANG Kuang-sheng (August 14).
(20) [Telegram] Reporting Pu Yi's activities after he arrived in Tokyo (August 27).
(21) [Telegram] Reporting that Pu Yi has returned to the Soviet Union on September 6 (September 9).
(22) [Telegram] Report presenting exhibits of Japan's military, political, and economic aggression against China, their atrocities committed,

and Japan's opium-related facts in China to the International Military Tribunal for the Far East; summoning Chinese, American, British and Japanese witnesses from July 1 to September 10; reporting the case of Japan's invasion of China has come to an end, and it is urgent to select political and economic experts who are proficient in English laws and familiar with the situation between China and Japan to come to Japan to help (September 12).

(23) [Official Letter] Continuing to report another 49 transcripts of the trial of the International Military Tribunal for the Far East from June 24 to September 10, 1946 (September 15).

(24) [Official Letter] Continuing to report another 13 transcripts of the trial of the Far East International Military Tribunal from September 11 to September 27, 1946 (September 30).

(25) [Telegram] Requesting experts who are proficient in law, English and China-Japan situations to Japan to help (October 3).

(26) [Official Letter] Reporting 29 trial transcripts of the International Military Tribunal for the Far East from September 30 to November 7 (November 8).

(27) [Official Letter] Reporting 15 trial transcripts of the International Military Tribunal for the Far East from November 8 to December 2 (December 3).

(28) [Official Letter] Reporting 14 trial transcripts of the International Military Tribunal for the Far East from December 3 to December 20, 1946 (December 28).

1947

(29) [Telegram] Reporting to postpone sending assistants (January 6).

(30) [Official Letter] Reporting that OKAWA Syumei was mentally ill and stopped appearing in court, MATSUOKA Yosuke and NAGANO Osami died of illness, and 25 others including TOJO Hideki were tried in court (January 7).

(31) [Official Letter] Reporting that the defense lawyers might take measures related to China in their extensive defense arguments, and hoped that China would weigh them properly and make preparations (January 10).

(32) [Telegram] Reporting that the court will adjourn for two weeks, and hoping the four consultants, including NYI, Judson T.Y., would rush to Japan for the new session (January 24).
(33) [Official Letter] Reporting 19 trial transcripts of the International Military Tribunal for the Far East from December 23, 1946 to January 20, 1947 (January 31).
(34) [Telegram] Reporting the Prosecution's evidence has all been submitted, and the four consultants NYI, AO, Wu, and KWEI are on the way to Japan (January 31).
(35) [Telegram] Reporting the trial will be adjourned for three weeks (February 10).
(36) [Telegram] Reporting the arrival of NYI, AO, Wu, and KWEI in Japan (February 10).
(37) [Telegram] Reporting the defense of the defendant who invaded Northeast China started this afternoon, and MATSUI Iwane was taken to hospital for treatment (March 18).
(38) [Telegram] Reporting Secretary Henry CHIU resigned due to illness, expecting to allow KAW V. P. to succeed him (April 3).
(39) [Telegram] Reporting that the war criminal OKAWA Syumei has not recovered from mental illness, and his trial comes to termination according to the law (April 10).
(40) [Official Letter] The trial procedure of reporting war criminal OKAWA Syumei has been decided to be terminated (April 10).
(41) [Telegram] Reporting that the defendant's defense about Northeast China was finished this morning, and about other parts of China started today (April 24).
(42) [Telegram] Requesting SHANG Chen in his special plane to bring the record of the negotiation for ceasefire in Shanghai (May 2).
(43) [Telegram] Appealing to Minister HSIEH Kuan-sheng for postponing NYI's return to Nanking (May 7).
(44) [Official Letter] Reporting 55 trial transcripts of the International Military Tribunal for the Far East from January 21 to May 5, 1947 (May 14).
(45) [Telegram] Reporting that the important task of NYI, Judson T.Y.'s will be completed in a few days, and he may return home for the first time at the end of the month (May 27).

(46) [Telegraph] Report that NYI, Judson T.Y. returned home for the first time. NYI has achieved excellent results, and still hopes that he will shoulder the heavy responsibilities in the Tokyo Trial (June 2).

(47) [Telegram] The "Changkufeng Incident" between the Soviet Union and Japan must resort to *The Protocol between China and Russia* in 1886 for verification (June 13).

(48) [Official Letter] Submitting the witness Shimizu's testimony in English and Japanese (handwritten with ink) (June 13).

(49) [Telegram] Reporting the witness Shimizu's statement in court (June 13).

(50) [Telegram] Reporting that the defense lawyer has requested a six-week recess, and plan to return to China to report on his work at the end of the month and continue to collect necessary evidence (June 20).

(51) [Official Letter] Reporting 31 trial transcripts of the International Military Tribunal for the Far East from May 6 to June 19, 1947 (June 21).

(52) [Telegram] Reporting the court session today, its contents and attendees (August 4).

(53) [Official Letter] Reporting the general work of the International Prosecution Section since its establishment (October 2).

**1948**

(54) [Letter] Following Keenan's suggestion to release a list of the second batch of suspects and ask the government's attitude (handwriting by pen) (January 7).

(55) [Telegram] Asking whether to extradite the 20 Japanese Class A War Crimes suspects, including NISHIO Toshizo, who were recommended for release by Keenan (January 19).

(56) [Telegram] Reporting that the article in *Mainland Evening News*, *Shanghai Evening Post and Mercury*, and *North-China Daily News* in Shanghai from the report by the Central News Agency in Tokyo on the 9th is inconsistent with the facts (January 22).

(57) [Telegram] Reporting to the Central News Agency to investigate the truth and ask for correction, that is, requesting assistance for a thorough investigation (January 23).

(58) [Telegram] Reporting that the Central News Agency reporter Li Chia admitted that the news he sent had not been interviewed by the procuration Section beforehand, and the content was false, and he apologized on the spot (January 23).
(59) [Official Letter] reporting that the article on January 10 by *Shanghai Evening Post and Mercury* from the January 9 news of the Tokyo Telegram is absolutely inconsistent with the facts, and expecting thorough investigation for verification (January 24).
(60) [Official Letter] Reporting the trial progress since January 12 for future reference (February 4).
(61) [Telegram] (Illegible handwriting) (February 10).
(62) [Telegram] Reporting that the phase of individual prosecution of each defendant began, and NYI serves for the argument about DOIHARA (February 19).
(63) [Telegram] Reporting that the summation of the personal crimes of the four defendants, namely, HATA Shunroku, HIRANUMA Kiichiro, HIROTA Koki, and HOSHINO Naoki, has been submitted one after another, and the report on ITAGAKI Seishiro was submitted today by HSIANG Che-chun (February 24).
(64) [Telegram] Reporting that the summation of the individual crimes of the five defendants, OKA Takasumi, OSHIMA Hiroshi, SATO Kenryo, SHIGEMITSU Mamoru, and SHIMADA Shigetaro, was submitted two days ago (February 24).
(65) [Telegram] Reporting that the summation of the personal crimes of the seven defendants, namely KAYA, KIDO, KIMURA, KOISO, MATSUI, MINAMI Jiro, and MUTO, has been submitted successively (February 26).
(66) [Telegram] Reporting that the summation of the International Prosecution Section on each defendant's personal crimes was completed on March 2, and the comprehensive defense of the defendant began on the same day. The prosecution actively discussed countermeasures and prepared to deal with them (March 3).
(67) [Official Letter] Reporting that the United States and the Soviet Union have different opinions on the reasons for the defendant's defense, and our compromise proposal was supported by Britain. It was agreed that

the prosecutors of each unit would meticulously study the defendant's pleadings. Presenting the current trial status for verification (March 4).

(68) [Telegram] Reporting that the defendant's debate has been completed, and the prosecution will start a brief debate today, which can be completed in two or three days (April 16).

(69) [Telegram] Reporting that the prosecution's cross-examination of TOJO and other war criminals has ended this afternoon. This morning, HSIANG Che-chun emphatically pointed out the main facts and sternly refuted the key war criminals who invaded China, such as DOIHARA and ITAGAKI. The cross-examination, in this case, has ended, and President announced in court that sentences would be pronounced on a future date (April 16).

(70) [Official Letter] Submitting two comprehensive defense statements of the prosecution and two final defense statements (April 20).

(71) [Telegram] Reporting to return to China to report on his work during the adjournment of the court for the verdict, and NYI, Judson T.Y. will handle the work in my absence (April 25).

(72) [Telegram] Reporting that prosecutors who do not need to stay in Japan are going through the departure formalities (June 26).

(73) [Telegram] Recommending NYI, Judson T.Y. as a judge to participate in the trial of major criminals such as NISHIO Toshizo and TADA Hayao by the GHO's Legal Section (July 3).

(74) [Express Mail as Telegram] Continuing with another three opinions on the case of the main war crime suspect, NISHIO Toshizo and others (handwritten in ink) (July 16).

(75) [Telegram] Reporting to return to China on August 14 (July 29).

(76) [Telegram] Reporting that on 14, together with Secretary KAW Vung-ping, he returned to Shanghai and transferred to Peiping by passenger ship *General Maggie* (August 14).

(77) [Letter] Thanking Director Huang Cheng-ming of the Ministry of Foreign Affairs for his thorough guidance, and hoping to forward the report to the Minister (handwriting in ink) (September 14).

(78) [Official Letter] Submit copies of all trial transcripts and documents of the International Military Tribunal for the Far East from prosecution to the end of cross-examination (October 20).

(79) [Telegram] Report the opening of the International Military Tribunal for the Far East today and the attendees (November 4).
(80) [Express Mail as Telegram] Stating that there are many errors in domestic newspapers' records about the trial of war criminals in the International Military Tribunal for the Far East (written in pen) (November 10).
(81) [Letter] Reporting the judgments pronounced by President Webb since November 4. It is speculated with Chief Counsel NYI that most of the defendants such as DOIHARA, ITAGAKI, MATSUI, and TOJO are expected to be sentenced to death, and as many as fourteen or fifteen defendants may be executed (handwritten in ink) (November 10).
(82) [Telegram] Pointing out that there is much misinformation about the Tokyo Trial in Shanghai newspapers (November 12).
(83) [Express mail as Telegram] Submitting the sentencing record of war criminals (handwritten catalogue in pen) (November 13).[2]

The letters and telegrams can be roughly classified into several categories. Those that fall into the first category include telegrams that were sent for the purpose of searching for evidence and witnesses. In Chapter 4, 6, 7, and 8 of this book, I have cited the relevant telegrams sent back home by HSIANG Che-chun.

The second category, the largest in number, is those that reported back home about the proceedings and developments of the Trial. Let's take as an example the following official letter sent by HSIANG Che-chun on October 22, 1947, which outlined the main work of the International Prosecution Office for the past one and a half years.

*An Overview of the Work of the International Prosecution Office*

*(i) The International Prosecution Office was established in December 1945, and the International Military Tribunal for the Far East was established in January 1946. The prosecutors representing our country arrived in Japan in February. HSIANG Che-chun, together with Keenan, the US prosecutor (also Chief Prosecutor), and others, arrived in Chungking on behalf of the prosecutors in early March to receive instructions from the Supreme Leader, and then went on to Shanghai, Peking, and Nanking to investigate and secure related evidence. On April 29, an indictment was filed against Hideki TOJO and two other suspects of war crimes for crimes of aggression, violation of rules of war, and violation of humanity. (MATSUOKA Yosuke and NAGANO Osami died of illness during*

*the trial, and OKAWA Shumei suffered from mental illness. Therefore, the trial proceedings for them were suspended.)*

*(ii) On May 3, 1946, the International Military Tribunal for the Far East began its sessions of a public trial. The prosecution will divide the very complicated cases into the following parts, for each of which evidence will be submitted: 1. Japanese Constitution and Japanese Government; 2. War Propaganda; 3. Japanese Invasion of Northeast China; 4. Japanese Invasion of entire China; 5. Implementing a Policy of Poisoning; 6. Economic Invasion; 7. Japan's Conspiracy of Aggression with Germany and Italy 8. Japanese Invasion of French Vietnam; 9. Japanese Invasion of the Soviet Union; 10. Japanese Invasion of the United Kingdom and the United States; 11. Japanese Invasion of Dutch Indonesia; 12. Violation of Rules of War; 13. Crimes against Humanity; 14. Individual Parts.*

*The prosecutors started the work of presenting evidence on June 4, 1946, and ended the work on January 24, 1947. We summoned 104 witnesses, collected 2,285 pieces of evidence, and produced 4.5 million words of court records, which exceeded all the records of the Nuremberg trials.*

*(iii) The Defense Team began presenting its evidence on January 14, 1947, in the following parts: 1. General Evidence; 2. Northeast China; 3. Entire China; 4. Soviet Union; 5. the Pacific Region; 6. Individual Defendants (listed in alphabetical order of their surnames). As of the 22 of this month, the Defense Team has summoned more than 300 witnesses, presented more than 1,000 pieces of evidence, and formed the trial records totaling 31,561 pages.*

*(iv) The general summations are expected to last two months starting from January 1948. After that, all the 25 defendants will be given final verdicts.*

*(v) Regarding the trials of the two defendants, DOIHARA Kenji and ITAGAKI Seishiro, I will report on separate occasions.*

*Chinese Prosecutor HSIANG Che-chun (seal)*
*International Military Tribunal for the Far East*
*Tokyo, Japan*[3]

## *Proposals for the Demand for Extradition*

In this type of correspondence, there was no lack of proposals to the government.

For example, HSIANG Che-chun once sent back a telegram, proposing that if senior officials would testify in court, they must be fully prepared both psychologically and materially. The timely suggestion ensured that CHIN Teh-chun and other witnesses completed the task successfully.

Another example shows that in early 1948, following the recommendation of Joseph Keenan, the Chief Prosecutor, the Allies released a number of detained war crimes suspects, including NISHIO Toshizo, the former Chief of Staff of the Kwantung Army and the Commander in Chief of China Expeditionary Army, and TADA Hayao, the Commander of the North China Area Army. HSIANG Che-chun sent two telegrams in succession to report the information and proposed that China extradite these war criminals and preside over the trial.

The telegram on January 17 stated,

> *I telegraphed a few days ago that Keenan proposed to Washington to release the second group of suspects. I hereby submit the list of suspects. In addition, what's the attitude of our government towards the two suspects—TADA Hayao and NISHIO Toshizo?" On January 19, the telegram read: "It is found that about 20 top Japanese war crimes suspects, including NISHIO Toshizo, after being detained for a long time without prosecution, have been released due to Chief Prosecutor Keenan's proposal to Washington. If our country intends to extradite them, it seems that we should contact Washington for negotiation."*[4]

A list of 20 people to be extradited is attached to the telegram:

1. *KISHI Nobusuke* (former Minister of Commerce and Industry).
2. *IWAMURA Michiyo* (former Minister of Justice).
3. *AOKI Kazuo* (former Minister of Great East Asia).
4. *TERAJIMA Ken* (former Minister of Railways and Lieutenant General of the Navy).
5. *ANDO Kisaburo* (former Home Minister, Army Lieutenant General).
6. *NISHIO Toshizo* (former Commander-in-chief of the Japanese Army in China and former Governor of Tokyo City).

7. *TADA Hayao* (former Chief of the General Staff).
8. *SHIMOMURA Sadamu* (former War Minister).
9. *TOYODA Soemu* (former Chief of Imperial Japanese Navy General Staff).
10. *TAKAHASHI Sankichi* (former Commander of the Combined Fleet).
11. *TANI Masayuki* (former Foreign Minister, former president of the Intelligence Agency, and former ambassador to the puppet government of China).
12. *AMOU Eiji, who issued the* Amou Statement, (former Chief of the Intelligence Section of Ministry of Foreign Affairs).
13. *HONDA Kumataro* (former ambassador to Germany and the puppet government of China).
14. *GOTO Fumio* (former vice president of the Imperial Rule Assistance Association).
15. *ISHIHARA Shoichiro* (former president of Ishihara Industry Co., military supply zaibatsu).
16. *KODAMA Yoshio* (former contractor of the Japanese Navy in Shanghai).
17. *RYOICHI Sasakawa* (former president of Patriotic People's Party).
18. *KUZUU Yoshihisa* (one of the leading members of the former Black Dragon Society).
19. *SUMA Yakichiro* (former Consul General and Counselor of the Embassy to Nanking, Ambassador to Spain).
20. *ABE Genki* (Superintendent—General of the Polie).

On January 21, YEH Kung-chao (YE Gongchao), Vice Minister of the Ministry of Foreign Affairs, wrote instructions on HSIANG Che-chun's telegram: "*Ministry of Justice and Administration and the Ministry of National Defense: No matter which criminals on the list should be detained or extradited, there must be well-prepared definitive evidence, otherwise nothing will come of the extradition.*"[5] It was right to make full preparations. Unfortunately, the National Government did not pay enough attention to it at that time, and finally rejected HSIANG Che-chun's proposal and decided not to extradite them. KISHI Nobusuke later served twice as Prime Minister of Japan in the 1950s. When HSIANG read the news of KISHI Nobusuke's appointment in the newspaper, he was very furious and exclaimed: "*How ridiculous! When a war criminal is appointed as Prime Minister, where is the law, and where is justice?*"[6]

There is also another letter worth pondering over. President Webb on November 4, 1948, started to read out the *Judgment*. Then again on November 12, the verdict was handed down on 25 Japanese Class A war crime suspects. Just two days before the sentencing, HSIANG Che-chun wrote a letter to Foreign Minister WANG Shih-chieh (Hsueh-ting), predicting the outcome of the sentencing.

The letter read:

> *Your Excellency Minister WANG Hsueh-ting* (courtesy name—the author's note)*:*
>
> *The Far East International Military Tribunal opened its session on November 4, and the president read out the judgment, which was telegraphed to you previously. The full text of the verdict, which has not been delivered to the prosecution yet, will only be issued one after another successively in sections before the announcement. I hereby submit the part already announced for you to read first. As far as this part was concerned, our prosecution's proposition was accepted in the court. Accordingly, most of the defendants, such as Doihara, ITAGAKI, MATSUI, TOJO, etc., are expected to be given a death sentence. After the debate on April 16, Chief Consultant NYI Judson T.Y. and I are convinced that as many as 14 or 15 defendants would be given the death penalty based on the prosecution's presentation of evidence. The court's judgment will be announced in a few days. The penalties in the verdict must be read out at the end of the sentencing. Please rest assured.*
>
> *Yours respectfully,*
> *HSIANG Che-chun,*
> *November 10, 1948*[7]

HSIANG made two predictions in this regard.

The first was that the defendants DOIHARA Kenji, ITAGAKI Seishiro, MATSUI Iwane and TOJO Hideki, the culprits of the invasion of China, "*may all be sentenced to death.*" Two days later, it was fulfilled.

However, the second prediction that "*As many as fourteen or fifteen defendants may be executed*" was not. Finally, only seven were sentenced to hanging. In addition to the four mentioned, the other three were KIMURA Heitaro, MUTO Akira, and HIROTA Koki. It should be noted that the Chinese Justice MEI Ju-ao had been informed about the verdict, but did not share it with HSIANG Che-chun and NYI, Judson T.Y. In fact, even though NYI had assisted Mei in writing part of *the Judgment* as arranged by the Minister of Foreign Affairs (see in the next chapter), he had no idea of the sentencing and the verdict to be given on the defendants. This reflects the independence of prosecutors and judges in trial arrangements and reveals the three jurists' ethical integrity.

The third type of correspondence was concerned with personnel arrangements and the evaluation of teamwork. For instance, it was mentioned in Chapter 8 of this book that on April 3, 1947, HSIANG sent a telegram to the Ministry of Foreign Affairs that as the secretary to Chinese prosecutor Henry CHIU had resigned due to illness, HSIANG proposed to the ministry that a young translator named KAW Vurn-ping with a Bachelor of Law from Soochow University, be his successor. He gave a very high evaluation of KAW.

> *The Foreign Ministry in Nanking: Our secretary Henry Chiu has resigned due to the illness. We have asked for permission for his resignation; we also asked for permission to have Mr. KAW Vurn-ping—Bachelor of Law of Soochow University, who has completed an assignment in the International Prosecution Section and is about to return to China—take up his post. We have yet to receive permission for this appointment and are worried the letter has been lost. There is an indication that TOJO and other war criminals have begun their active defense. There are few people in our department, but there is much to be done. KAW was a top student and can offer much-experienced support. Please give approval to the above proposals.*[8]

HSIANG complimented the chief counselor NYI even more on his contributions many times in his letters and telegrams. For example, "*Chief Counselor NYI will complete his important work soon and be allowed to return to China at the end of the month.*" (May 27, 1947) "*Mr. NYI has accomplished his tasks in Japan and is highly regarded. Our prosecutors still have important official tasks that need to be conducted back in China, and have asked for permission for him to perform both duty. Please give assistance to him. I am looking forward to his coming to Japan so that we can shoulder heavy responsibilities together.*" (June 2, 1947) HSIANG also recommended to WANG Shih-chieh that NYI be assigned to participate in the trial of war criminal suspects such as NISHIO Toshizo and TADA Hayao organized by the GHQ. "*Excelling in the prosecutions with his legal expertise and competence, Mr. NYI is highly respected by all parties.*" (July 16, 1948)[9]

The fourth category of documents relates to the submission of all the transcripts of the Tokyo Trial from the prosecution stage to the end of the debates and other important documents. In his official letter written on October 20, 1948, HSIANG classified the materials submitted by the Chinese prosecution team.

*(1) Trial transcripts from the prosecution stage to the end of the debates (48,412 pages in 26 volumes).*
*(2) Excerpts from the trial transcripts of the International Military Tribunal for the Far East.*
*(3) Comprehensive debate papers of the International Prosecution Office.*
*(4) Final Rebuttals by the International Prosecution Office to the defendants' comprehensive debate papers.*
*(5) Manuscripts of the documents submitted by the prosecutors and the defendants to the International Military Tribunal for the Far East (2282 from the Accounting and Prosecution Office and 163 from the defendants, 3915 altogether).*
*(6) The index book of the above. "Together with the official letter was a list of the documents and four large wooden crates. China Travel Service was entrusted with their transportation to Nanking for submission."*[10]

There was also a special type of correspondence that twice refuted the false reports by the media. The first occurred at the end of the prosecution phase. On January 10, 1948, newspapers published in Shanghai, such as *North China Daily News* and *Shanghai Evening Post*, and *Mercury* carried the information provided by a reporter from Central News Agency in Tokyo that the evidence presented by Chinese prosecutors was scanty or even less than that from New Zealand. This was a serious distortion of facts. HSIANG was outraged. He and NYI tracked down the reporter to clarify the facts and sent three telegrams to the Ministry of Foreign Affairs within three days.

> *I have just heard that on January 10, China Press, North China Daily News, Shanghai Evening Post, and Mercury in Shanghai carried telegraphed news published by Central News Agency in Tokyo on January 9 regarding the evidence of the Japanese Army's atrocities committed in China. However, investigations find that the prosecutors did not make such statements at the aforementioned talk, and the news is false. I will make a statement to the agency for correction and a probe into the source of the false information. I would like to inform the Ministry of Foreign Affairs about it immediately. (January 22)*

> *The information is absolutely inconsistent with the facts, and the reporter of the agency has contacted no one from the Chinese Prosecution Office about the above news. Such a reversal of right and wrong is extremely shocking and misleading. In addition, it contains some points involving judges, and therefore, it is even more necessary to look into the sources. I have contacted the Agency about the distortion and required correction. Now I am writing to inform you about the case. (January 23)*
>
> *Counselor NYI and I have just questioned a certain Mr. Li, the Tokyo correspondent for the Central News Agency. He admitted that he was responsible for the news. As for the news about the evidence provided by the Chinese Prosecution Office of the International Military Tribunal for the Far East, it indeed had not been verified by the prosecution office in advance before it was issued and contained many errors. He made an apology on the spot and promised to re-issue another report about the truth immediately for the sake of correction. (January 23)*[11]

On January 24, HSIANG wrote a long letter demonstrating that the report from Central News Agency was "*inconsistent with the facts*" in many aspects. Actually, from the opening of the court to the end of 1947, it received a total of 3,686 documents, of which the prosecutors proposed 2,391." *In the case of the Japanese army's atrocities in China alone, there are 99 cases collected in our country and submitted by our office to the court. Most of the other documents are proofs of each defendant's conspiracy of aggression, as well as that the defendants should be held responsible for the atrocities committed by the military due to their positions. The above documents can only be found in court records. As of January of this year, the 30-odd documents submitted by NYI and me in the rebuttal phase have not been included. Central News Agency reported on the 9th of this month that the Chinese only provided approximately 30 documents for the entire case, of which only 17 were concerned with the Japanese atrocities, which is simply not the case.*"

Moreover, after verification, the Chinese prosecution team found that only one piece of New Zealand's evidence recorded as No. 1880A was accepted by the Tribunal. HSIANG said indignantly: "*Central News Agency reported that some judge had pointed out that New Zealand could submit 300 proofs of the atrocities, which is so inconsistent with the facts.*"

Having elucidated the truth, HSIANG Che-chun then stated in the letter that the prosecution staff's resolve to keep their eyes on the big picture and their determination to work with diligence:

> *Since I came here as China's Prosecutor by order of the Government, I've found our team overworked and understaffed. Night and day, I work with all the team members, daring not to slacken off.... This time, under groundless accusations, my colleagues are all filled with apprehension. When news travels afar, it's bound to lose authenticity and stir up a misunderstanding. With my gentle persuasion and constant encouragement, they have carried on with their hard work as usual. This incident, of course, is better kept between us.*[12]

The second episode happened when the judges were deliberating on the sentence and judgment. Since September 1948, reporters from the *Chinese Central News Agency* had again written a series of essentially untrue reports and commentaries on the Tokyo Trial. As a result, Judge MEI Ju-ao poignantly pointed it out in a telegram addressed to the Ministry of Foreign Affairs on September 16, 1948:

> *The report is rife with shallow comments and implausible hearsay, most of which are miles away from the truth. Therefore, it seems that the reporter intends to sound sensational. Those words are probably not said out of pure spite, but they are superficial, subjective, and mostly impertinent. For example, the account that "The Court has confirmed the start of the war as Japan's attack on the Pearl Harbor rather than the capture and occupation of China's northeast city of Shenyang during the Mukden Incident" is total rubbish. This is in direct contradiction to the sections in the verdict approved by the majority. In the meantime, Justice MEI felt quite frustrated, "According to common judicial practice and judge's professional ethics, I cannot make a public statement to right the wrong. There is nothing I can do but wait for the official announcement of the verdict soon. Only then can the truth be revealed."*[13]

As mentioned above, HSIANG Che-chun and MEI Ju-ao worked independently and did not exchange information with each other. However, the press's reports were public. On November 4, 1948, the Tribunal President William Webb began to announce the *Judgment*; on November 5 and 6, *Ta Kung Pao* and other Chinese papers were busy predicting the verdict findings. Thus, seeing much misinformation circulating around, HSIANG Che-chun felt he must speak up. He twice sent telegrams to the Ministry of Foreign Affairs:

*Regarding the sentencing of the International Military Tribunal for the Far East (IMTFE), Shanghai-based newspapers published many untrue stories on November 5 and 6.... In a word, on the one hand, reporters are not proficient in legal terms and procedures; on the other hand, since they cannot peruse the rest of the unread verdict, those reporters mainly come up with conjectures of their own about the findings of the whole case. And the editors then write editorials based on those reports. No wonder misinformation passes on from one to another, causing misunderstanding for all parties. That's why I'd like to send a telegram to clarify the situation. (November 10) And "it's hard for the outsiders to guess what crimes each defendant will be held responsible for and how they will be sentenced. All remain to be disclosed by the verdict. According to those Shanghai newspapers, a certain section of the Judgment was deleted; one defendant was rarely mentioned and such, which were all inconsistent with the truth."(November 12)*[14]

## *Interviews with the Media*

Despite these two less-than-pleasant episodes, during the whole duration of the Tokyo Trial, China's prosecution team and Chinese media had worked with each other rather well. As a matter of fact, the third way for the former to leave behind important comments was from media reports and interviews.

According to incomplete statistics gathered from three Chinese newspapers, *Central Daily News*, *Shun Pao*, and *Ta Kung Pao*, there were as many as 150 reports and interviews with HSIANG Che-chun and his prosecution team before and after the Tokyo Trial, covering the whole process of their work.[15] A case in point is the many reports published before the opening of the court sessions:

*Our government has sent distinguished jurists MEI Ju-ao and HSIANG Che-chun as the first group of representatives. Mr. HSIANG will be China's Prosecutor and Mr. MEI China's Judge for the IMTFE. (January 5, 1946)*

*The Chief Prosecutor of the Shanghai Supreme Court, HSIANG Che-chun, has arrived with his secretary Henry CHIU today as China's Assistant Prosecutor for the IMTFE set up by the General Headquarters (GHQ) of the Allied Powers. (February 9, 1946)*

*Joseph Keenan and others will join forces with China's Prosecutor HSIANG Che-chun, to probe the evidence against the war criminals and consult with the witnesses in Shanghai. Mr. HSIANG just flew to Shanghai four days ago. After a short stay, Keenan and Mr. HSIANG will fly to Chungking to call on President Chiang (Kai-shek). They'll return to Tokyo as scheduled in ten days. (March 17, 1946)*

*To gather evidence against criminals in Nanking Massacre and find witnesses, Special Prosecutor Colonel Morrow [i.e., American Deputy Prosecutor (Thomas) Morrow], Special Investigator Cole [i.e., American Deputy Prosecutor (Roger F.) Cole] and Secretary Henry CHIU from China's Prosecution Division arrived in Nanking on April 4 and stayed at No. 73 on Shanghai Road. Their investigations are already in motion. (April 7, 1946)*

There are other similar reports.

After the court was in session, more reports appeared in the papers. They are too many to be enumerated in this book.

What's worth pointing out is that Prosecutor HSIANG Che-chun had shown Chinese delegates' clear-cut attitude and steadfast stance on numerous occasions via his talks with the media.

The first one is an interview published on Shun Pao on March 17, 1946:

*The Tokyo Military Tribunal is about to try war criminals next month. Thus the reporter hastens to interview Mr. HSIANG Che-chun in Cathay Mansion and inquire about the organization of the IMTFE and the latest events. According to Mr. HSIANG, the IMTFE was set up by the GHQ. Nine countries, including China, the United States, Britain, the Soviet Union, France, Canada, Australia, and New Zealand, are invited to participate, and each country shall send one inspector and one justice respectively to make up the body. As long as the leading Japanese war criminals are guilty of one of the three crimes, i.e., crimes against peace, violations of the laws and customs applicable in international armed conflict, and crimes against humanity, they will be arraigned by the IMTFE and sentenced accordingly. At present, the IMTFE is engaged in preparing for the indictment against each war criminal. The court session is going to be officially opened next month. The IMTFE will then try its best to ensure the defendants get their chance of defense. For in developed countries, under the rule of law, defendants enjoy certain rights within the purview of the law. Consequently, war criminals due to stand trial are entitled to retain lawyers to argue for their case; those without a lawyer will be assigned one by the court. I hope every single war criminal will be*

> *legally held accountable for all the crimes committed because warmongers must be published to secure the everlasting peace of the world and the welfare of mankind.*[16]

Mr. HSIANG Che-chun made his second remark on April 27, 1946, when interviewed by *Shun Pao* during his business trip to Shanghai.

> *Shun Pao News reporters were told yesterday that there are as many as 11 countries participating in the Tribunal. In addition to the nine countries that have accepted the Japanese surrender, India and the Philippines have recently joined the court. In about ten days, the court is to be opened. Once the hearing has started, the trial may be adjourned so that the defendants are given enough time for their defense. This trial session would take roughly five to six months, and after that time if the case cannot be finished as expected, it will be prolonged. We have gathered a large amount of evidence, which is currently being translated into English without delay. Mr. HSIANG is staying in Shanghai briefly before flying back to his duties in Tokyo within two or three days.*[17]

Mr. HSIANG made his third remark on January 29, 1948, proposing that the Chinese National Government should extradite Class A Japanese war criminals like KISHI Nobusuke to China for their court trial sessions, which was published in *Central Daily News* the next day.

> *Mr. HSIANG Che-chun, the Chinese prosecutor at the International Military Court for the Far East, proclaimed that the release of the 20 Class A Japanese war crimes suspects from Sugamo Prison would not affect China's right to extradite any of them to China. Mr. HSIANG continued that the Chinese government and its people are very much concerned about the release of such war crimes suspects. These 20 Class A war suspects Mr. Keenan proposed to be released include a few infamous military officers and notorious politicians who were active in the conspiracy to conquer China. KISHI Nobusuke (Commerce Minister of the TOJO Hideki Cabinet and one of the five rulers of Manchukuo), ANDO Kisaburo (former Commander of Japan's South China Area Army), NISHIO Toshizo (former Japanese Supreme Commander in China), TADA Hayao (former Deputy Chief of Staff of the Japanese Army), KODAMA Yoshio (Head of the Shanghai Branch of "KODAMA Agency," a secret service organization of Japanese Navy, responsible for the looting of Central and South China), TANI Masayuki (former Japanese ambassador to WANG*

*Ching-wei's puppet government), and SUMA Yakichiro (former Japanese Consul-General in Nanking and active spy. Finally, Mr. HSIANG expected the Chinese government to take into consideration these facts and take proper countermeasures so that any Japanese who has committed crimes against peace and crimes against humanity in China is subject to legal judgment.*[18]

After the conclusion of the prosecution phase, Mr. HSIANG made the fourth remark, demanding tough punishments for the eight war criminals, including DOIHARA Kenji and ITAGAKI Seishiro. Carried by *Central Daily News* on April 21, 1948, it went as follows:

*After the two years court trial, when speaking to Central Daily News, Mr. HSIANG remarked that China insisted on its demand for tough punishment for DOIHARA Kenji and ITAGAKI Seishiro, two of the 25 leading war criminals in custody. He also pointed out that six other war criminals ought to be severely punished on the ground that they incited and participated in the aggression against China: HASHIMOTO Kingoro (founder of Sakurakai, a militaristic club), MINAMI Jiro (War Minister during the Mukden Incident), ARAKI Sadao (successor to MINAMI Jiro who completed the occupation of Northeast China and Jehol Province), MATSUI Iwane(chief culprit of the Nanking Massacre), HATA Shunroku (successor to MATSUI Iwane as commanding general of the Central China Expeditionary Army), KOISO Kuniaki (Chief of Staff of the Japanese Kwantung Army and successor to TOJO Hideki as Prime Minister of Japan). In the end, Mr. HSIANG expressed his belief that the International Military Tribunal for the Far East will set an example by proving that wars of aggression will eventually lead aggressors to the guillotine and jail instead of places of honor.*[19]

As reported by multiple papers, Mr. HSIANG Che-chun made his last remark on December 2, accusing the U.S. Supreme Court of illegally accepting the appeal from the HIROTA Koki, DOIHARA Kenji, and others:

*Our Prosecutor, Mr. HSIANG Che-chun said today that the Supreme Court of the United States has no right to accept the appeal from HIROTA Koki, DOIHARA Kenji, and others; he also pointed out that the trial of the 25 Class mentioned above A war criminals is an international matter. The Supreme Court of the United States is not qualified to inspect the verdict made by the International Military Tribunal for the Far East.*[20]

## *Evidence of Biological Weapons*

Another contribution made by the team of Chinese prosecutors was the gathering of evidence of the research and use of chemical and biological weapons in China by the Japanese army.

The infamous Unit 731 was the leading Japanese organization of studying and manufacturing bacteria war weapons in cold blood. This unit was stationed in Pingfang District of Harbin as "the Epidemic Prevention and Water Purification Department of the Kwantung Army." Under the name of epidemic prevention and water purification, this army unit carried out live experiments with biological and chemical weapons on Chinese and Korean civilians and POWs. This army unit was described as having the largest research, experiment, and manufacturing camp of bacteriological weapons the world had ever seen. Unit 731 had many branches, including the Institute of Bacteriological Weapons at Tokyo Army Medical School and many other biological warfare units across China, among which Army Unit Ei 1644 dispatched 12 teams to Shanghai, Nanking, Yueyang, Kingmen, and to a few other places.

The Japanese militarists blatantly violated international conventions and carried out outrageous live experiments with frostbite, bacterial infection, and poison gas on humans. This is another hard evidence of Japanese aggression and expansion, looting resources, and tramping on China's sovereignty.

Before and after the Tokyo Trial, Mr. HSIANG Che-chun and Mr. Henry CHIU, together with Assistant Prosecutors Sutton and Morrow, launched on-the-spot investigations into the Japanese use of biological weapons in China and produced special reports based on their findings. In the context of the emerging Cold War, however, the United States government offered immunity from prosecution to the leading members of Unit 731 headed by ISHII Shiro, in exchange for submitting to the American government all the research data, including those on live human experiments. Some key researchers were even sent to America to continue their "research." With the help of the United States government, ISHII Shiro and his gang escaped the trial of the military tribunal and the condemnation of human conscience and morality.

However, solid evidence of crimes can never be erased.

The original site of Unit 731 in Pingfang District of Harbin had been made into the Exhibition Hall of Evidence of Crimes Committed by Unit 731 of the Japanese Imperial Army.

After many years of investigation and identification of the objects among the facility's remains, the Exhibition Hall contains 643 precious historical objects as strong evidence that exposed the crimes of the Japanese Imperial Army.

There are also many people in Japan who respect history and adhere to conscience. MOROMORA Seiichi, a well-known Japanese writer, discovered the criminal facts of Unit 731 in China when he interviewed Japanese veterans. After many rounds of investigations in China and Japan, in 1981, he published a book named *The Devil's Gluttony: Unmasking Unit 731, the Japanese Germ Warfare Unit.*

The chapters are titled as follows:

*"Special Military Zone—20 km South of Harbin City"*
*"The Cruel Inspection— Specimens of Nightmares"*
*"Little Dark Place— Unit 731"*
*"Why is 'Unit 731' the Devil?"*
*"Fighting for Being a Man—The 'Maruta' Riot"*
*"The Technical Secrets of Germ Warfare"*
*"The Devil's Sister—Unit 100"*
*"The Devil in Gluttony All Day"*
*"The Illegitimate Child of the Japanese Army—the Struggles of the First Class of Teenage Soldiers"*
*"The 'Army God' under the Mask"*

The book sent shock waves through Japan.[21]

In March of 2015, the Medical Crimes Exhibition, which aims to expose the crimes committed by the Japanese Imperial Army's Unit 731 during World War II, was on display at the International Peace Museum of Ritsumeikan University in Kyoto, Japan. The exhibition details Unit 731's brutal live human experiments on colonial subjects for germ warfare and weapon research. It also introduces the development of Japanese medicine during and after the war, interspersed with testimonies from Japanese military doctors and victims.

On the evening of August 13, 2017, the eve of the 72$^{nd}$ anniversary of Emperor Hirohito's surrender decree, Japan's NHK TV broadcast a documentary titled The

Truth of Unit 731 – Elite Doctors and Human Experimentation, which lasted about 50 minutes and aroused public concern in Japan. In the documentary, NHK, for the first time, unearthed the audio recordings of trials held in the Soviet Union shortly after the end of World War II and used a live recording of participants and interviews with witnesses to reconstruct the reality of core members of Unit 731 developing bacteriological weapons. According to the documentary, during World War II, Unit 731 secretly developed bacteriological weapons and used them in combat in China. After the war, Unit 731 completely destroyed all evidence at the facility, while former members of the unit remained tight-lipped. As a result, the truth was hidden. At the end of the documentary, it revealed a doctor and a former member had committed suicide due to remorse, implying that all Japanese people should face the truth and reflect upon history.

It is important to note that the efforts made by Chinese prosecutors and international colleagues in those years did not fade into oblivion. The evidence and reports gathered by Sutton, Morrow, and others remain in the U.S. archives. In 2017, Columbia University Press published the book *Hidden Atrocities*, written by Jeanne Guillemin, a well-known American biological warfare researcher. The book cites the reports from Sutton, Allan Waitt, Commander of the U.S. Chemical Weapons Force, and Chimba Osamu, a defector from Unit 1644 in Nanking, et al., it revealed the war crimes that Unit 731 and other Japanese Germ Warfare Units had carried out experiments on humans, including cholera, typhoid, anthrax, plague, and a dozen other pathogens, as well as Japanese Imperial Army had used bacteriological weapons in Hunan, Jiangxi, Zhejiang, and other places.

The book recounts twice the details of HSIANG Che-chun submitting evidence to the International Prosecution Section in 1946:

> *In addition to these reports, Sutton received valuable information intermittently from the Chinese prosecutors' team. On May 9, he found a note left by the prosecutor HSIANG and several pages of translated evidence on his desk.*
>
> *The prosecutor also left Sutton additional documents about the use of chemical weapons by the Japanese—incidents, types of weapons, chemical agents, and casualties, including seven attacks in Changteh in 1943 in which hybrid bombs of mustard gas and sneezing agents were dropped.*

In a word, although the team of Chinese prosecutors was in an "*under-staffed but overworked*" situation, they were "*devoted to official duties day and night and cannot afford to slacken our efforts.*"(Excerpt from HSIANG's letter) They made an indelible contribution and should be forever remembered in history.

## *References*

[1] Xiang, Longwan. 2010. *The Tokyo Trial, Chinese Prosecutor Hsiang Che-chun.* Shanghai Jiao Tong University Press, 5–6 (272–277 of the English court records).
[2] Xiang, Longwan. 2014. *HSIANG Che-chun's Letters, Telegrams, and Statements at the Tokyo Trial.* Shanghai Jiao tong University Press, 3–77.
[3] Ibid., 48–49.
[4] Ibid., 50.
[5] Official Letter Received No. 37-192. Ministry of Foreign Affairs of the National Government.
[6] Xiang, Longwan. 2010. *The Tokyo Trial, Chinese Prosecutor Hsiang Che-chun.* Shanghai Jiao Tong University Press, 330.
[7] Xiang, Longwan. 2014. *HSIANG Che-chun's Letters, Telegrams and Statements at the Tokyo Trial.* Shanghai Jiao tong University Press, 75.
[8] Ibid., 37.
[9] Xiang, Longwan. 2010. *The Tokyo Trial, Chinese Prosecutor Hsiang Che-chun.* Shanghai Jiao Tong University Press, 42–43, 69.
[10] Xiang, Longwan. 2014. *HSIANG Che-chun's Letters, Telegrams, and Statements at the Tokyo Trial.* Shanghai Jiao Tong University Press, 53–57.
[11] Ibid., 51–53
[12] Mei, Xiao-ao, and Mei Xiaokan. 2013. *The Tokyo Trial Manuscript of MEI Ju-ao.* Shanghai Jiao Tong University, 21.
[13] Xiang, Longwan. 2014. *HSIANG Che-chun's Letters, Telegrams and Statements at the Tokyo Trial.* Shanghai Jiao tong University Press, 74–76.
[14] Ibid., 73–74, 76.
[15] Ibid., 192–285.
[16] Ibid., 197–198.
[17] Ibid., 198–199.
[18] Ibid., 263–264.
[19] Ibid., 270–271.
[20] Ibid., 281–282.
[21] MOROMORA, Seiichi. 2014. *The Devil's Gluttony: Unmasking 731, the Japanese Germ Warfare Unit (three complete volumes).* Academy Press.

CHAPTER 12

# More to Remember

### *A Sword for a Hero*

In the Tokyo Trial, the Chinese judge's team led by MEI Ju-ao also made indelible contributions, examples of which include that justice MEI strove to occupy a central seat on the bench before the trial, that he actively assisted President William Webb during the trial, that he took the lead in submitting the draft judgement on Japanese aggression against China at the stage of preparation for the conviction and sentencing, and that, above all, he unified the majority, persuaded and coordinated with them, and finally succeeded in imposing death penalty to seven heinous Class A war criminals including TOJO Hideki, DOIHARA Kenji, ITAGAKI Seishiro, MATSUI Iwane, MUTO Akira, KIMURA Heitaro and HIROTA Koki. All these made a significant mark in history. The contents of the *Judgment* cited in this book were mostly written by a team led by Justice MEI, and YANG Shou-lin and NYI, Judson T.Y. made great contributions. Particularly, NYI, chief adviser to the Chinese prosecutor assisted in the work of MEI even after his assignment to the prosecution was completed, at the request of the Ministry of Foreign Affairs. He was the main author of the part on Japanese aggression against China in the *Judgment*.

In NYI's letter to the Foreign Minister WANG Shih-chieh on November 28, 1948, he mentioned this experience:

> *Although the prosecution work came to an end this spring, I, as requested, have stayed on in Japan for the legal work. During the past summer and autumn months, I systematically studied the entire court files of 48,000 pages and prepared a draft judgment on Japanese aggression against China, totaling 255 pages. In response to each point of dispute on the facts, I cited the relevant evidence to support our claims with evidence.*[1]

Justice MEI kept a diary, and his descendants have retained a diary book containing entries of more than 50 days from his departure to Tokyo to a few days after the opening of the trial sessions. Here are a few quotes to give the reader a glimpse of how MEI Ju-ao felt at that time.

MEI arrived in Tokyo on March 20, 1946, in a U.S. military plane. He wrote in his diary that day:

> *I set my foot on Japan's soil... My general impression is that all the factories in Yokohama and Tokyo were bombarded and burned down. The war criminals we are about to try must be held responsible for it! They disrupted the world order, caused great damage to China, and ruined their nation's future. How dangerous it was for a country to be run, not by statesmen but by a bunch of military men with neither political mind nor global vision! An ever-promising nation has been doomed; as the saying goes, "You must reap what you have sown." It is a tragedy in human history and also an important lesson.*[2]

On March 29, a famous scholar, Dr. KU Yuh-hsiu (GU Yuxiu), who had participated in the Surrender Ceremony held in Nanking and was awarded the "China War Memorial Medal," and WANG Tan-ju (WANG Danru), the Chinese Chief Liaison Officer in Japan came to visit MEI Ju-ao.

MEI vividly described their meeting:

> *Dr. Ku and General Wang have come back from Kyoto... They bought a beautifully decorated sword about three feet long as a gift to me and presented it in a small "ceremony." I said, "An ancient saying goes, 'face-powder for a beauty while a treasured sword for a hero,' but I am not a hero, unfortunately." Dr. Ku said, "You represent the 450 million Chinese people and millions of our compatriots who were killed in the war, to come and punish the prime culprits in the capital of their country. What in the world can be more heroic than this?" I said, "In the Peking*

*opera, the official with a sword bestowed by the emperor could execute the criminals first and then report to the emperor. But we are now living in an age of the rule of law, where all arch-criminals must be tried before execution; otherwise, I wish I could behead a few to appease my hatred of the evil war criminals!"*[3]

*This morning, another judges' meeting was held to discuss the fourth draft of the Rules of Procedure. After the discussion, each judge signed our oath as follows: "We affirm that as Members of the International Military Tribunal for the Far East, we will duly administer justice according to law, without fear, favor or affection, according to our conscience and the best of our understanding, and that we will not disclose or discover the vote or opinion of any particular member of the Tribunal upon findings or sentence but will preserve inviolate the secrecy of the counsel of every member." Our oath was signed in the following order: The United States, China, Britain, the Soviet Union, Canada, Australia, France, the Netherlands, and New Zealand. I signed my name in Chinese, followed by an English translation.*

Since the seating arrangement of the bench was not stipulated in the Charter of the Tribunal, it was reasonable to seat the judges in the same order as the signatories of the Allied Powers accepting Japan's Instrument of Surrender, that is, the United States, China, Britain, the Soviet Union, Australia, Canada, France, the Netherlands, and New Zealand. However, President William Webb wanted to have the British and American judges sit by his left and right sides, and then those from China, the Soviet Union, and the rest of the countries. He even claimed that "the Supreme Commander required this arrangement for the Allied Powers." But MEI Ju-ao refused to submit to the threat and protested:

*I can never accept such an arrangement with no proper grounds, in law or facts.... China was inflicted by the most disastrous Japanese aggression, fought the longest war of resistance, and suffered the greatest losses. It is inconceivable that China's deserving place in an international tribunal against Japanese war criminals will be lower than that of Britain, a nation that only surrendered during the wars."* MEI Ju-ao solemnly pointed out: *"The only solution is to apply the sequence of signatures on Japan's Instrument of Surrender for the rehearsal. If the Supreme Commander does not agree, we can convene a conference to discuss it tomorrow. If things are not done like this, I will definitely not join this rehearsal."*[4]

Fortunately, he was supported by the Canadian and French judges, and President Webb finally agreed so that the Chinese Judge sat on his left-hand side throughout the trial. Regarding the significance of this debate over the seating arrangement, MEI expounded his views in his late years in the book *The International Military Tribunal for the Far East:*

> *First of all, we should realize such struggles, open or closed, occur frequently and sometimes unavoidably, on any international occasion. They should not be treated lightly because they concern a country's status and honorability in the international community. Secondly, despite being ranked as one of the Five Powers after World War II, China had to deal with oppression and discrimination. Determination and persistent efforts of China's representatives in the international arena were thus necessary to safeguard China's rights and interests. Last but not least, a legitimate reason to fight for national interests is paramount to display one's resilience and courage; with that, one should hold on straight to the end.*[5]

As a matter of fact, it was not unusual for the President to encounter problems during the court sessions of the Tokyo Trial due to the long history of Japanese aggression against China, his lack of knowledge of the Chinese language, and the complex situation in China. To ensure smooth conduction of the Trial. MEI would often communicate with Webb by whispering or passing notes to him during the sessions, as we can see in photographs and documentary footage. For example, on August 23, 1946, defense attorney Blakeney submitted Pu Yi's notes as evidence, which caused a dispute in court. "*Since they are not in a language commonly understood by both the Court and the prosecution, I submit that they are tendered to any Member of the Tribunal who care to look at them,*" the Chief Prosecutor Keenan said. "*We have a representative of China on the bench. The representative of China would like to see those notes,*" the President responded immediately. Then the notes were handed over to Justice MEI as a court document, which facilitated the smooth conduction of the trial.[6] As another example, when the problem of inaccurate translation occurred as mentioned in Chapter 3 of this book, Justice MEI agreed to have his secretary FANG W.F.S. step forward so that the difficulty was easily solved.[7]

## *The Hard-won Victory*

As a result of the fact that the judges' meetings were held behind closed doors and that the judges signed an oath of confidentiality, the heated arguments among the eleven judges during the sentencing preparation phase were hardly reflected in the media coverage. Fortunately, Justice MEI Ju-ao sent a dozen telegrams[8] to the Foreign Ministry during his stay in Tokyo. Chapter 11 of this book has quoted one of his telegrams refuting a groundless news report. The following correspondences are quoted to help readers understand the actions and contributions of the Chinese judge's team.

> *The trial of war criminals by the International Military Tribunal for the Far East ended at 5:00 p.m. yesterday. The President declared the court adjourned and the date for the official judgment to be announced later. The "Tokyo Trial," which lasted nearly two years, held open sessions for four hundred and nineteen days, and produced records of more than forty-eight thousand pages, has now come to a conclusion. The judges' review meetings will begin next week, and how long these will take cannot be predicted, a rough estimate being two to three months, with the judgment to be delivered in late June or early July.* (April 17, 1948)
>
> *Now that the end of the whole case is in sight, as my responsibility, I should do what I can and spare no effort to win the final victory for our country in this unprecedented battle for international legal justice. However, the drafting of the Judgment is still at an initial stage and is now being carried out in groups, starting with the part on historical facts of the 17 years of Japanese aggression.* (April 24, 1948)
>
> *(1) Since my return to the office, I have been working on the first draft of "Part One of Fact-findings of Japan's Full-scale Aggression against China," which was presented to a majority judges' meeting last week and was adopted successfully after the examination. The draft is about 150 pages long and contains a clear and informative account of the purpose of Japan's invasion of China and the rights and wrongs involved, and also a conclusion in favor of China, which is quite comforting to me. Consequently, this will not only facilitate the determination of the various defendants' responsibilities for the invasion of China but will also prevent future historians from making far-fetched interpretations or distorting the truth. (2) Among the eleven judges, based on their respective legal propositions and different opinions on the composition of the judgment, the majority has taken on*

*the responsibility of drafting the entire judgment. The majority consists of seven members from China, the United States, Britain, the Soviet Union, Canada, New Zealand, and the Philippines. (The President holds an opinion only slightly different from ours, indicating that he will still join us after the meeting. It is also possible for the French and Dutch judges to participate, thus leaving as the only exception the Indian judge Pal, who is stubbornly old-fashioned and has indicated that he would never cooperate with us. Pal is busy writing his own dissenting opinion, which is supposed to be a thousand pages long.) Our group is working hard, with a fine division of labor and a good sense of team spirit. (3) The parts of the majority's draft (i.e., the sole text of the future judgment in the name of the Tribunal) which have gone through our review process are the following three: (a) preamble; (b) invasion of China's four Northeastern provinces (Manchuria) and (c) the full-scale aggression against China. There are more parts being drafted and yet to be reviewed, including: (d) Japan-Soviet relations; (e) preparations for an overall aggressive war; (f) initiation and expansion of the Pacific War; and (g) Japanese atrocities (i.e., violations of international laws and customs of war and of humanity during the war).* (June 1, 1948)

*However, the drafting of the judgment has progressed quite slowly, mainly because the case is huge and court documents are voluminous, and the judges from 11 countries have different opinions, which often leads to a deadlock and takes a lot of time to negotiate and coordinate. I fully understand that our people, quite naturally, are extremely concerned about the Tokyo Trial and have the greatest expectation for it. I will definitely try hard within reach of my influence to speed it up and will rack my brain and make every effort to achieve what we deserve in this struggle for international legal justice, rather than disappoint our people in the long-awaited results. To this day, I am paying more attention to the contents of the judgment than the speed of its preparation. A speedy conclusion is certainly what we hope for, yet the ultimate victory is what we must strive to win. With only moderate virtue and ability, I will do my very best and will never be negligent in the fulfillment of my duty.* (July 23, 1948)

*The International Military Tribunal for the Far East began to deliver its judgment on November 4, 1948. The judgment is about 1,200 pages long with more than 200,000 words. It is a full and accurate account and a straightforward resolution of the Japanese warlords' dictatorship and preparations for war and their step-by-step execution of the aggression. A special chapter is dedicated to the*

*Japanese atrocities in various places, which the Nanking Massacre constitutes the most extraordinary section and occupies a prime position. Of the over 400 pages describing the facts of Japan's external invasion, the section on "aggression against China," which was drafted by myself, is about 250 pages long and takes up more than half in length. With its detailed elaboration of the complex Sino-Japanese relations over 17 years, the rights and wrongs, and the truth and falsehood, will be revealed to the world and the future generations, which makes me feel relieved and pleased.* (November 10, 1948)

*Following this will be our final program, that is, the pronouncement of each defendant's individual verdict and sentence. This program has been decided through voting by all the eleven judges after long discussions and heated debates. The other parts were presided over by the majority. The process was complicated and peculiar, which cannot be described in a few words, nor can it be disclosed at this time. The only thing I can report as consolation is that the culprits who were most infamous for invading China and most hated by the Chinese people have been condemned to severe penalties. Please understand and forgive me for not explaining further. In addition, the judgment was prepared by the majority of seven judges from China, the United States, Britain, the Soviet Union, Canada, New Zealand, and the Philippines. Although I do not fully agree with some of the details, as they are insignificant to our main principles, I do not intend to express a personal dissent for the sake of maintaining the unity of the majority and the strength of the judgment.* (November 11, 1948)

On November 12, 1948, in accordance with Article 15(h) of the Charter of the International Military Tribunal for the Far East, President Webb pronounced the sentences of the 25 defendants charged in the indictment: all were guilty of one or multiple counts; seven were sentenced to death by hanging: DOIHARA Kenji, HIROTA Koki, ITAGAKI Seishiro, KIMURA Heitaro, MATSUI Iwane, MUTO Akira, and TOJO Hideki; 16 were sentenced to imprisonment for life: ARAKI Sadao, HASHIMOTO Kingorou, HATA Shunroku, HIRANUMA Kiichiro, HOSHINO Naoki, KIDO Koichi, KOISO Kuniaki, MINAMI Jiro, OKA Takasumi, OSHIMA Hiroshi, SATO Kenryo, SHIMADA Shigetaro, SUZUKI Teiichi, KAYA Okinori, SHIRATORI Toshio, and UMEZU Yoshijiro; two were sentenced to imprisonment for a fixed term: SHIGEMITSU Mamoru (7 years), and TOGO Shigenori (20 years).

## *To the Japanese People*

On November 14, 1948, MEI Ju-ao published "*Letter to the Japanese People*" on *Asahi Shimbun*, under the title "*Peace for the Future—From Justice Mei,*" and the subtitle "*Chinese Representative Justice MEI Ju-ao Sent the Letter (Manuscript) to Our Press through His Secretary Lo.*" Justice MEI made a solemn statement as follows:

> *The trial of Japanese Class A war criminals has demonstrated the establishment of a principle in international law that anyone who planned and launched war will be regarded as a criminal and subject to legal sanctions. This is a fact made very clear by the Nuremberg and Tokyo Trials. During the trial, all the brutal acts of the Japanese army in various countries for more than ten years were presented to the Japanese people, who thereby can certainly realize the iniquities of the Japanese warlords and their false propaganda to the public.*

MEI also looked forward to the future of Sino-Japanese relations:

> *Due to their close ties in history, geography, and culture, China and Japan should have had an intimate relationship and peaceful cooperation. Nonetheless, the desirable situation was obstructed by the Japanese militarists and ambitious aggressors. Their evil conduct made the two countries suffer from decades of hostilities, triggered wars in East Asia, and disturbed world peace. I firmly believe that the sentences delivered by the Tribunal on November 12 will not only promote international justice, humanity, and the development of international law but will also contribute to the peace and cooperation between China and Japan in the future.*[9]

On November 16, MEI Ju-ao telegraphed the Ministry of Foreign Affairs again:

> *I would not discuss the sentences here since the judgment of the International Military Tribunal for the Far East was completely pronounced and the details reported in newspapers. Whether or not the public opinion at home shows satisfaction is beyond my knowledge. However, searching my conscience, I have indeed made my utmost effort and perhaps can feel worthy of our people, regardless of praise or blame.*[10]

On November 28, NYI, Judson T.Y. also commented on the judgment in his letter to the Foreign Minister:

> *The result of the judgment turned out that seven criminals were sentenced to death, of whom four, DOIHARA Kenji, ITAGAKI Seishiro, MATSUI Iwane and HIROTA Koki, were all major aggressors against China, and the other three, MUTO Akira was a prime culprit of the Nanking Massacre and the Manila Massacre, KIMURA Heitaro was a principal offender in the invasion of Burma, and TOJO Hideki was the common enemy of all countries. The American side was quite dissatisfied as they considered that the judgment gave "preference" to the aggression against China. When the sentence was being read, the U.S. prosecutor whispered "surprise" to himself.*[11]

It can be seen that through the joint efforts of the Chinese prosecutor's and judge's teams, they successfully accomplished their mission at long last.

However, the sentencing of the Tribunal was not the end of the story. On November 29 and December 2, 1948, seven defendants, including TOJO, HIROTA, and DOIHARA, successively appealed to the U.S. Supreme Court through their American lawyers to overturn the judgment of the International Military Tribunal for the Far East. Surprisingly, the U.S. Supreme Court accepted the appeal on December 6, which caused public opinion worldwide uproar and the extreme resentment among most prosecutors and judges who had participated in the Tokyo Trial.

HSIANG Che-chun took the lead in making a statement to the reporter of the Central News Agency. On December 1, the Central Daily published a special dispatch from Tokyo:

> *HSIANG Che-chun, the prosecutor, representing China at the IMTFE, said today that the U.S. Supreme Court has no right to consider the appeal of TOJO, DOIHARA, and others. He pointed out that the trial of the 25 Japanese Class A war criminals was an international matter, and the U.S. Supreme Court is by no means qualified to review the judgment announced by the International Military Tribunal for the Far East.*[12]

Immediately afterward, the Central News Agency reported twice on the solemn and just statements of the Chinese judge MEI Ju-ao.

On December 2, a special dispatch stated:

> *MEI Ju-ao, the judge, representing China at the IMTFE, told the Central News Agency reporter this afternoon that the U.S. Supreme Court has no right to review or modify the judgment made by the International Military Tribunal for the Far East against the 25 Japanese prime war criminals. This action taken by the defense lawyers, similar to the motions they submitted at the beginning of the Tokyo Trial, is, in fact, a "strategy for protraction" and will have no effect on the sentence by the Tribunal.*

On December 7, another special dispatch further stated:

> *The Chinese judge MEI Ju-ao stated that should make the judgment of an international tribunal that represented 11 countries be subjected to review by the court of one country, then any international decision or action in the future could also be changed or revoked by one country alone. This dangerous precedent would have a profound impact on international cooperation and mutual trust among different countries. MEI expressed his shock at the decision of the U.S. Supreme Court.*[13]

On December 20, under the pressure of international public opinion, the U.S. Supreme Court rejected the appeal of the Japanese war criminals by a 6-to-1 vote. On the late night of December 22, the death penalty against the seven criminals was executed in the order of DOIHARA, TOJO, MUTO, MATSUI, ITAGAKI, HIROTA, and KIMURA. These evil warmongers had come to their rightful end. SHANG Chen (SHANG Zhen), head of the Chinese delegation in Japan, witnessed the execution.

On December 23, the Central News Agency reported on MEI Ju-ao:

> *MEI Ju-ao, the Chinese judge of the International Tribunal, made a statement after the execution of TOJO and six other war criminals. He said that the execution of the seven prime culprits symbolizes the victory of international justice and manifests the futility of invasion. There is no vengeance in this matter, but it showed that aggression is a road to gallows, not a road to glory. The death penalty against those offenders is a comfort to the people of China and other countries who suffered greatly from Japanese aggression. MEI believes that the trial and sentences are only*

*symbolic since thousands of Japanese war criminals are still at large. MEI concludes that the world progress can only be made by changes. After World War I, only a few war criminals were tried, and no one was severely punished. The end of World War II led to the trial of thousands of war criminals, of which the Nuremberg Trial and the Tokyo Trial were the most significant ones.*[14]

This book will not further discuss the contributions made by the Chinese judge's team. Readers can refer to *MY PERSONAL EXPERIENCE AT THE TOKYO TRIAL* (Shanghai Jiao Tong University Press, 2016) and *THE TOKYO TRIAL MANUCRIPTS OF MEI RU'AO* (Shanghai Jiao Tong University Press, 2013), written by MEI Ju-ao himself and edited by his daughter and son, MEI Xiaokan and MEI Xiao'ao.

Apart from the Japanese aggression against China, the International Military Tribunal for the Far East also dealt with Japan's crimes of aggression against other allied countries in the Asia-Pacific region. Details of the latter will not be reported here, and readers can refer to *THE TOKYO TRIAL: FOR WORLD PEACE* (Shanghai Jiao Tong University Press, 2017), by Professor CHENG Zhaoqi, and *THE TOKYO TRIAL: LEGAL CONTEST BETWEEN JUSTICE AND EVIL* (Third Edition), by Professor HE Qinhua (The Commercial Press, 2016).

Seventy years have passed since the Tokyo Trial. As a trial with the largest number of participating countries, the largest scale, the longest court proceedings, and the vastest volumes of archives, its importance is self-evident. While being a historical event, it still has profound practical significance today.

The trial of Japanese war criminals by the International Military Tribunal for the Far East upheld international justice, safeguarded human dignity, penalized the prime culprits who had launched the war of aggression with their hands bathed in the blood of the people of all countries and nailed the war criminals to history's pillar of shame forever. The Tokyo and Nuremberg Trials not only reflected the victory of the world anti-fascist war but also laid the cornerstone of the post-war international order.

### Beyond "Victor's Justice"

Since the beginning of the Tokyo Trial, there has been a view that the Tokyo Trial was "Victor's Justice," which is translated into Chinese as "victor's trial," or "victor's righteousness." In a sense, Tokyo Trial was indeed a trial against the defeated country by the victorious countries. If the Fascist Axis Powers had not been defeated, it would have been impossible to bring them to trial. However, those who hold the view of "victor's justice" believe: "Losers are always in the wrong. The accusations against the defendants in court are imposed by the victorious countries."

The originator of this view was TOJO Hideki himself. From December 26, 1947, to January 8, 1948, during the stage of the defense presenting rebuttal evidence, he spoke in court as a witness. In his long testimony read in court by his American lawyer George F. Blewett, TOJO denied all his crimes from the "Manchurian Incident" to the launch of the Pacific War. In December 1948, about a month after the judgment was delivered by the Tribunal, he said: "*In the last analysis, this trial was a political trial. It was only victors' justice.*"[15]

In fact, around the time of the Tokyo Trial, positive evaluations dominated the mainstream in Japan's academic circle and media. TOTANI Yuma, a Japanese scholar, summarized the following six points of consensus reached in the Japanese intellectual community at that time:

1. *Introduction of the judicial theory of crimes against peace had epoch-making significance in the history of the legal system;*
2. *The attempt to pursue individual criminal responsibility for war crimes should also be regarded as a great contribution to the Tokyo Trial;*
3. *HIROTA Koki and SHIGEMITSU Mamoru, former members of the Cabinet, were not military men but still found individually responsible for war crimes, which enlarged the original boundaries of pursuing such responsibilities;*
4. *The Tokyo Tribunal recognized the suspects' right to defense, which had often been neglected;*
5. *The Tokyo Tribunal adopted advanced technologies used in British and American courts;*
6. *It was determined as an unshakable fact that Japan had carried out wars of aggression against China and surrounding areas.*[16]

However, with the ending of the American military occupation, the outbreak of the Korean War, and the rapid economic development in Japan, the Tokyo Trial gradually slipped out of media concern, and the Japanese people's attitude towards the Tokyo Trial changed gradually.

One of the important reasons for the ideological confusion was the long-delayed publication of the *Transcripts of the Proceedings of the International Military Tribunal for the Far East*, of over 48,000 pages, and the *Judgment* of over 1,000 pages. It was not until 1968, 20 years after the end of the Tokyo Trial, that the Japanese shorthand version of the court records was published in Japan under the title of *International Military Tribunal for the Far East*. The most authoritative English version of the transcripts of proceedings, *The Tokyo War Crimes Trial* co-edited by British scholar R. John Pritchard and Sonia M. Zaide, did not come out until 1981 in the United States and the United Kingdom, 33 years after the Tokyo Trial was closed. In sharp contrast, *Dissentient Judgment*, written by the Indian judge Radha Binod Pal was published as early as the 1950s in India and Japan, respectively.

Around 1970, the Vietnam War left the United States in the lurch. In 1971, Richard H. Minear, an American scholar, published a book entitled *Victors' Justice: The Tokyo War Crimes Trial*, in which he quoted the above comment from TOJO Hideki. Although it contained only less than 200 pages, the book exerted a tremendous influence because of its early publication and sharp criticism of the Tokyo Trial. In the following year, its Japanese translation was published in Japan, which gave impetus to the emerging trend of criticizing the Tokyo Trial. Minear strongly opposed the U.S. Government's policy toward Vietnam, holding that the Asia-Pacific strategy of the United States was derived from the concept of the Tokyo Trial. He also declared: "*This book is political scholarship. It is political in its choice of subject. It is political in its tone. It is political in the implications I draw for the present day.*" Due to the fact that the book was based on the author's viewpoint of the then-current affairs, with a tunnel vision, there is not even a word of narration on Japan's invasion of Asian countries, particularly China. We have reason to wonder whether the author had read the entire trial transcripts carefully as first-hand material before writing his book.

The publication of the English version of the Tokyo Trial transcripts of proceedings in 1981 significantly clarified the historical truth. Donald Water, a famous British historian of international relations, wrote the foreword to it, where he pointed out: "*The issues that he* [Minear] *has raised are generally irrelevant because, for John Pritchard, the Trial itself was among the most important and meaningful historical databases in the 20th-century history.*"

Since then, a series of original archives and research writings have been compiled and published. That the Tokyo Trial was a just trial, a civilized trial, and an international trial has become the common consensus of more and more scholars.

In 1983, an international symposium on the Tokyo Trial was held in Tokyo. Thereafter new achievements have been reached constantly in the study of the Tokyo Trial, with young scholars being the main contributors. And the claim that the Tokyo Trial was "victors' justice" has been seriously challenged by more books and thesis.

As a matter of fact, it is quite clear from the transcripts and documents that the results of the Tokyo Trial were indeed based on evidence and solid facts. A lot of such evidence and facts have been cited in the previous chapters of this book. Among them, two sets of numbers are worth noting: the Tribunal admitted as many as 3,915 pieces of evidence from both the prosecution and defense and appearing in court were more than 300 witnesses for the defense, far exceeding the number of witnesses for the prosecution, the latter being 104. Had the Tokyo Trial been just a "victors' trial" or a mere formality, why should it have bothered with all these procedures?

The lengthy *Judgment* covers 1446 pages of the transcripts of proceedings, which President Webb readout for seven whole days from November 4 to 12, 1948, excluding one weekend. Out of the seven days reading Chapter 10, Verdicts took only part of the afternoon on November 12. This chapter is just 86 pages long and constitutes only 5.9% of the *Judgment*. This further illustrates that the Tokyo Trial was by no means a mere punishment of the war criminals.

## *Warnings from History*

*The Judgment of the International Military Tribunal for the Far East* reveals and elaborates on the rise, expansion, predominance, and devastation of Japanese militarists. Among its ten chapters, Chapter 4, The Military Domination of Japan and Preparation for War Introductory, is the longest, with 494 pages accounting for 34.2%, or more than a third, of the total. This chapter analyzes the rise and expansion of Japanese militarists in detail, offering an elaborate warning for the world. The first paragraph of its Preface points out clearly:

> *In dealing with the period of Japanese history with which this Indictment is mainly concerned, it is necessary to consider in the first place the domestic history of Japan*

> *during the same period. In the years from 1928 onwards, Japanese armed forces invaded in succession the territories of many of Japan's neighbors. The Tribunal must deal with the history of these attacks and with the exploitation by Japan of the resources of the territories she occupied. But its most important task is to assess the responsibility of individuals for these attacks, in so far as they were illegal. This responsibility cannot be measured simply by studying Japanese activities abroad. Indeed, the answers to the questions, "why did these things happen?" and "who was responsible for their occurrence?" will often only be found in the contemporaneous history of Japanese domestic politics is known.*[17]

Therefore, based on the structure of Chapter 4 of the *Judgment,* the following is a summary of Japan's aggressive conspiracy history.

The first step was to "make gods."

Around 1920, in order to build up support and courage for the extreme militarists and to find a theoretical basis for the territorial expansion, some "theorists," represented by OKAWA Shumei, a Class A war criminal, wantonly advocated the principles of "Hakko Ichiu" and "Kodo."

"Hakko Ichiu" originates from ancient Chinese classics; Hakko reads "BAHONG" in Chinese, where "BA" means eight and "HONG" originally refers to the belt of a crown tied underneath the chin and has a transferred meaning of "dimension." "Kodo" is the "imperial way" or "kingly way." It is said that in Japan, "Hakko Ichiu" and "Kodo" first appeared in an Imperial Rescript issued by the first Emperor, Jimmu Tenno, which gradually developed into the concept of moral goals or ways to achieve them. The so-called "Hakko Ichiu" meant bringing together all corners of the world under one roof or making the world one family. This was the moral goal. The so-called "Kodo" meant loyalty to the Emperor and was the road that led to "Hakko Ichiu." After the Meiji Restoration, Emperor Meiji proclaimed these ideas in an Imperial Rescript issued in 1871. In the decade before 1930, those Japanese who urged territorial expansion did so in the name of "Hakko Ichiu" and "Kodo." They repeatedly advocated military aggression under these two ideas, which eventually became symbols of world domination through military force.

OKAWA ShuMei stated in his book, *Study on the Japanese Spirits* published in 1924, that since Japan was the first state created on earth, it was therefore Japan's divine mission to rule all nations. He advocated the Japanese occupation of Siberia and the South Sea Islands and predicted a war between East and West around

1925. In 1926, he organized a patriotic society, which promoted the unification of the world in accordance with Japanese morality. At the invitation of the Army General Staff, he often lectured to them along these lines.

Another fanatical protagonist of these ideas was HASHIMOTO Kingoro, a Class A war criminal, who was one of the initiators of the Mukden Incident, an active participant in the Nanking Massacre, and a founder of the radical society "*Sakura Kai*" (the Cherry Society). He claimed that "*the first step in unifying the world is to unify the people of Japan itself directly under the Emperor.*"[18] The Tribunal found: "None of the conspirators held more extreme views than he did; none was more outspoken in his statement of these views." The *Judgment* states, "He was an ardent admirer of government by a military dictatorship. ... He was a principal in the formation of the conspiracy and contributed largely to its execution."[19] This kind of apotheosis with the feel of an evil cult incited the fanatical narrow nationalism and produced such freaks as "Kamikaze Brigade" (suicidal air fleets).

The second step was to "foment troubles."

Around 1930, Japanese militarist radicals were mainly junior officers. They conspired to create disturbance and make it a fait accompli in order to force the senior Army officers and the government to acquiesce. In the Tokyo Trial, the crimes of those Japanese war criminals began in 1928, the year of the "Huanggutun Incident," when Marshal CHANG Tso-lin, then Commander-in-chief of the Chinese Armies in Manchuria, was murdered. The success of this incident further encouraged the arrogance of those militarists.

On July 1, 1929, the Tanaka Cabinet was forced to resign. Soon afterward, the militarists fomented troubles again, including the "Wanpaoshan Incident" on July 1, 1931, the "Nakamura Incident" on July 17, 1931, and especially the "Mukden Incident" on September 18, 1931. In the series of conspiracy activities, the worst "trouble-makers" were ITAGAKI Seishiro, DOIHARA Kenji, as well as OKAWA Shumei, and HASHIMOTO Kingoro.

The third step was to "force the Cabinets to resign."

One of the major obstacles that prevented the rise of the Japanese militarists was the Cabinets based on elections by the political parties. In order to clear up this obstacle, the Army adopted the policy of "letting those who follow us thrive and those who resist us perish." On January 17, 1932, HASHIMOTO Kingoro published an article entitled "*On the Reform of the Parliamentary System*," which argued: "*Responsible government—Party Cabinet System—runs absolutely counter to the Constitution. It is the democratic government that ignores the 'Tenno' government,*

*.... When we consider their dangerous anti-national structure, political ideology, and their aggressive evils, we believe it most urgently necessary first to make a scapegoat of the existing political parties and destroy them for the sake of the construction of a cheerful new Japan."*[20] At that time, TANAKA Giichi was the Prime Minister. During the 17 years from 1928 to 1945, there were as many as 16 cabinets in Japan! Only seven Prime Ministers were elected from political parties, three of whom, namely HIROTA Koki, HIRANUMA Kiichiro, and KONOYE Fumimaro, supported the Army's lines, while the rest came to no good end. For instance, TANAKA Giichi and WAKATSUKI Reijiro were forced to resign. Even worse, HAMAGUCHI Osachi and INUKAI Tsuyoshi were assassinated by the young radical officers. In October 1941, when TOJO Hideki, the fascist leader, became the Prime Minister, he was concurrently the War Minister, Home Minister, Minister of Education, Minister of Commerce and Industry, and Minister of Military Supplies, with all powers concentrated in one person.

The fourth step was to "implement obscurantism."

In order to deceive and manipulate public opinion, the militarists implemented crazy obscurantist policies to fool the Japanese people, especially adolescents and young adults. In June 1933, ARAKI Sadao, a Class A war criminal who was the then War Minister, delivered a speech, saying: *"Japan is eternal and is destined to expand. The true spirit of the Japanese race lies in finding order amid chaos and in realizing an ideal world, a paradise for East Asia." "The path for the Japanese people to follow is the 'way of the Emperor,' and the Army of Japan is the Emperor's Army. It will therefore fight against anyone who opposes it in its task of spreading the 'Imperial Way.'"*[21]

ARAKI Sadao did not just talk about it as an abstract theory but also linked this fallacy with the invasion of Northeast China. He openly advocated: *"The foundation of Manchukuo is a revelation from heaven, which has reawakened the national spirit of the Japanese people. If the zeal which the Mukden Incident has engendered is sustained, the new order will be achieved."* At that time, all Japanese schools were forced to carry out military training conducted by the instructors from the Ministry of War in an attempt to mobilize the belligerent spirit and blind obedience among the Japanese youth.

In addition to miseducation, the Japanese militarists spared no effort in manipulating public opinion. On May 20, 1936, the War Ministry set up the Intelligence Bureau. Its task was to misguide and manipulate all communications to the public and facilitate through the media execution of the government policies. The *Judgment* states:

> *Freedom of the press had always been limited in Japan.... The police enforced the censorship laws in connection with every form of public expression.... After the Manchurian war, the government and the Army launched an organized campaign to justify Japan's position on the continent, and to stifle criticism at home. Material dealing with military matters could be printed only after it had been approved by the Police Bureau of the Home Ministry.*[22]

The fifth step was to "expand armaments."

The Japanese militarists were aware that expanding armaments was a "hard power" in realizing their aggressive ambitions. They did not conceal that the purpose of military expansion was to prepare for war, not only against China but also against the Soviet Union, Britain and the United States. Japan was a resource-poor island country; therefore the militarists made every effort to plunder the resources of China and other Asia Pacific countries. The *Judgment* also revealed more than once Japan's industrial development plans in Northeast China after the Mukden Incident and in Northern China and the whole country after the Marco Polo Bridge Incident (the beginning of the full-scale war of aggression against China in 1937). On March 11, 1942, SATO Kenryo, Chief of the Military Affairs Bureau of the War Ministry, admitted in his speech that the purpose of the national defense plan formulated by the Army in 1936 was to greatly expand armaments and productivity in order to consolidate and advance the achievements reached in the Mukden Incident. The Japanese Army held that since the arms expansion and rearmament of European powers would be completed in 1941 or 1942, Japan must greatly expand its arms and productivity before 1942 at any rate.

The sixth step was to "breach treaties."

Another obstacle to the Japanese militarist expansion was the constraints imposed by international treaties, which were signed by the Japanese government around World War I. In the *Judgment*, Chapter 3, "*Obligations Assumed and Rights Acquired by Japan*," begins with a list of these treaties, including *the Nine-Power Treaty of 1922* signed in Washington for the protection of China's territorial and administrative independence; the *Opium Conventions of 1912 and 1931* for the prohibition of production, distribution and use of opium and similar drugs; *the Four-Power Treaty of 1921* for the respect of territorial interests of countries in the

Pacific region; *the Hague Convention V of 1907* for the maintenance of inviolability of the territory of neutral powers; *the Pact of Paris of 1928* for the solution of international disputes through diplomatic means, mediation and arbitration; *the Geneva Red Cross Convention of 1929* and *the Geneva P. O. W. Convention of 1929* for the humanitarian behaviors in war, and other treaties. Consequently, after the Mukden Incident, *the Lytton Report* of the League of Nations condemned Japan's aggression and expansion, which exasperated the militarists and led to Japan's withdrawal from the League of Nations. A Japanese spokesman said that Japan could no longer cooperate with such an organization and withdrew from the above-mentioned treaties one by one. Without treaty constraints, Japan's military expansion and invasion of the various Asia-Pacific area became even more unscrupulous and rampant.

The seventh step was to "form an alliance."

The "Axis," an alliance formed by Japan, Germany, and Italy, was a source of evil for waging wars and was the common enemy of the whole world. Japan was very active in the establishment of this tripartite alliance. On November 25, 1936, and November 6, 1937, the Privy Council of Japan approved the German-Japanese Anti-Comintern Pact and the German-Italian-Japanese Ant-Comintern Pact, respectively; on September 27, 1940, Japan concluded the Tripartite Alliance with Germany and Italy, which was a necessary step for Japan to prepare for its invasion of Southeast Asia and the South Seas by force. MATSUOKA Yosuke, a Class A war criminal who was then the Foreign Minister, clearly pointed out that the main target of the Alliance was the United States.

The foregoing analysis shows that the rise and expansion of Japanese militarism were not accidental.

From the perspective of international law, the Tokyo Trial, like the Nuremberg Trial, has brought about many innovations. First, it started the practice of international criminal law. Second, it established the principle of pursuing individual criminal responsibility for international crimes. Third, it implemented the principle of no exemption from one's criminal responsibility based on his official position.

These principles constitute the historical source of modern international criminal law. The purpose of international criminal law is to safeguard the common interests of the whole international community. The world consists of different countries, but all countries have common needs in political, economic, and cultural areas. The modern international community forges a bond of common interest and pursuit, building common moral standards and values. Both Nuremberg and Tokyo Trials prosecuted three types of crimes, namely "conventional war crimes," "crimes against humanity," and "crimes against peace," which were considered as crimes against all mankind in addition to crimes against the direct victims. In this respect, the two Trials played a preventive role in safeguarding the common interests of the entire international community, thus contributing greatly to modern international law's development.

Regrettably, words and deeds that negate the Tokyo Trial have constantly existed in Japan. With the declassification of Japanese archives, it can be seen clearly that the Japanese government, as a driver behind public opinions, has been trying for a long time to repudiate the conviction of the Tokyo Trial. For example, KAYA Okinori, one of the 28 Class A war criminals, who had been sentenced to life imprisonment, returned to politics after early release. On June 1, 1954, as Minister of Justice, he entrusted some scholars to "study" the Tokyo Trial from the "legal" perspective, and one of the four entrusted scholars, surprisingly or unsurprisingly, was BANNO Kunkichi, a former defense lawyer of ITAGAKI Seishiro. What is more worrisome is that the trend of negating the Tokyo Trial is not limited to the academic circle. On March 13, 2013, Mr. ABE Shinzo, then Japan's Prime Minister, publicly stated in the House of Representatives that "the Tokyo Trial was victors' trial." Moreover, the Liberal Democratic Party established a special agency to "review" the Tokyo Trial.[23] We must now ask: What is the intention of the Japanese government? Does it plan to remove this cornerstone of the post-war international order? We are convinced that any attempt to deny and distort the history of aggression will be repulsive to the general public. The peace-loving people from all countries will never allow militarism to bounce back and historical tragedies to replay!

Finally, let us recapture the powerful and resonating words of our two great predecessors, to conclude this book.

MEI Ju-ao said in 1961:

> *I am not a revanchist. Neither do I intend to ascribe the debt of blood owed to us by the Japanese imperialists to the Japanese people. I believe, however, that to forget the suffering of the past is to be vulnerable to tragedy in the future.*[24]

HSIANG Che-chun pointed out in an interview in 1985:

*Since the Opium War in 1840, among the countless wars of aggression by western powers, only the War of Resistance Against Japanese Aggression, for the first time, ended with China's real victory. Only the Tokyo Trial enabled the Chinese people to feel really proud and elated!*[25]

## References

[1] Official Letter No. 37-333. Ministry of Foreign Affairs of the National Government.

[2] MEI, Ju-ao. 2016. *My Personal Experience at the Tokyo Trial.* Edited by MEI Xiao'ao and MEI Xiaokan. Shanghai Jiao Tong University Press, 282.

[3] Ibid., 289–290.

[4] Ibid., 335–337.

[5] MEI, Ju-ao. 2005. *International Military Tribunal for the Far East.* Law Press; People's Court Press, 71–72.

[6] Cheng, Zhaoqi, and Xiang Longwan. 2017. *Transcripts of the Proceedings of the International Military Tribunal for the Far East (Chinese version), First Series.* Vol. 4. Shanghai Jiao Tong University Press, 204 (4227 of the English court records).

[7] MEI, Ju-ao. 2016. *My Personal Experience at the Tokyo Trial.* Edited by MEI Xiao'ao and MEI Xiaokan. Shanghai Jiao Tong University Press, 348–352.

[8] MEI, Xiao-ao, and MEI Xiaokan. 2013. *The Tokyo Trial Manuscript of MEI Ju-ao.* Shanghai Jiao Tong University, 1–29.

[9] *The Asahi Shimbun,* November 14, 1948.

[10] MEI, Xiao-ao, and MEI Xiaokan. 2013. *The Tokyo Trial Manuscript of MEI Ju-ao.* Shanghai Jiao Tong University, 28.

[11] Official Letter No. 37-333. Ministry of Foreign Affairs of the National Government.

[12] Xiang, Longwan. 2014. *HSIANG Che-chun's Letters, Telegrams and Statements at the Tokyo Trial.* Shanghai Jiao tong University Press, 281.

[13] *Central Daily News,* December 3&8, 1948.

[14] *Central Daily News,* December 24, 1948.

[15] Minear, Richard H. 1971. *Victors' Justice: The Tokyo War Crimes Trial.* Princeton University Press, 3.

[16] TOTANI, Yoma. 2015. "The Historical Significance of Research of War Criminal Trial." Translated by Chen Aiguo. *The Restudy on the Tokyo Trial.* Compiled by the Tokyo Trial Research Center, 49.

[17] *The Judgment of the International Military Tribunal for the Far East.* Translated by Zhang Xiaolin, retranslated by Xiang Longwan and Xu Xiaobing (2015). Shanghai Jiao Tong University Press, 47.

[18] Ibid., 79 (48586 of the English court records).

[19] Ibid., 591–592 (49780–49782 of the English court records).

[20] Ibid., 288 (pp49085–49086 of the English court records).

[21] Ibid., 57 (48537 of the English court records).

[22] Ibid., 80–81 (48590–48591 of the English court records).

[23] Cheng, Zhaoqi. 2017. *The Tokyo Trial: For World Peace*. Shanghai Jiao Tong University Press, 7–76.

[24] MEI, Xiao-ao, and MEI Xiaokan. 2013. *The Tokyo Trial Manuscript of MEI Ju-ao*. Shanghai Jiao Tong University, 418.

[25] Xiang, Longwan. 2010. *The Tokyo Trial, Chinese Prosecutor Hsiang Che-chun (Xiang Zhejun)*. Shanghai Jiao Tong University Press, 7.

# Index

## S



## T



## U



## W

## ABOUT THE AUTHOR

**XIANG Longwan** is a mathematics professor at Shanghai Jiao Tong University (SJTU). He was one of the founders of the Center for the Tokyo Trial Studies (CTTS) of SJTU in 2011 and has served as Honorary Director since then. He is the son of HSIANG Che-Chun, the prosecutor representing China to the International Military Tribunal for the Far East, also known as the Tokyo Trial, from 1946 to 1948. The family connection inspired his interest and early research into the history of the Tokyo Trial. This field had barely been researched in China and initiated the establishment of the research center. He has been teaching and exploring mathematics for nearly 40 years and previously served as Provost of SJTU. He has published more than ten textbooks and monographs as well as about 70 research papers in both fields of mathematics and studies of the Tokyo Trial.

## ABOUT THE TRANSLATORS

**YANG Aijun**, an English professor at Zhejiang Yuexiu University, is researching translation practice and studies. He has published over 20 journal articles and two books in the past years, including *Dr. Zha's Diary of Fighting the COVID-19* (second translator).

**LI Dan**, a lecturer at Zhejiang Yuexiu University, specializes in translation and has more than ten years of experience translating English and Chinese subtitles. She has translated dozens of works such as Bojack Horseman, Narcos, Chicago Fire series, etc., and subtitles for world-famous stream media platforms such as Netflix, Amazon, and Disney. Her translation is well-received among the viewers.

**HUANG Danhua**, an English associate professor at Zhejiang Yuexiu University, is currently researching the application of translation technologies. He has been translating for Contemporary International Relations since 2017. In the past years, he has published more than ten journal articles.